I0755074

DANIEL,

A MODEL FOR YOUNG MEN.

A Series of Lectures.

BY THE

REV. W. A. SCOTT, D. D.

NEW ORLEANS.

NEW YORK:
ROBERT CARTER & BROTHERS,
285 BROADWAY.
1854.

Entered according to Act of Congress in the year 1854, by
ROBERT CARTER & BROTHERS,
in the Clerk's Office of the District Court of the United States for the
Southern District of New York.

TOBITT'S COMBINATION-TYPE,
181 *William st.*

PRINTED BY
JOHN A. GRAY
95 & 97 Cliff St.

DEDICATION.

To the Young Men of the South and South-West, and especially of New Orleans, this volume is most respectfully inscribed, as an expression of the author's admiration of their enterprise and noble bearing in business. And in making this dedication, he cannot withhold his fervent prayer, that, like Daniel, they may by an enlightened piety and patriotism serve their country and their God faithfully, and attain at last to everlasting life and glory.

RECOMMENDATORY NOTICE.

BY W. B. SPRAGUE, D. D.

The Lectures that compose this volume, have manifold claims on the patronage of the Christian public. That these claims will be acknowledged and honoured, in due time, there is no reason to doubt; but meanwhile it may not be amiss just to advert to some of the grounds on which they rest.

In the first place, these Lectures are invested with great interest, in consideration of the class to whom they are addressed. They are *young* persons, who have just entered the great school of life; whose characters are yet but partially formed, and around whom Christian philanthropy would naturally desire to throw every influence, favourable to their intellectual and moral culture, with reference to both the life that now is, and that which is to come. They are young *men*—in whom are prospectively bound up both the civil and Christian well-being of society; on whom it will devolve a few years hence to settle great problems of weal or woe, that will tell on the destinies of the world. They are more especially the class of young men who *reside in cities;* where, more than anywhere else, the tempter holds his throne; where the opportunities for doing good or evil are multiplied indefinitely; insomuch that it takes but little time for a young man in these circumstances to work himself into a model of Christian activity, or a monster of vice and crime. Any well-directed effort then to form the characters of young men, especially in large cities, to virtue and piety and honourable usefulness, is worthy of all praise, and will be sure not to lose its reward.

In the next place, the portion of Scripture which forms the subject of these Lectures, is, on many accounts, one of remarkable interest. In its historical details, nothing can exceed it—it records events which stand out in the world's history, and form some of the most impressive illustrations of the Divine character. Its prophecies also are worthy of the most profound and earnest inquiry; though, as these Lectures were designed to be of altogether a popular character, it was not fitting that they should include any elaborate investigation. Then the character of Daniel is one of the purest and most exalted of which even the inspired record has preserved an account. In respect to intelligence, industry, integrity, consistency and devotion, he shone with almost unequalled lustre; and there is no condition of prosperity, or adversity, or temptation, in which a young man can be placed, but that the example of Daniel, duly considered, may either shed some light upon the path of duty, or suggest some motives for diligently pursuing it.

There will be little difference of opinion, it is presumed, on the question, whether the author has done justice to his noble theme. No intelligent and candid reader will doubt that he has brought out the mind of the Spirit with great clearness and force. He has discussed a great variety of questions—historical, theological and practical, that naturally suggest themselves; and has shown himself at every point thoroughly at home. One very important feature of the work is, that it furnishes incidentally a vast amount of evidence of the Divine authority of the Scriptures—a point upon which young men, especially at this day, need to be enlightened and strengthened, in order that they may resist the insidious and multiform assaults of skepticism. Dr. Scott has left upon every page of his work the impress of a vigorous, discriminating, independent mind. Without any affectation of originality, he has his own way of saying things; and a terse, striking and effective way it is. Without apparently thinking of the graces of composition, his style is always perspicuous and manly, and sometimes radiant with beautiful imagery. You feel that you are in contact with a mind of bold and lofty impulses, and with a heart that is in unison with every measure for the promotion of human virtue and happiness.

There is yet one other circumstance to which I cannot but allude, that seems to me to bespeak for these Lectures a more than common share of attention—I refer to the fact that Dr. Scott's position as a minister in New Orleans, rendered it peculiarly fitting that he should perform just such a service as this: it is doubtful whether there is any other place in the United States in which he could speak to so large a number of young men, especially those who are thrown out of the range of the endearing associations of home; and the instructions and counsels which he would address to the young men of his own charge, must of course be equally adapted to others of the same class in similar circumstances. And I cannot forbear to add that, to my own mind at least, the work gathers additional interest from the fact that its author was prevented from giving it the revision he intended, by having been kept so constantly in contact with sickness and death during the last summer. His readers, while they will be well contented to take the work as it is, will hardly fail to have their gratitude awakened, that such a life as his was preserved amidst such self-denying and perilous labours.

There is one circumstance pertaining to the history of this publication which I cannot forbear to note, as strikingly illustrative of the care which Providence often takes of our concerns, through indirect and apparently undesigned instrumentalities. The publishing of this work was originally undertaken by the Harpers; and the sheets, as they were printed, were sent to me, by the author's request, with a view to my writing an introductory paragraph or two, after I had read them. As the printing was nearly finished, I had written all that I thought necessary, and had forwarded it to the publishers on the very day before the fire swept away their immense establishment. Not only my humble contribution, but the MS. of the Lectures, and even the stereotype plates, which were nearly completed, perished in the conflagration; and the only copy of the Lectures that remained was that which had been sent to me in the proof-sheets, and which, by the merest accident, had escaped destruction. I congratulate myself on having been thus instrumental in the preservation of a work, the good effects of which I confidently expect will reach far beyond the present generation.

It is due to myself to state that the only consideration that has seemed to me to justify, in any degree, the writing of these paragraphs, is that the respected author of this work resides in a part of the country so distant from this, that there may be some circles at the North, and especially in New England, in which he is not so familiarly known as to supersede the necessity of an introduction from some one more immediately identified with this region. It was this circumstance, I am sure, that drew from him the request with which I have now complied; and if what I have written shall procure an additional reader to the book, I shall feel quite satisfied. I will only add that he and I have never yet seen each others' faces; nor will he have read this brief notice, till the printer has rendered it useless for either his judgment or his modesty to suggest corrections. I am glad of the opportunity thus to give him the hand of fraternal fellowship even a thousand miles off; and I pray God to cause his course as an author as well as a Christian minister, to shine more and more unto the perfect day.

Albany, March 2, 1854.

PREFACE.

It has been my custom for more than ten years to devote my Sabbath evenings, during the winter and spring months, to young men. On such occasions I have delivered above *one hundred and fifty* different discourses. During this portion of the year I have to preach three discourses each week, the Sabbath evening discourse being one of them. The lectures now presented to the public are not a selection out of these hundred and fifty, but the Sabbath evening series of the last season. It will be understood, therefore, that these lectures were prepared from week to week amid the pressure of the duties, cares, and anxieties inseparable from a large city congregation. They were listened to by crowded assemblies, and with increasing interest to the close of the series. When these lectures were promised to the publishers, it was my intention to revise them during the leisure moments of summer. But it is well known that early in June the yellow fever became epidemic in our city, and has continued to prevail, with perhaps unparalleled fatality up to the present time. More than ten thousand persons have died in this city since its ravages began in June; and among them, many of the precious youth who listened to these lectures have fallen its victims, and are now sleeping their long sleep with the dead, in a soil that knows not the dust of their fathers, and from which the trumpet of the last day alone can awaken them. It may be readily supposed that in filling my pulpit, and in visiting the sick, in burying the dead, and in attempting to instruct, encourage, and comfort the living and the bereaved, and alleviate the miseries of the suffering poor, I have had but little time or heart for the work of revision. And now with the autumn a new campaign opens, that imperatively requires *day by day* all my time and all my strength. These lectures, then, must be published as they are, or not at all. With the humble hope that they may do good, I have ventured to send them to the publishers.

Whoever looks into this volume will see that I do not enter upon the prophecies of Daniel. If it were desirable for me to give the public my views of them, it does not fall within the scope of this effort to do so. The plan of these lectures requires that they should be read with an open Bible, and that the portions of Scripture indicated in each lecture should be read at the same time with the lecture. One great object in view, in this and in all my labors as a minister of the Gospel, is to give prominence to the Scriptures of God, which are the testimony of the Holy Spirit concerning Jesus Christ our Lord, and are intended to lead us to a saving apprehension of His Truth and Grace. *I am persuaded that the young men required for our times must be thorough Bible men.* They must be brought up on the pabulum of Bible truth. And I know of no more effectual method of imparting such truth to them than by explaining and enforcing the doctrines, precepts, and duties set forth in the lives of Bible heroes.

The authors that have fallen in my way, and to which I am more or less indebted for help in preparing these lectures, are the following: Prælectiones Joannis Calvini in Librum Prophetiarum Danielis, published in 1571; Diodati's Notes; Works of Plutarch and Josephus; Orton's Exposition; Layard's Nineveh; Vaux's Nineveh and Persepolis; Herodotus; Rich's Babylon and Persepolis; Fletcher's Assyria; Kitto's Bible Illustrations; Gausen's Lectures; White's Providence, Prophecy, and Popery; and especially do I desire to acknowledge my obligations to the first-named above, the immortal Calvin, and, next to him, to Prof. Stuart, for his Commentary on Daniel, and to Hengstenberg, for his work on the Genuineness, &c., and to Tregelles on Daniel, and to the lectures of Dr. Cumming, of London, on Daniel. As in the delivery of these lectures, it was my earnest endeavor, with God's help, to do good to the multitudes of young men that attended my ministry, so now they are committed to the press with the hope that by the Divine blessing they may be useful in directing such to the proper performance of their duties to their country, their fellow-men, and their ever blessed Creator; and to Him, through Jesus Christ, be all the praise. Amen.

W. A. Scott.

New Orleans, 20th September, 1853.

CONTENTS.

LECTURES ON DANIEL.

LECTURE I.

"To be ignorant of the lives of the most celebrated men of antiquity, is to continue in a state of childhood all our days."—PLATO.

"Social life is the aggregate of all the individual men's lives who constitute society. History is the essence of innumerable biographies."

SUPERIORITY OF BIBLE BIOGRAPHY FOR GIVING LESSONS TO YOUNG MEN OF THE NINETEENTH CENTURY.

Rom., xv. 4: For whatsoever things were written aforetime were written for our learning, that we, through patience and comfort of the Scriptures, might have hope.

Scriptures suited for all Ages.—Reflection on the Period of early Youth.—The Bible a Picture-gallery.—William von Humboldt.—Bible to be read Earnestly.—Superiority of Example illustrated.—Origen, Cicero.—Wellington, Webster.—Field open to all.—No possible Excuse for low Attainments in personal Piety and Christian Character.—Fountain-men wanted in our Times.

THE apostle alludes here to the Old Testament Scriptures, and assures us that they were not intended merely for the Jews, nor for those generations in which they first appeared, but also for the instruction of succeeding generations of mankind. *That we, through patience and comfort of the Scriptures*—that is, through those remarkable examples of patience exhibited by the saints and followers of God, whose history is given in the Scriptures, and by seeing the comfort which they derived from God, in their sufferings for the truth and in maintaining their piety in the midst of a wicked world—*might have hope* —that we shall be upheld and blessed as they were, since we worship the same God and adhere to the same faith with them. The apostle, in writing to the Hebrews, uses the same allusion. In the eleventh chapter to the Hebrews, he enumerates a host of Old Testament worthies, and then says: *Wherefore, seeing we also are compassed about with so great a cloud of witnesses, let us lay aside every weight, and the sin which doth so easily beset us, and let us run with patience the race that is set before us, looking unto Jesus, the author and finisher of our faith.*

"Whoever," says Sir Charles Bell, "has sat on a sunny stone in the midst of a stream, and played with the pebbles, and osier-twigs, and running waters, must, if he have a soul, remember that day, should he live a hundred years; and to return to such a spot after twenty years of a struggling life in the great world of man's inventions, is a still greater epoch. In age to go back thus to childhood—to Nature in her simple guise—to look upon the same scenes, and again to behold the same trees, still in their youth and freshness, and the same clear-running waters and soft, sweet-looking grass-plots that we looked on in our dewy youth—it is impossible to do this, and not feel something of the deep marvelousness of this ever-changing life, and something of an earnest longing for clearer communings with the unseen world. If, with such reflections we seem, on the one hand, to be little better than corks floating on the stream, still, on the other hand, this very deep consciousness of earth's unsatisfying nature preaches to us that this stream of life may bear us onward and upward to GLORY, HONOR, and IMMORTALITY.

Perhaps most of you, after years of absence, have revisited the scenes of earlier youth; or, if not the scenes of your own childhood, you have visited the birth-places and residences of great men; and every remarkable object, every street and corner, tree, stone, and running brook, seemed to have a tale to unfold, and to bring to your recollection some circumstance important to your own or their times, and you seemed to yourself to be walking in a city of tombs.

The Bible is just such a city of tombs. It has nothing, however, of the gloomy sadness of tombs about it. It is fragrant as the spicy groves of "Araby the Blest!" It is a historical gallery that stretches across the waste of far off centuries, and delivers us from false conjectures, wild fablings, and vague theories. By opening up a system of pure Theism, it emancipates the world from degrading superstitions; and by revealing the origin of our race, and incidentally communicating their dispersion over the globe, we are taught that all men are brethren. At Hampton Court there is a gallery of the beauties of Charles the First and Second; at Holyrood House, in Edinburgh, there is a gallery of all the kings of Scotland; and in the City Hall of Frankfort-on-the-Maine, there is a gallery of all the emperors of Germany; and in Versailles, in the collection of pictures, statues, and the like, which is dedicated to all the glory of France,* a large suite of rooms is devoted to likenesses of the marshals of France. Now we have the privilege, young men, of opening a gallery containing more beauty, more sprightliness, more intellect, more courage, and more sublimity of character, a thousand times told, than Hampton Court, Holyrood House, Frankfort, and Versailles can show. Our gallery of paintings begins with the first man and woman, and comes down from Eden to Patmos —a long array of patriarchs, prophets, and apostles, sages and kings, and their mothers, wives, and daughters. The pictures are drawn by hands as unerring as the rays that now give us our daguerrotypes. And these pictures, while life-like and flesh-colored, are always salutary in their influence. They feed no idle and licentious thoughts. They awaken the intellect and sanctify the affections. They regulate the passions, and point to themes ever elevating and noble. They save us from much that is evil, and inspire us with earnest desires for that which is good and holy. These are the pictures our fathers and mothers looked on for so many years, until they assumed their likeness, and have gone to their communion above. When traveling in a foreign land, it was always a delightful thought to me that my beloved ones at home might look at the same sun and moon, and gaze on some of the same stars that shone on me; and whenever I caught sight of the ocean, there was relief to the sadness of separation, in reflecting that its waters washed

* "À toutes les gloires de la France."

the shores of my own native land. So there is something affecting, deeply affecting, in the thought that the Bible portraits, which have been made by the direction of the Holy Spirit, are our family pictures—our household ornaments and furniture from generation to generation. The good in every age before us have admired and imitated the faith of Abraham, the patience of Job, and the benevolence of the New Testament.

A profound scholar and great statesman, William von Humboldt, minister of the King of Prussia, says of the Scriptures, that "among the strongest, purest, and finest tones in which the voice of antiquity has reached us, may be reckoned the books of the Old Testament; and we can never be enough thankful that in our translation they have lost so little of their reality and strength of expression." He speaks of Luther's translation from the Hebrew into the German language, which is, indeed, one of the finest translations ever made. Happily for us and our children, the same simplicity and strength characterizes our English version. "I have often," continues the Prussian statesman, "reflected with pleasure on the existence of so much that is exalted, rich, and varied, as is contained in the Bible, in the books of the Old and New Testaments; and if this be, as is very frequently the case, the only book in the hands of the people, yet have they in this a compendium of human thought, history, poetry, and philosophy, so complete, that it would be difficult to find a feeling or a thought which has not its echo in these books. Neither is there much in them which is incomprehensible to a common, simple mind.

The learned may penetrate deeper, but no one can go away unsatisfied."*

The Bible, my young friends, is indeed, as your honored parents have taught you, the gracious gift of God to mankind. The Holy Scriptures are an invaluable blessing to our race. They bear upon their front and within themselves the indubitable marks of their divine Original. The attempts of unbelievers to weaken or destroy the evidences in their favor, have only brought out the more clearly the many "infallible proofs" that they were "written by inspiration of God." But while the outworks of Revelation have been ably defended, too few have searched out with honesty and diligence the treasures deposited therein. It is *something* to be well established in the faith—to receive the Bible as the Word of God, but so far as a personal salvation is concerned, we are no better than the heathen, if we remain ignorant of what the Bible contains. A crude, undigested notion of divine things is a very unsatisfactory way to receive God's revelation to us for our salvation. We may assent to the truth, excellence, and importance of the Scriptures, yet not give our serious attention to know what they teach, whereby we may glorify God and enjoy Him forever. Curiosity alone might be deemed sufficient to prompt us to a diligent perusal of the sacred Volume. But our duty in this matter is not left to the promptings of mere curiosity. We are *commanded* by the very highest authority

* Religious Thoughts and Opinions of William von Humboldt. Boston: 1843.

to search the Scriptures. Nor can we remain in ignorance of the sublime knowledge they reveal without a manifest contempt of God. Nothing should be more interesting to us than the WILL of God which is revealed to us, and requires of us unfeigned obedience. Who is the Lord, that I should serve Him? What would He have me do? May I obtain His favor? Should I not dread His anger? These are questions, which to us, as sinners hastening on to death and judgment, it is of very serious consequence we should have answered in a proper manner. But these are questions which the Bible alone fully and faithfully resolves. It is something to insist on our duty to read the Bible from its beauties of language, the surprising facts it relates, the grandeur of its representations, and the sublimity of its doctrines; but the highest recommendation for its study is: That it is the WORD OF THE LIVING GOD, which is able to make us wise unto salvation. "But that which stamps upon the Scriptures the highest value," says Bishop Porteus, "that which renders them, strictly speaking, inestimable, and distinguishes them from all other in this world, is this, that they, and only they, contain the words of eternal life. In this respect, every other book, even the noblest composition of man, fails; they cannot give us that we most want, and what is of infinitely more importance to us than all other things put together—ETERNAL LIFE." But lest we should fail to see the practical tendency of Revealed Truth, much the greatest part of it is taken up with the records of history, and the description of remarkable lives. Nor are these to be passed over carelessly. They are written for our admonition. 1. The narrative of striking facts and the delineation of celebrated characters, is perhaps, of all methods of instruction, *the most effective.* Important truths are hereby conveyed to us in the most pleasing form, and deep impressions are made upon the mind beyond any thing that mere dry doctrines or precepts can produce. No one is ignorant of the power of example both for good and evil. Such is man's nature, that he is more guided by the practice of others than by his own reason. A child writes more easily after a copy than by rule. Men are prone to imitate whatever they see done, be it good or bad, emulating the one and aping the other. Men love to be in society. You know the proverb says: "As well be out of the world as out of the fashion." Hence men will go any whither in company, presuming on defense, support and justification in the countenance of their fellow-men. Hence men will do as a *mob* what they could not be prevailed upon to do as *individuals.* Hence it is more difficult to make men behave with gravity and decorum in large assemblies, even in deliberative bodies, legislative and ecclesiastical, than in their social circles or as individuals. They satisfy their own minds, and justify their doings partly by dividing the responsibility, and partly by pleading the authority of others. They are prone to think that laudable, allowable, or at least excusable, for which such precedents can be alleged.

2. *Examples inform and impress the mind in a manner more compendious, easy, and pleasant than precepts or any other instrument or way of discipline.* Precepts

are abstract, naked, powerless—without a hold on either the fancy, sense, or memory; like the shadows of a passing cloud, too subtle to make any great impression, or leave any remarkable footsteps. But example comes home with irresistible power and strikes out its likeness. Precepts are but a skeleton, dry, meagre, lifeless, exhibiting nothing of person, place, time, manner, or individuality—things in which chiefly consist the flesh and blood, the colors and graces, the life, and soul, and ideality of both men and things. These are the very things that please, affect, and move us; and example is their embodiment. It gives us the body in its full, and proper, and beauteous proportions, preserved amid trials and in spite of temptations—life as it is and must be, just in the same kind of world we now live—life in moving tableaux—transforming a notional universality into the reality of individual existence. Precept is the man chiseled out, standing mute in the awful majesty of a statue of Praxiteles; example is the man with the life-speaking eye, the grace of living motion, and the lips parted with instructive lessons. The most successful professors of arts and sciences explain, illustrate, and confirm their general rules and precepts by particular examples. Mathematicians *demonstrate* their theorems by schemes and diagrams; orators *back* their enthymemes with inductions; philosophers *urge* the reason and nature of things, and then throw themselves aback on the practice of Socrates, Zeno, and such like personages. Politics is more easily and clearly drawn out of veritable history than out of books *De Republica*. Plato,

More, Sidney, and Harrington, had never dreamed their republics and commonwealths in the fairy land of Utopia if they had had the example of the United States of America in reality before them. Artificers describe models, and set patterns before their learners with greater success than if they merely delivered accurate rules and precepts to them. A man can more readily learn to build by looking at and carefully examining the parts and frame of a well-contrived house while it is constructing, than he can by ever so studious an inquiry into the rules of architecture ; or he may learn to draw by setting a good picture before him, than by merely speculating upon the laws of perspective ; or to write fairly by imitating one good copy, than by listening to a thousand oral directions. Nor is the case at all different when these principles are applied to morals. Seneca* says " that the crowd of philosophers which followed Socrates derived more of their ethics from his manners than his words."

It is said of Origen, the most learned man of his age, the author of a Hexapla—a man that employed seven amanuenses at once—" that he recommended religion more by his example than by all he wrote." One good example may represent more fully and clearly the nature of virtue than a thousand eloquent descriptions of it. It is good in God to give us food ; but it is a still higher proof of His benevolence to give us a taste for and a relish in our food, so that we enjoy it. It is a proof, both of Divine wisdom and goodness, that we have a Reve-

* "Plus ex moribus, quam ex verbis Socratis traxit.—*Ep.* ii.

lation of the Divine will; but it is still a higher proof of Supreme goodness that so much of the Divine will is given to us illustrated by examples. We have in the Bible examples of all the Christian virtues. Is it *faith* we have to acquire? Then we have but to look at Abraham. Is it wisdom, constancy, humility, and resolution? Behold Moses. Is it zeal, patience, perseverance, and piety? Then look at Peter, Paul, and John. Is it self-denial, courage, steadfastness, integrity, and devotion to high and ennobling principles of duty that we seek? Then we have only to study the histories of Joseph, John the Baptist, Nehemiah, and Daniel.

3. Good examples are powerful, because they persuade and incline us to follow them by plausible authority. That prudent, wise, and pious persons do any thing, is itself a very probable argument that we are under obligations to do the same thing; and if we err, it is a great comfort to be found in such company. "Will you," says the great Roman orator, "will you commemorate to me the examples of Scipio, and Cato, and Lelius, and say they did the same thing? Though the thing displeases me, yet I cannot withstand the authority of such men: their authority is so great, that it can cover even the suspicion of a fault."*

In a word, examples incite our passions and impel us to duty. They raise hope, influence courage, provoke emulation, urge up timidity, awaken curiosity, and affect the fancy, and set in motion all the springs of activity.

* Cicero in Verrem.

The examples of the Bible instruct and warn, encourage, admonish, and comfort. They teach principles and duties. They show us what to believe and what to do, that we may inherit eternal life.

It is by reading and studying the lives of those who have distinguished themselves above the rest of mankind, that we may both amuse and instruct ourselves. History has, therefore, done well in immortalizing those men who have, by their talents or genius, or by their enterprise and benevolence, done much for the well-being of their fellow-men. The Supreme Being sends into the world, from time to time, and in every age, men who distinguish their day by eminent services done to their generation and to posterity. The private and public lives of such men should be carefully treasured up, and perused with universal interest. God, of his goodness, has so constituted our world, that great benefactors to our race, though dead, continue to speak to us. Although all that is mortal of Daniel Webster is gone to the grave, yet, in his own immortal words, HE STILL LIVES!

But if biographical studies in general are thus greatly valuable, and especially to the young, they become much more so when they are applied to the lives, characters, and principles of holy men, of divinely inspired men—such as prophets and apostles, and lives and characters written by them. Between ordinary biography and that of the Bible there is this remarkable distinction. In perusing the lives of eminent statesmen and warriors, or of those whose names have been celebrated in the paths of science, philosophy, or literature, we usually derive all the benefit which they are calculated to confer, when we have thereby gained a better acquaintance with the varieties of human character and the springs of human action—when we have gathered some gleanings of information upon the subjects or modes of life, and splendid achievements with which they were most familiar, or for which they were renowned. We do not seem to have the courage to make an application of their glorious deeds, and discoveries, and principles, to ourselves. We never dream that we ourselves may, through their example and agency, become warriors, statesmen, artists, poets, philosophers, or philanthropists. We may admire, and not attempt to imitate. It was therefore gratifying to see, in the remarks of Lord John Russell in Scotland, and of Lord Brougham in England, on the death of Wellington, that they both took occasion to remind their countrymen, and particularly young men, that while Providence might deny to them the circumstances that could make them heroes, like the great duke, still it was in their power to imitate him in the essential elements of all true greatness—purity of principle and fervent devotion to the welfare of his country. Integrity and patriotism are virtues not patented to any sect or age. It is greatly to be regretted that the duty of selecting the available virtues of the great should be so generally overlooked. But even were it otherwise, biography in general falls far short of Christian biography. When the faith, or the piety, or the benevolence, or the endurance of trials for the truth's sake, or the noble deeds of a disciple of Jesus is the object of our admiration, we ought not to rest satisfied with yielding our esteem and approbation—we ought to follow in his footsteps, since our safety and happiness, as well as our duty to ourselves and our country, lie in the same path. Two important particulars are worthy of being mentioned here and remembered; namely, *that the field is open to all*, and that *special divine energy is promised to all that will trust in God, and walk in the way of his commandments.* Each one of us is invited to walk in the same way of life in which the patriarchs, prophets, apostles, and martyrs have travelled home to God and glory. Each one of us is freely invited to come and take of the fountain of God's sanctifying grace. God's word, moreover, warns us that all the by-paths of man's own devising communicate with the broad way that leadeth to destruction.

Again, in studying Bible biographies, we should be careful to separate the peculiarities of individual character and experience, and the extrinsic circumstances by which these may have been called into action, from the grand general outlines which characterize the whole family of the good and pious. In natural temperament and external circumstances there may be a great distance between men of the same age, and much more between different ages and countries. But all the pious are *new creatures* in Christ Jesus. All the virtues, in every age, and under all circumstances, are alike in their adherence to truth and attachment to principle. In reading the lives of prophets and apostles, "holy men of old," and of eminent servants of God in modern times, we must guard against sheltering ourselves in our own littleness, indolence, and impiety by saying to ourselves that if we had been endowed with equal talents, or had been placed in similar circumstances, we should have developed equal heroism, and have shone with equal light. It is not so. *Circumstances aid great men, but do not make them.* On the contrary, great men make circumstances. They lay a contribution on every thing around them, and make it lie at their feet, obedient to their will. As there is no situation in life in which we may not serve God—no trial under which his grace cannot impart peace and strength to enable us to endure and conquer, so no circumstances can be found so favorable to the development of genius or of piety, as that its rise or progress can be ascribed to mere chance or caprice, or to any other source than GOD'S HELP IN UNION WITH HUMAN EFFORT.

We must, then, guard against the excuse for our sloth, and for our low attainments in the knowledge of divine things, that we are not inspired as were the prophets and apostles. True, we are not, but the mere gift of inspiration was not always connected with saving grace. Saul was among the prophets, but did not yield the fruits of sincere obedience to God. Balaam prophesied, and was slain in battle by the people of God. Isaiah, and Paul, and John were eminently pious, not because they were inspired, but because they were partakers of divine grace; and it is in their experience of pardoning mercy, and attainment of *personal* holiness, and not in prophetic phrensy, that we are to be like them. True piety is the same in all ages. There is but one Gospel, one Lord, one faith, one baptism. Christ is the essential figure of all time, past, and to come. Before the Incarnation, the pious looked forward to the coming of the Son of God; since the Advent, the pious look back to Calvary, to the lifting up of the Son of Man. The Gospel is alike addressed to the learned and to the unlearned—to the Sabbath-school child and the believer of fourscore years—to the soldier on the tented plain, the operative in the mill, and the slave in the field—to the dwellers in palaces and the tenants of cottages. It is God's message of mercy and good-will to all men, of every tribe, kindred, tongue, people, and nation, under the whole heaven. Are the truths of God's word, then, precious to you, as they were to the servants of God in olden time? The work of the Spirit is in every believer, a renewal of the whole man after the image of God, enabling him to die unto sin and to live unto righteousness. The varieties of individual characters produced by any outward circumstances are but the distinctions of time, and shall pass away when time shall be no more. It is of infinite moment, then, that Christ be formed in your heart, the hope of glory. There is no reason why you should not receive the grace of God—no reason why you should not be among the number of the faithful, who, having "turned many to righteousness, shall shine as the stars, for ever and ever."

"When a man turns to the Lord," says an old Jewish writer, "he is like a fountain filled with living water, and rivers flow from him to men of all nations and tribes."

It is just such men, my young brethren, you are called to be. Your age and your country call for fountain-men—men of deep original experience in the grace of faith and in the knowledge of God's Word. God has given you bodily constitution, health, and nerves, the education and the style of mind, and the social and political status in the world, which with fixity of thinking and sincerity in praying will make up such an aggregate of character as will be a blessing now, and an honor forever. Your country and your God require of you to be men like Joshua and Caleb, to whom the giants of Canaan—all the adversaries of truth—*shall be but as bread.* We want men of large minds and warm hearts—men of sound understanding and of sincere faith; then "shall our peace be like a river, and our righteousness like the waves of the sea."

The development of character which we have to study in the biographies of the Bible speaks volumes of encouragement and hope, warning and admonition. Like the pillar-cloud of the Hebrews, one side is bright and glory-revealing, while the other is dark and full of terror. The lives of God's servants tell us there is a beauty and excellence which the wicked do not prize nor seek to obtain—that there is a blessedness, both here and hereafter, in which the ungodly have no interest; tell us there is danger around the unbelieving and impenitent, doubt and darkness before them, while they are without the ark of safety or without the light of hope. But the lives of Old Testament worthies, and of all true Christians, speak to us also the language of encouragement. They tell us there is forgiveness with God, that He may be feared—that the grace of God is sufficient for all the trials of life—and that Heaven makes amends for all the sorrows of earth.

LECTURE II.

DANIEL A TRUE BIBLE PROPHET.

On Dan., viii., 1–3; Ezek., xiv., 14, and xxviii., 3.

Personal History of the Prophet true.—Expositors of Daniel.—The Scope and Definiteness of his Prophecies.—Sir Isaac Newton a patient Student of his Writings.—Porphyry refuted.—Mysteries and Miracles no Objection.—Proofs of the Authenticity of the Book of Daniel.—Daniel is its professed Author.—Monumental Proof.—The Book was received by the Jews.—Josephus' Testimony.—Incidental Allusions, such as Mode of capital Punishment, reckoning of Time, Style of Houses, Presence of Females at Festivals, personal Incidents, Food, Change of Name, and the Language of the Book itself.—Convenience of small Change.—Ready to give an Answer for your Hope.—Man's personal Responsibility to God.—The Atonement of the Bible Man's only Hope.

AMONG the Hebrew prophets, Daniel's celebrity is next to that of Moses. There are none whose wisdom, and dexterity, and elevation, and influence have been more celebrated among the Jews. It would be as reasonable to deny the personal existence and reign of David or Solomon, as to deny either the personal history or extraordinary prophetic character of Daniel. Yet there are not wanting those who deny both. And this is the more remarkable when we consider the evidence in support of his personal history. There is no more reason to doubt that such a distinguished man, a Jewish exile, lived and flourished at Babylon during the captivity, than there is to doubt the existence of Nebuchadnezzar himself. Indeed, as a mere matter of history, the proof in favor of Daniel is stronger than that in favor of Nebuchadnezzar. None of the Greek historians mention such a king as Nebuchadnezzar of Babylon. But surely this is not sufficient proof that there never was such a king.

Recent discoveries on the banks of the Euphrates, even if we set aside all traditions and all ancient history on the subject, have brought to light the absolute certainty of the existence of such a king as Nebuchadnezzar, and that he lived and did just as the Bible says he did. The Jews have always considered Daniel as one of their greatest prophets. See Josephus, Antiq., lib. x.

But the only authentic source whence we can learn the true history of Daniel is the book which bears his name. There are many apocryphal narratives respecting him, but they belong to a later period, and are not trustworthy. The simple profession of the author of the book before us, that he was *Daniel*, a prophet in the Babylonish captivity, is *prima facie* proof that this is the fact. The *onus probandi* may be fairly thrown on those who deny it. How do we know that a monument pointed out to the traveler at Rome is the arch of Titus? The monument speaks for itself. It says it was erected in honor of Titus after his destruction of Jerusalem.* The inscription itself, standing on a public edifice, is proof of the fact it relates. And we know from history and tradition, and the nature of the monument itself, that it is both genuine and authentic. It is true, antiquarians are sometimes deceived. Inscriptions are sometimes forged. But *this*

* The inscription on the arch of Titus:

SENATUS.
POPVLVSQVE. ROMANVS.
DIVO. TITO. DIVI. VESPASIANI. F.
VESPASIANO. AUGUSTO

proves the general principle of evidence which I insist upon to be true. "If," as Tregelles has well stated it, "ancient inscriptions had not been admitted as carrying with them much weight of evidence, forgeries would not have been attempted. The existence of counterfeit coins proves that coins in general pass current as genuine." You are aware that men of thorough acknowledged piety and scholarship, such as Sir Isaac Newton, Bishop Newton, Faber, and Calvin, devoted a considerable portion of the best part of their lives to the elucidation of the book of Daniel. The most recent works on this book that I am acquainted with are from the pens of the late Professor Stuart, of Andover, Dr. Cumming, of London, Dr. Tregelles, of England, and the works of Professors Hengstenberg and Havernich, of Germany. I have named these authors, because, as many of you are blessed with a liberal education, you may be inclined to devote some portion of your time to mental and moral improvement by giving your attention to some of them. The late Moses Stuart's "Commentary on Daniel," Dr. Tregelles' "Defense of the Authenticity of the Book of Daniel," and Hengstenberg's "Genuineness of Daniel," leave but little more to be said on the authority of this book as a true part of the inspired Word. Hengstenberg and Stuart state and answer the objections that have been made to the authenticity of the book that seem to deserve refutation; and Tregelles sets forth the arguments that establish the claims of the book of Daniel to its place in the blessed Volume. All expositors of the Bible have testified to the excellence of the book of Daniel. In at least one point of view, it is regarded as one of the most interesting books of the whole Bible; namely, as an exposition of the GREAT PRINCIPLES on which God governs the world, and as a running commentary in advance upon the history of things and nations that are now passing over the stage of time. This book comprehends so many events, and extends through so many successive ages, that it presents to us an astonishing proof of divine Providence and of divine Revelation. Who but the omniscient and omnipotent God could thus declare the things that shall be, with their times and their seasons? Surely he who could thus foretell the dispensations of Providence must have been an honest and truthful servant of Him, whose dominion is an everlasting dominion, and whose kingdom endureth from generation to generation. Sir Isaac Newton, "who explored the firmament with unwearied wing, and made an apocalypse of the stars," felt that he was sounding a greater depth, and rising to a loftier height, when he sat down a patient student of this book, to ascertain the mind and meaning of the spirit of God therein, and make it plain to less gifted souls, than when engaged in his loftiest astronomical studies. There is no part of divine prophecy so definite, so reduced to facts and figures, as the book of Daniel. No prophecy, if false, could, therefore, be more easily exposed. And yet there is no part of the divine Volume that has given more trouble to the unbelieving Israelite and the skeptic than the prophecies of Daniel. The Israelite sees plainly that if Daniel's chronology be of God, then the Messiah must have come, and that it is in vain to look for another; and the infidel only gets over the difficulty by denying that there is any divinity in the

Old or New Testament. Genesis and Malachi, Matthew and Revelation are alike to him. He receives none of them as true, although he is not able to give any satisfactory solution of their origin, character, preservation, and influence. In the face of the most astonishing body of evidence that has ever been produced to prove any thing, in favor of the inspiration of the Scriptures, he sets them aside as fables and fictions without any authority. And in rejecting what God has said as unworthy of credence, he believes more than he is required to believe in receiving the Bible as the Word of God. Infidels are, after all, the most superstitious and the most credulous.

One of the earliest opponents of Daniel and of Christianity was Porphyry, who saw so clearly the fulfillment of part of his prophecies, that he declared the book must have been written by some one who lived in the days of Antiochus Epiphanes—that is, that the prophecies, so called, are but narratives of events fulfilled. The answer to this is very simple and easy. The book of Daniel is found not only in the Hebrew Bible, just as we have Isaiah, Ezekiel, and the other prophecies and histories, dating back to the time when it is believed they were respectively written, but also in the Greek translation from the Hebrew, called the Septuagint, which was made and scattered throughout the Greek empire at least *one hundred* years before Antiochus Epiphanes was born. Josephus and the whole Jewish nation are witnesses of this fact.

If it should be said there are too many *mysteries and miracles* in this book, we answer, there are mysteries in it that we are not able to solve, nor shall we now attempt to explain. It is not my purpose, in the present course of Lectures, to enter upon any discussion of the prophecies of Daniel, but mainly to pursue the narrative, so far as it shall suit our design—which is, to present the private and public life of Daniel, as far as we can ascertain what it is, as a model for the young men of our age and country—taking also, as we proceed with it, such a survey of the monuments and histories of those times and countries as may elucidate the divine record, or serve to prove its genuineness and authenticity. The manifestations of God found in this book seem to have been necessary for the peculiar times and trials of his servants. The Jews were then in captivity, their temple was destroyed—their sacred rites, their sacrifices, and their ceremonies had ceased. Their priests and their Levites were gone. It would seem, therefore, natural to expect, when all the outward signs of their religion were thus removed, that God should manifest more of himself to them, in order to keep up the light of religion in the absence of its outward and visible ordinances. We may sum up some of the main points that prove the authenticity of the book of Daniel and set forth his claims to be considered as a true prophet, in the following order:

1. *The book of Daniel was received as authentic by the Jews before the coming of Christ, and before the Maccabean Age.* Its place in the canon was never disputed by them. As it existed in the Hebrew Bible, so we find it translated with the other books of the Old Testament into Greek, by the learned Jews of Alexandria, about three hundred years before Christ. Accordingly, we have it in the Septuagint translation to this day. Jose-

phus, the learned and distinguished Jewish historian, bears honorable testimony to the character of Daniel and the authenticity of this book. The point of his testimony which I cite relates to the authority of the book called the Prophecy of Daniel. Josephus, speaking of this book, says, "All these things did this man leave behind him, writing as God had showed to him; so that those who read his prophecies, and see how they have been fulfilled, must be astonished at the honor conferred by God on Daniel." This is the testimony of the distinguished Jewish historian, who was bitterly hostile to Christianity. In his antiquities, he shows how each prediction of Daniel had been fulfilled in regard to the Babylonian empire, and the Persian and the Medean. And if it be asked why he does not also speak of the fulfillment of Daniel's prophecies concerning the last of the four great monarchies, we answer: Josephus was a servant of the Roman empire, and he had not the courage to proclaim that Daniel's prophecies relating to Rome, the then existing empire, would be as certainly fulfilled as they had been concerning the three former empires.

Again, 2. *Jesus Christ and His apostles expressly refer to Daniel as one of the prophets of the Old Testament.* In Matthew, xxiv. 15, the Saviour says: "*When ye shall see the abomination of desolation, spoken of by Daniel the prophet, stand in the holy,*" &c. This allusion of our Lord proves that He and the Jews of his time regarded Daniel as a real prophet, just as they did Moses, and David, and the other prophets, and proves also that Daniel prophesied of the judgments of God upon Jerusalem and the Holy Land subsequent to the crucifixion of the Messiah. In like manner, there are allusions scattered through the New Testament which clearly point to events, and things, and expressions contained in the book of Daniel, though the prophet himself is not named.

We find the apostle saying of some of the Old Testa ment hero saints, "By faith they stopped the mouths of lions," and "quenched the violence of fire." These are evidently allusions to Daniel's deliverance from the lion's den, and to the escape of his three friends, Shadrach, Meshach, and Abednego, who were thrown into the fiery furnace by Nebuchadnezzar, and had not even their garments singed by the flame. These allusions to Daniel and his prophecy show that the book of Daniel was known to our Lord and his apostles, and received by them as inspired.

Time at present does not allow me to dwell on these allusions. The most remarkable fact about them is, the wonderful harmony that runs through them and through the whole Word of God. "You cannot touch, as it were (Dr. Cumming,) a note in Daniel, but all the apostles of the New Testament respond to it. You have noticed sometimes in a building, in a church or a hall, that if a certain note or tone be given by the speaker, the whole building will instantly vibrate in harmony or in unison. In the same way, you cannot touch a truth in Daniel, but tones of harmony will burst from the lips of Paul and from the writings of Peter. The whole Bible is a grand harmony, revealing the mind, the will, and the glory of God."

3. Daniel's truthfulness as a writer is seen in the record he has made of the capital punishments inflicted in

his time at Babylon. Casting into a heated furnace was a mode of practising cruelty known only to the Chaldeans; while casting into a den of wild beasts was a punishment peculiar to the Medes and Persians. In our age, the historian of Cuba does not say that the victims of some unfortunate attempt at revolution are bastinadoed, or put to death by the bowstring or the silken cord; he does not speak of the mode of inflicting death in Turkey, Persia, China, or Japan; but he does tell us that Crittenden and his brave but ill-fated companions, who, like true Kentuckians, would kneel to none but God, were slaughtered by a file of soldiers with Spanish muskets, and that Lopez was put to death by the *garoté vil.* This *garoté vil*, I believe, is a refinement upon any thing known in Spain in the days of Columbus. It would, therefore, be a great mistake to say that any suspicious gentleman of Spain was put to death three hundred years ago by Spanish officials as Lopez was at Havana. We have, therefore, a plain argument in favor of the truthfulness of the history of Daniel, that, in speaking of the infliction of capital punishment under the Chaldeans, he mentions that of the fiery furnace; and when speaking of capital punishment under the Medo-Persian dynasty, he, without saying a word about the change, relates that it was performed after the national manner, namely, by casting into a den of lions. It were difficult to conceive a more striking proof of the simple straightforwardness of the writer, and of his perfect acquaintance with the manners and the customs of his age, than we have in the narrative.

4. The *method* of reckoning years is also a proof that

the record before us is in perfect harmony with the age and country *when and where it was made.* Thus we read in chap. ii.: "In the second year of King Nebuchadnezzar." The writer then lived in the age and kingdom of Nebuchadnezzar. From the way in which a traveler speaks or writes of longitude, we can tell to what country he belongs. For as each country reckons longitude from its own meridian, so each traveler would allude to his own sovereign and meridian whenever occasion requires. An Englishman would reckon his longitude from Greenwich, under the reign of her Majesty Victoria. A Frenchman reckons his longitude from Paris in the time of Louis Napoleon. An American says: In such a year of the Independence of the United States of America, and such a degree of longitude west from Washington, the star-spangled banner was planted on such a fortress or island. Thus, as the mode of reckoning longitude, and the mention of the sovereign or government found in some distant shore or island, would show the country to which the discoverer and writer belonged, so the allusion here made to the mode of reckoning time shows that the narrative comes from the pen of one who was well acquainted with the habits and customs of the people among whom he lived, and of whom he wrote. Another proof of the same kind is found in ch. ii., v. 5, where the king commands their houses to *be made a dunghill.*

Now, if their houses had been built of stone or brick, or even of wood, as in this country, it would be difficult to see the propriety of such a decree. But when you remember that the houses of the Chaldeans, as also the houses of the ancient Egyptians, were made of bricks of clay hardened in the sun, there is no difficulty in understanding it. Such bricks might easily be dissolved by violent rains, and soon be reduced by moisture and rain to a pulp or mass of soft clay. Our Saviour refers to such houses in Matthew vii.

5. *The presence of females* at the great festival of Belshazzar is another proof of the same kind in favor of the claims of this book. Such a statement made now, concerning a great festival of the Sultan of Constantinople, would be pronounced at once to be false. But the ancients were not Moslems. The ancient Egyptians, Chaldeans, and Persians did not exclude their females from their feasts. Abundant proof to the contrary can be collected from history and monuments. Xenophon, the historian of Cyrus, says that it was a custom peculiar to Babylon, and unknown among subsequent nations. He was mistaken in part. Such a custom prevailed among the Jews and Egyptians, as well as with the Chaldeans. Our record accords minutely with the actual peculiarities of the age and country concerning which it is made. Xenophon further corroborates the statements of Daniel about Belshazzar, for he tells us that the "last king of Babylon was cruel, cowardly, and voluptuous, who despised the Deity, and spent his time in riot and debauchery." This is precisely the character which Daniel gives to Belshazzar, who was the "last king of Babylon." And again, it is known that the Cyaxares of Xenophon is the same with the Darius of Daniel. The character is similar. Xenophon says he was weak, cruel, and pliable, yet furious in his anger, and tyrannical in the exercise of

his power. This corresponds to his conduct as recorded by Daniel. He tells us that, as king, he allowed his nobles to make laws for him which were unalterable, and afterward repented and endeavored to retract them. He casts Daniel into the den of lions for non-compliance with his orders, and then spends the whole night in lamentation and remorse at the consequences of his cruelty. It is thus that we catch, sounding along the lapse of centuries, and from the ruins of Persepolis and Babylon, now being brought to light, echoes of the great original—proofs that the Prophet Daniel was truthful, both as a historian and as a foreteller of future events, and that, like the other holy men of old who wrote the Scriptures, he was moved thereto by the Holy Ghost.

6. And we have still other similar proofs that Daniel is the author of this book, and that it is a truth-telling book, and was written at the time assumed, and that he was a living participator in the events which he records. For example, it is here stated that the Hebrew youths were fed from the royal table. Is this fact sustained by the history of the Chaldeans? Was there any such custom among them? It is alluded to here as a common and a well-known fact, just as an eye-witness would record a custom prevailing at the period when he lived. And inquiry satisfies us that such a custom did prevail at that time among the Chaldeans and Persians, but that it was a custom peculiar to them, and common to no people besides.

The CHANGE of their names from Hebrew into Chaldee is another proof of the genuineness and authenticity of the book. This was in accordance with a custom universally prevalent among the Chaldeans. In 2 Chron., xxxvi., 4, we find the King of Babylon changing the name of Eliakim into Jehoiakim. See also 2 Kings, xxiv., 17.

The fact stated is in harmony with the age and the country in which it purports to have been penned.

An argument, also, in favor of the authenticity and genuineness of the book is derived from the *language* in which it is written. The book of Daniel, as also the book of Ezra, was written partly in Hebrew and partly in Chaldee, a language that differs in its forms and structure from the Hebrew about as much as the Italian or Spanish differs from the Latin. Now a historian of Italy, writing the history of his country two centuries ago, would contain allusions to passing events and things that had happened before, and would contain peculiarities of style belonging to the language of Italy at that time; and if he lived at Florence, Bologna, or Naples, he would most likely betray the peculiarities of the language and customs prevailing where he resided. If a liberally educated man, he might refer to events in the past history of Asia, Greece, and Rome, but he could not allude to the electric telegraph, steam-ship, or the crowning of Louis Napoleon as Emperor of France. And so clearly are these things understood, that scholars can determine quite accurately *where* and *when* a book was written by its style, allusions, and facts. So we find the internal evidence of the book of Daniel just what we have a right to expect. It is written in Hebrew and Chaldee, just such as a well-educated Hebrew, well acquainted with Chaldee, would use, and in just such Chaldee as prevailed in his time on the banks of the Euphrates, but such as did not prevail before nor since, nor at any other place. This is precisely one of the arguments which prove the genuineness and authenticity of the New Testament; namely, we find the language of Matthew, John, Peter, and Paul, just such as their history would lead us to expect—a Syro Chaldaic Greek. The Greek of the New Testament is not the Greek of Homer nor of Xenophon, nor is it the Greek of Chrysostom nor Athanasius. The New Testament is written in the language that prevailed among the Jews in their own country in the age of the Cæsars—a language that never prevailed before, and did not prevail after the destruction of Jerusalem, and a language that never existed any where, as a living tongue, but in Judea—a language, which, indeed, none but Jews under Greek-Roman emperors would have used. There is, then, in this fact strong presumptive proof that the New Testament was written by the men, and at the time, and in the country that we claim for its authors, and that its authors were, as they profess to have been, inspired by the Holy Spirit to write as they did. The same argument avails for Daniel.

Possibly there may be those who are saying in their hearts, you are dwelling too long on the introductory part of the series—we want to get at once to the dreams, and the image of gold, and the lions' den. *Why prove to us what we already receive as true?* True, you believe the Scriptures, and it is a great blessing that your minds are not tainted with the poison of infidelity. But there are many precious young men in all our cities who are not so fortunate as you are in this respect. They have not been so well educated, or have been thrown into unfavorable circumstances, or have been led astray by wicked companions. And even you will find yourselves sometimes in nests of Infidels, who will taunt, and jeer, and scoff at the simplicity of those that believe in the Bible. Is it not well, then, to have you armed for such emergencies? The boldness of our age, the exigencies of our times, demand thorough conviction of the truth of what we profess. It is both reasonable and scriptural that I should endeavor to make you intelligent, and able to give a reason for the faith that is in you. As we cannot live this year upon the provisions consumed last year, so it is well to ply the mind and conscience day by day with evidences of spiritual realities. You may be convinced in your hearts—and nothing is so convincing that the Bible is really the Word of God, as an inward, experimental knowledge of its precious teachings applied to ourselves—and nothing is so well calculated to convince one of the truth of the Bible as the honest, prayerful, regular waiting upon a minister of the Gospel, who expounds divine truth from his own knowledge of its preciousness. But you will need as you go your way through the world, not only what will convince your own hearts that the Bible is from God, but you need to be so well rooted, and established, and furnished, that you may be able to convince others also. It is most important to have money with your banker; but you will lose many little comforts and many solid advantages if you have not a little change in your pockets. I found, in traveling in the East, that the circular notes of our countryman, banker in London (Mr. Peabody,) were generally, and among civilized people, even better than French or British gold; yet it was exceedingly convenient to be able to save ten per cent. commission and exchange from an Egyptian or Asiatic banker by having a little ready money on hand. So it is most important to have deep convictions in your own soul—a bank of faith at communion seasons and in the solemn assemblies of Sabbath congregations; but it is not less valuable, in this strange railroad and lightning-speed world, and amid its multitudinous excitements, and amid its strange mixture of society, to have a little ready argument which you can employ—a little mother wit, that you may answer therewith a fool according to his folly. Religion is not a thing to hang up at the church door or in an antiquarian hall, along with the armor of past ages. It is not to be left in the vestry as a clergyman does his gown, to be put on only on Sabbath. True religion is a cosmopolite. It is to be seen on our highways and in our market-places, and should be honored in our halls of science, commerce, and justice.

In concluding this discourse, remember that the grand distinctive feature throughout the whole book of Daniel is to depress all that is *human*, and unfold and lift up the glory of all that is *divine*. The great object seems every where to be to make man feel what the late Mr. Webster considered the greatest thought he ever had in his mind—*man's personal responsibility to God.* It is regarded as an evidence of an able address to a jury by an attorney, that he lodges in their bosoms the conviction he desires for his client; so it is a good sermon that converts the hearer—that places the creature in the dust, and exalts God upon his throne. If, then, the book of Daniel humbles man, and exalts the Creator and the Redeemer of man, it must be in keeping with the Gospel of Christ. In reading the book of Daniel, we see kingdoms, and monarchs, and statesmen—their councils, their armies, their great men, their magnificence and glory, as the dust of the balance, and GOD ALONE IS GREAT. Throughout the book we have these two grand ideas developed; man, even the mightiest of men, are poor, frail, short-lived, guilty, miserable; and God is wise, and good, omnipotent, supreme, and glorious.

In this, as in every portion of the Word of God, we find great saving truths. "Amid the foliage of prophesy—amid the flowers of poetry—in the details of biography, and in the long annals of national or universal history, truths profitable, or refreshing, or sanctifying to the soul, flash forth continually. God in providence never omits to feed the minutest insect in his provision for the greatest and the most important of created intelligences."* In his Word there is living bread for the soul of the humblest, as well as warning, and instruction, and reproof, for kings, and presidents, and nations. In the pages of the prophets, as truly, if not as fully as in the pages of the evangelists, such truths are written as unfold to us our true condition as sinners, and our hope of pardon and eternal life. The whole Bible is an intensely practical book. Christianity is an intensely practical thing. It is the one thing needful for all men. It is the great want of the human soul. It is not a dead, lifeless

* Dr. Cumming's Preface to Daniel.

body; but a living, earnest, expansive, heartfelt, progressive thing. Man has sinned, and therefore he suffers. Sin has entered our world, and death by sin. The conscience, intellect, and heart of man—all is morally diseased. The great question then is, How can we escape the consequence of sin? This question the Bible answers promptly and fully. Jehovah laid upon His Son our iniquities; He made Him who knew no sin to be sin for us, that we might become the righteousness of God in Him. The moment man sinned Jesus stood between the living and the dead—He offered himself as a victim in our room and stead, and was accepted. Being without sin, and exempt from obligations of his own, he had a right to assume our place. We as sinners were without holiness and without strength. No man can save himself. All the popes, bishops, prelates, poets, philosophers, and councils in Christendom can no more change the heart of man than they can create a fixed star, or soar to the sun. They can no more pay the price of human redemption than they can create a universe. Yet it is true that the history of the world without God is nothing but a history of successive efforts and successive failures to regenerate and save itself without Christ. What are all the thousand smoking altars, and the ten thousand bleeding victims of heathenism, rude and refined, ancient and modern, but so many efforts of man to redeem and save his own soul? What is Pantheism, but man's vain effort to regenerate man, and perfect his character and happiness without Christ? What are Popery and Puseyism but priestly and abortive efforts to regenerate man without Christ? Aristides, Socrates, Plato, Alfred, and other names of the like character are not types of humanity. They are the exceptions to the general character and condition of our race—they are the few tall trees seen from a distance; while beneath and around them we find here and there, and everywhere, the pestilential swamp, and all manner of vile and worthless things. The mass of terrible corruption which lies and festers in the mass of the heathen population of our globe may be estimated from the first chapter of Romans, and from the lanes, and alleys, and dens, and Bridewells, and Tombs of the large cities of the earth. The lower stratum of society is not a basket of flowers, but a terrible reality that calls for help. It were painful enough to see the ancient heathen worshiping Mars, a sort of cannibal, who drank the blood of his victims; Mercury, who was a thief; and Jupiter, who was a monster. But it is more painful to see the depravity, corruption, and wretchedness of modern times—to see the Gospel, itself pure, precious and Godlike in all its influences, perverted and made the patron of cruelty and persecution—made to set up inquisitions for the murder of saints, for the plunder of widows, and its ministers spies of the police, through the Confessional, for the suppression of freedom and the enslavement of mankind. It is more painful still to see young men of the nineteenth century, enjoying the blessings of Christianity, surrounded and urged by every honorable inducement to noble conduct, throw away all their privileges, and destroy themselves by indolence or dissipation, or by following false principles. In the very outset of life, my young friends, you feel your need of religion; you feel your need of a guide and protector. Let this holy Volume be your guide, and God your protector. The Gospel is not a mere directory nor rule—it is a *prescription also.* It directs the living and healthy, and it also cures the diseased, and gives life to the dead. Calvary is not a mere composite of Sinai. It is the spot on which the Son of man was lifted up, and the Son of God in human nature died—died for us! God gave his Son for us. The great Redeemer left the robes of majesty and beauty for the vile refuse garment that Pilate cast upon his shoulders. He left the admiration of angels for the execration of the mob. He exchanged a diadem of glory for a wreath of thorns—and why? It was for us—that our ruined souls might be redeemed, and live forever with God and holy angels.

It is not enough, then, that you are intelligent, and honest, and industrious, and high-minded—you must have a personal interest in the salvation of the Cross. You must receive Christ, and rest upon Him alone for salvation, as He is offered in the Gospel. The Gospel is the power of God unto salvation to every one that believeth. And when it shall prevail over our globe, then there will be an end to all bitterness and pride, sectarianism, selfishness, and vain-glory—to all insubordination among subjects, and to all despotism on the part of rulers. The great rainbow of the covenant, that started from the cross and vaulted into the sky from Jerusalem, and now sweeps over the throne of Jehovah, shall complete its orbit, and rest again on the ground, and Christ shall reign supreme over all nations and people. It is for you now to choose the Lord's side and be found with his conquering hosts, or by refusing to accept of his mercy, make your everlasting destruction sure. The old year is gone and is now numbered with your earliest years.* Passion's fervid hopes and fears for another year are gone.

> "The dream of youth is broken—
> Gone are the voices once so sweet;
> Friends too dear shall never meet—
> Treasures of the heart's young day,
> Vain delusions—pass away;
> All earthly things are flying."

Heaven only is sure. FLY NOW TO CHRIST AND LIVE FOREVER. Amen.

* Delivered at the beginning of the year 1853.

LECTURE III.

DANIEL AS A MAN—A MODEL.

On Dan., i.

Affairs in Judea.—Shinar.—Three Carryings-away to Babylon.—Sketch of Daniel's History and Character.—Why refused King's Fare.—Benefits of early Education.—Ashpenaz a cunning Politician.—Melzar a sharp Contractor.—The Experiment.—Attainments of Daniel and his Friends.—A Model for his Intelligence, high Bearing, and Steadfastness in his Religion.—King's Efforts to seduce him all fail.—Reflections. 1. Appreciate a good Education.—Lord Dartmouth.—Webster's Eulogy. 2. Duty of immediate personal Piety.—Solemn Questionings.

READ verses 1–5.

From 2 Kings, xxiii., 34–36, we learn that Jehoiakim was raised to the throne of Judah by Pharaoh-Necho, King of Egypt. He continued tributary to Egypt three years, but in his fourth year, which was the first year of the reign of Nebuchadnezzar, a great battle was fought near the Euphrates between the Egyptian and Babylonian kings, and the Egyptian army was defeated. This victory placed all Syria under the Chaldean government; and thus Jehoiakim, who had been tributary to Egypt, now became a vassal of the King of Babylon. See also, Jer., xxv., 1, and xlvi., 2; 2 Kings, xxiv., 1.

After three years, the King of Judah rebelled against the King of Babylon, who came against Jerusalem, and besieged and took it, as soon as his engagements with other wars allowed him to direct his attention to Jewish affairs. *The land of Shinar* was the ancient name of

Babylon. *And brought the vessels into the treasures of his god.* His god was Bel, the tutelar guardian of the Babylonish empire. To carry away the richest and finest vessels of the temple of a conquered people was a common custom among conquerors. What, however, was necessary to carry on the worship of Jehovah, he left. The King of Babylon did not attempt to alter the civil or religious constitution of the land. He left Jehoiakim on the throne, and the religion of his God in His temple. He only laid the land under tribute.

The Chaldeans carried away the vessels of the Lord's house three different times. 1. In the war spoken of in the text. 2. In the taking of Jerusalem, a few months after.—See 2 Kings, xxiv., 13. 3. Eleven years after this, when Zedekiah was king in Jerusalem, and when the temple and city were destroyed. 2 Kings, xxv., 8–15.

Among the captives of the *children of Israel* we find Daniel and his three friends. *They were of the king's seed and of the princes.* Various opinions have been expressed as to Daniel's age when he was carried to Babylon. The term applied to him and his friends (יְלָדִים) means boys, lads, or youths. We are in the habit, after the manner of the Apocrypha, of speaking of the three Hebrew *children*, but without any authority. The term should be considered as signifying young men, in this place. Ignatius thinks Daniel was twelve years of age when he was carried to Babylon. Chrysostom says he was eighteen. These and similar statements of the Fathers are but guesses. They are probably, however, near the truth. Daniel and his friends were given in charge to Ashpenaz, the master courtier of the Chaldean conqueror, to be fed and educated, so that in time they might become personal waiters and attendants of the monarch. It is known that it was the usual custom of Oriental monarchs to prepare for themselves active and sprightly waiters from the highest classes of society, and that these waiters were usually put in training at about fourteen years of age. The history also renders it probable that Daniel was of regal descent, of the royal family of David. You perceive that he and his three friends are said, in the 3d verse, to have been "of the king's seed and of the princes." They were drawn from the upper classes of society at Jerusalem, and retained in Babylon as *hostages*, to secure the quiet and submission of the Jewish king and his nobles in their tributary condition. Daniel's good education, fine intelligence, amiability of manners, his knowledge of his own language and nation, and the rapidity with which he acquired a knowledge of the Chaldee tongue and customs, soon rendered him a person of distinction at court. When, by the interpretation of the king's dream, he is raised to be the head of the Magi, and of all the learned men in the kingdom, he does not forget his old friends, nor despise the religion of his fathers. He had nothing of the spirit of jealousy and self-exaltation. He made his friends participators in the honors and emoluments that he gained by being placed over the Magi and astrologers of Babylon. He has, moreover, perpetuated the memory of his friends as among the noblest of martyrs for truth that stand recorded on the pages of sacred history. The history which he has given of his three pious and distinguished companions in the 3d chapter consigns them to the heartfelt applause and perpetual remembrance and admiration of mankind.

A second dream of the king is the occasion of his being again raised to honor, which he seems to have retained during the interregnum. Next we find Belshazzar on the throne, and, in the midst of his Bacchanalian tumult, heathenish impiety, and contempt, he is alarmed by the mysterious hand-writing on the wall; and when his Magi and astrologers were summoned in vain to give him the interpretation, his mother tells him what Daniel had done in the days of Nebuchadnezzar. Daniel is forthwith sent for, and large promises of reward are made to him, in case he should read and explain the writing on the wall. He did so; and the explanation was, that the death of the king, and the extinction of his dynasty, was near at hand. And in that very night Cyrus made himself master of the city, and the king was slain. Belshazzar, however, complied with his promise. Daniel was clothed with most costly decorations, and made the third ruler in the kingdom. But this honor lasted only an hour. The prophet's elevation was followed by the fall of the kingdom, the king's death, and the extinction of his dynasty. Darius the Mede now assumed the throne of Babylon; and Daniel's talents and honors so disturbed his companions, that they succeeded in having him cast into the lions' den for his steadfastness in his religion. Jehovah did not forsake his servant, but sent his angel to heep Daniel in safety, even among the hungry lions. When the king discovers this, he takes Daniel out and casts his persecutors into the den, and they were instantly torn in pieces. Of his visions I shall not here speak.

He lived to be upwards of eighty-four years of age. And, as his name is not found among those Jews who returned to Palestine after the proclamation of Cyrus, it is probable that his age, and perhaps his office, prevented him from leaving Babylon. He probably died in Chaldea. His tomb, it is said, has been discovered at Shushan. Never was there raised up a truer patriot, a warmer and more faithful and constant friend than Daniel. His visions close with kind and comforting assurances. It has been beautifully suggested that this was appropriate. He needed them. His life had been one of care and labor, study and prayer. His bosom had beat so high and so long with patriotic and devotional feeling, that now, when the liberation of his countrymen was at hand, it was very trying for him to bear up under the future miseries and vexations which, *as a prophet*, he saw were coming on his nation. It was fitting, therefore, that his last days should be cheered with strong faith and personal assurance of Divine favor. Daniel's character is pre-eminently worthy of our attention. His life was not only conspicuous, but singular and difficult. A Hebrew—a Hebrew prophet—and yet prime minister at a heathen court, which then governed the world; and yet never did he fail in his duties, either as a statesman or as a true disciple of Moses. Amid all the luxury, and splendor, and honors of the Babylonish court, he preserved an incorruptible integrity and spirituality of character. The length of time that he acted as prime minister of state is proof of the ability and fidelity with which he discharged the duties of his high station. The whole of his life presents in high relief the fearlessness of his spirit and the fervor of his heart. He ever cherished humble views of himself, but the warmest emotions of patriotism toward his country. What is more pathetic and powerful than his intercessions in behalf of his suffering countrymen! What more heroic than his ever life-long simple obedience to and trust in his God! Such is a summary of the life and character of Daniel, the prime minister, and the prophet of Jehovah. I desire you to take him as a model. He is eminently worthy of your profound study and earnest efforts.

Read from the eighth to the sixteenth verse.

Why did he firmly refuse to eat of the king's meat or drink of the king's wine? The temptation to do so was certainly very strong. Did he refuse because it was sinful in itself to eat meat and drink wine, or to eat and drink with a king? Did he refuse because he had no taste for meat and wine, like other young men? His refusal was doubtless for other reasons.

1. The Chaldeans probably ate such unclean beasts as hares, swine, and the like animals, which were not lawful for a Jew to eat. 2. The Chaldeans, as the heathen generally did, and do still, probably ate animals which had been strangled, or not properly cleansed of their blood. According to the law of Moses, a Jew could not eat of such flesh. 3. It was a heathen custom to offer the animals that were eaten first as victims to their gods. Among the Romans these oblations were called *libamina.* The provisions then set apart for Daniel and his friends, coming from the king's table after this dedication to idols, were to be looked upon as offerings to heathen deities, and could not, therefore, be eaten by them, either as

Jews or as worshipers of the only true God. The case was plain. The King of Babylon was in the habit of doing just what is equivalent to our "asking a blessing at table." And in "saying his grace," he took a portion of his food and of his wine and offered them to his idol before he tasted it himself. This offering consecrated the whole of his subsistence to his god. Daniel and his friends could not participate in such worship to idols. They could not thus deny their country and the religion of their parents. They were prepared to run all hazards, rather than appear to compromise themselves with heathenism. In our velvet and morphine churches and latitudinarian age, it may seem difficult to decide the course of action. In flying from Charybdis we fear to fall upon Scylla. But Daniel did not hesitate. He could not comply with the wishes of the great king, for, by so doing, he should offend his God. But will he not offend so mighty a monarch, whose servant, captive, and slave he is, and give up all hope of advancement, for the sake of his religion? And might he not excuse himself by saying, this has an air of exclusiveness and of self-righteous arrogance about it—I do not like to set myself up as too good to eat of the king's provisions? But it was not thus Daniel reasoned. The case seems scarcely to have admitted of debate in his mind. *He purposed in his heart that he would not defile himself with the portion of the king's meat, nor with the wine which he drank.* Young, high-minded, sensitive, and well bred as these Hebrew youths were, they shrunk not from the task, odious as it seemed to be, of adhering with unwavering steadfastness to their religion. Daniel was the leader in this matter; and God had given him peculiar fitness for the trial (verse 9.) Their conscientious scruples were supported by their education, and the favor of the God whom they served. The result would have been very different if these young men had not received a religious education. But, happily for them, they had not been brought up in public "godless" schools, where there was no regard for God, and none for his Word. They had not been educated in such schools as the Socialists and Infidels of our day would establish, where Pantheism and Atheism are either taught directly, or allowed to occupy the young mind by withholding from it the knowledge of the true God. On the contrary, they had been brought up—though in a wicked, apostate age of their country—still they had been brought up at their fathers' home to a knowledge of the God of Abraham, and the writings of Moses and the early prophets. Their early education was, under God, the means of their preservation. "The deep engraving of truth upon the heart of the young is never altogether effaced. Those impressions of divine truth that are made on our hearts in youth often emerge in after years with all the freshness and the beauty of yesterday! Silenced they may be, overshadowed they may be, but they are rarely extinguished."—*Dr. Cumming.*

The goodness of God is seen in their education, and in bringing to bear upon its impressions such a train of circumstances as brought forth its fruit. The characters of Ashpenaz and Melzar, and their respective conditions, concur in allowing an experiment that resulted triumphantly.

Daniel, seeing at once the necessity of action, determines to follow the plainest, strictest, most honest, boldest mode of proceeding, as, in the end, the safest and the best. He goes, therefore, at once to head-quarters, to Ashpenaz, who has already conceived favorable impressions of him. The answer of this high functionary is both kind and cautious. It amounts to this, that he would willingly grant his request, if he could; but he was afraid to do so. He was appointed by the king to take care of these youths, and to prepare them for his service in a given time. The king had also appointed the fare, and, if the result desired was not attained, his head was in peril, and especially if it should appear that the failure was owing to his not having strictly obeyed orders. Daniel at once saw how the matter stood. He saw that Ashpenaz was an old politician. This great man, like many of his successors in high places, was willing enough to share any advantage that might accrue from disobedience of orders, but not willing to take the responsibility. He would wink at any thing a subordinate might do in the matter, who chose to risk his head. Daniel goes next, therefore, to *Melzar*, who was either the master of the boarding-house where the young men were served, or he was an officer under Ashpenaz, whose duty it was to attend to the food, clothing, &c., of the royal captives. As in Turkish seraglios, so it seems to have been the custom at Babylon, that every three or four lads should have one eunuch to take care of them; and Daniel, now understanding how the matter stood, makes his address accordingly. He proposed they should make an experiment of ten days, and, if they did not look worse, then the experiment was to be continued. To this Melzar consented. One reason of his consenting, no doubt, was, that he could keep the young men on pulse and water cheaper than on such fare as the king provided, and he could abstract and sell the king's portions sent to the young Hebrews, and thereby drive a profitable speculation; for it is to be observed, they did not demand to be fed on Hebrew luxuries, such as they might have used without doing violence to their religious scruples. They only asked for the simplest, cheapest, and most easily-prepared diet. And the result of the experiment was triumphant. See 15th and 16th verses. *Pulse* means grain, such as barley, wheat, rye, peas.

A vegetable diet may have been healthful, and have had a tendency to produce a fine complexion and pleasant countenance; yet, as this spare diet was chosen from conscientious scruples, no doubt God gave them his special blessing. They were sincere and faithful in their adherence to religious principle, and God rewarded them. They became not only more handsome than the other lads, but grew more comely than they themselves had been before; and in the examination at the *end of the days*, (*i. e.*, of the three years,) they are found fit to stand before the king. It seems, from verses 18--21, that of all the noble captives from different nations, only four were wanted to stand before the king, and that Daniel and his companions were found ten times better than all the magicians and astrologers that were in all his realm.

The learning and the tongue of the Chaldeans. The Chaldeans were then more renowned for learning and wisdom than the Egyptians. In three years Daniel became as celebrated in the Chaldean court for his knowledge of their science and literature as for his deep piety. Even in his own lifetime his reputation for wisdom became a proverb. *Thou are wiser than Daniel.* Ezekiel and Daniel are ranked with Noah and Job for exemplary conduct. Daniel's writings give abundant evidence of his scholarship. His style is pure and correct. He wrote in Hebrew, where he delivers to us a bare narrative of events; but in *Chaldee*, where he relates the conversations which he had with the wise men and the kings. Nebuchadnezzar's edict, after Daniel had interpreted his dream concerning the great metallic image, is given in Chaldee. It is probable that the ancients knew more than we are in the habit of ascribing to them. However this may be, Daniel, being a Hebrew, was brought up to a knowledge of the arts, customs, laws, and religion of his nation. With him science was associated with religion, and the more he knew of science and literature, of men and things, under the control of religion, the greater were his advantages of gaining influence. And so it should ever be. Learning should be the handmaid of devotion. The spoils of Egypt should beautify the temple of Salem.

Another feature of Daniel's circumstances at this time, that makes his steadfastness to his country and his country's God the more worthy of perpetual remembrance, is, that he was of noble, if not of royal birth.

He was of the royal tribe of Judah. It is true, not *many* mighty, not *many* noble are called, but some are. Piety has friends among the friends of science and learning. Some men of the highest rank and the most gigantic intellect have been and are sincere believers in the Gospel. The prophets of the Old Testament and the apostles of the New Testament were of different callings and rank in society. David was a shepherd-boy; Isaiah and Daniel were of the royal tribe; Amos was a herdsman; Zechariah, a captive from Babylon; Elisha was a plowman; Matthew was a fisherman; Luke a physician; and Paul a learned man. There is a sense in which rank and wealth, power and station, do not affect the value of the soul. In the Gospel, every soul is regarded as of transcendent worth; still, it is true that some men are in positions that render their piety of more value to the world than others.

The King of Babylon desired to detach Daniel from his Hebrew associations, and to unteach him his Christianity, and for this purpose he not only required him to eat from his table, but changed his name. The good education and family religion of Daniel and his three friends were sadly in the way of the king's purpose. He had to pull down a noble structure before he could begin to build. He had to root out what tradition and parental training had implanted, before he could hope to make them heathens like himself. Each of their names had "God" in it, and thus their names served to remind them of their religion, and, at the same time, doubtlessly annoyed the king. He had strong reasons, therefore, for changing their names; and, profiting by their example, he gave them names that were either merely civil and social, or contained an allusion actually idolatrous. Collateral history proves that such a custom did prevail in ancient Babylon.

The change of names was a mark of dominion and authority. It was customary for masters to give new names to their slaves. The same custom prevailed in Egypt; and all know that then, as now, rulers, on ascending the throne or coming into power, often assume a name different from what they had before.

Daniel signifies God is my Judge. Changed into Belteshazzar, which means, the Treasure of Bel; or, the Depository of the Secrets of Bel.

Hananiah signifies the Lord has been gracious to me; or, he to whom the Lord is gracious. Changed into *Shadrach*, a Chaldee word, which has been variously understood. The chief meanings attached to it are: The Inspiration of the Sun; the God who is the author of evil, be propitious to us; let God be propitious to us, and preserve us from evil.

Mishael, one that comes from God. Changed into Chaldee, *Meshach*, which means one that belongs to the goddess Sheshac, a celebrated deity among the Chaldeans, mentioned by Jeremiah, xxv., 26.

Azariah signifies the Lord is my helper. This was changed into *Abednego*, which means the servant of Nego, who was one of their divinities; which was the Chaldee name for the sun, or the morning star.

As the king did not like their religion, he sought, by heathenizing their names, to heathenize their hearts.

It may be true, as the poet says, that "A rose by any other name would smell as sweet"—still there is much in a name. A happy *soubriquet* may make a president. Abstractedly and logically, there may be nothing in the names we give to our children, but practically it is of importance to give them such names, and to apply to them, as they are growing up, such epithets, as may bring to their minds high and noble examples, and give them worthy associations.

The king was delighted with Daniel's scholarship, but not with his religion. He would have Daniel's good face and deep science in his court, but not his piety. And so it is now with many people. They hear, like Herod, gladly, but do not obey. They are pleased with the Gospel, but do not bring forth fruits meet for repentance. They like Christianity for its decencies, but do not like the urgency of repentance.

In changing the young Hebrews' names, the king, however, as we have seen, did not yet get rid of their religion. Their creed and character remained the same. It is true, they seem not to have resisted their new appellatives. They quietly submitted to be called by heathen names, because this was a matter they could not control. And so Christians have in all ages patiently submitted to the reproach of the world, and have borne them joyfully. There are several *great principles* raised from the history of Daniel and his companions, which I shall reserve for the next discourse, accommodating the history before us to the DUTY AND MEANS OF SELF-IMPROVEMENT, and apply it to the design of the young men's Christian Association, at whose request and in whose behalf it will, God permitting, be delivered.

With two reflections I close:

I. From the example before us, we should learn to appreciate a Christian education. These young men of the best families of Jerusalem were brought up to know and serve the God of their fathers. And they did not disgrace their education. As they had been carefully brought up in the institutions of Moses, so they continued to regulate their conduct by them, even in the court of a heathen king, where they were prisoners and slaves. They were not ashamed to acknowledge their principles. An incident of Lord Dartmouth is related that is worthy of being remembered by young men from home. You know that one of our New England colleges is named after him. He gave a large sum of money to endow it. A fine picture of him still graces one of its halls. He was a young English nobleman, rich, and handsome, and accomplished; but he had something far better than all these things. He was sincerely pious; "he loved and honored his Saviour; and although, at the time when he lived, it was the fashion to mock at serious things, he was never ashamed of his religion. The king and some noblemen agreed, on one occasion, to take an early morning ride. They waited a few minutes for Lord Dartmouth. On his arrival, one of the company seemed disposed to call him to account for his tardiness. '*I have learned to wait upon the King of kings before I wait upon my earthly sovereign,' was Lord Dartmouth's answer. No matter what he had to do, or who wanted him, reading the Bible and secret prayer were duties which he never put off.*" Remember his example, and be faithful to God, as he was.

Mr. Webster, in closing a beautiful eulogy upon a young gentleman of the bar, who had recently died, said: "Gentlemen, and he did what I fear many of us have not done—he achieved a religious character."

II. The other point that I would have you seriously consider IS THE DUTY OF BEING PIOUS NOW. Responsibility and eternity stand connected with the flight of time. Our present life gives coloring to our whole future eternity. Like a mighty river, time flows on noiselessly in its course, and we approach nearer and nearer to the judgment-seat.

> "'Tis greatly wise to talk with our past hours,
> And ask them what account they bore to heaven."

Many of your days are past—your days of infancy, of childhood, and early youth. Many days of instruction, too, are past. Days when God's voice was heard—days of conviction, when His Spirit strove with you—when your companions united with the Church—days, too, of judgment, when His arm was stretched out to you in affliction and warning—and what has been the result? Has your instruction produced conviction, and your conviction resulted in conversion? Have you come to Christ as a poor sinner, and received forgiveness? The weeks, months, and Sabbaths of another year are gone! What is the net result or gain to your soul of all your past years? Does your heart—does the closet, the family, the Church—your every sphere of duty, show that you have been *doers* of the Word, and not *hearers* only? During the past year, some of you have had days of prosperity—when new relationships were formed, and new schemes of business were brought to maturity, and new hopes were fulfilled. These days are gone, and their remembrance is now like a pleasing vision. But were the *causes* and *measures* of your prosperity such as God approves? Did holy angels sympathize with you in your pleasures and pursuits?

Perhaps, my dear friend, your review of the past year is filled with sorrows. You may have had stroke upon stroke. Days of pain, of losses, of bereavement, of disappointment, may have filled up the year. Well, they too are gone, and will return no more. And did the Saviour support you by his power? cheer you with his promise? animate you by his own bright example and glorious victories? Then are you prepared to bless Him for the days of your sorrow. Then you are living in the cheerful expectation that the day will soon come when it shall be found that your trials and sorrows were the seeds of an abundant harvest of joy. Or is the storm still beating upon you? Are the heavens still dark around you? Then, while you humble yourself under the mighty hand of God, He will exalt you in due time. Ask of the days that are past where happiness is to be found. Time past is a chronicle and an oracle. Look into this chronicle and see, ask this oracle and know. Is sin profitable? Is there a single instance of one, registered in the hoary chronicles of the past, who hardened himself against his God and prospered? Hark! The answer is prompt and unequivocal, "The way of transgressors is hard." "The wages of sin is death." Millions of the votaries of fashion, of the slaves of Mammon, and of the worshipers of Fame, have tried to find happiness apart from God, but all have failed. It is a delusion to seek happiness in the things of the world. It is a scheme of the Evil One to allure souls down to eternal death. But does the oracle and chronicler of the mighty past show aught against the goodness of God? NOTHING. Not a syllable. No sincere penitent has ever been repulsed—no true mourner was ever sent away without comfort—no praying soul rejected—no trusting believer forsaken.

Man's manner of life describes his character, and foretells his end. Young man, immortal you are—you must live when time is dead. Answer, then, in the sight of God and in prospect of eternity, What is your course of life? on what is your heart set? about what have you been most anxious? What do you labor most to possess? Which has been esteemed most in your estimation—the favor of God and the pardon of sin, or the pleasures of this world and the possession of riches? *By your soul's preference and pursuit is your state for eternity to be judged.* Answer these questions honestly to yourselves, and let not time's oracle speak in vain. Pray, then, with the pious poet:

"Teach me, O thou sacred Power,
Every pulse, and every hour,
At Thy hallowed cross to lie,
On Thy promise to rely!"

LECTURE IV.

PRINCIPLES AND LESSONS FROM THE EUPHRATES.*

On Dan. i.

Young Men's Christian Association: its Subjects.—Dangers of Young Men in Cities.—Lessons from the Euphrates to the Mississippi.—Young Hebrews in Exile at Babylon teaching young Men from home at New Orleans: 1. *To adhere to right Principles.* 2. *That a Man is no Loser for maintaining right Principles.—True Expediency.—Use of Public Lecturing.* 3. *Decided, avowed religious Principles.—General Cass's Testimony.—True Piety eminently Social.—Regular Church-going.*

The Rev. Dr. Scott read the first chapter of Daniel, and then said:

Respected Hearers,—The vigilance of the Argus-eyed daily prints of the city have already informed you of the formation of the "New Orleans Young Men's Christian Association," and that it is, moreover, at their request that I have the honor of delivering before you this evening their opening address, which, I am happy to be informed, is to be followed by addresses from other gentlemen of acknowledged eloquence and ability. I have read the first chapter of Daniel in the introductory portion of the services this evening, for two reasons: 1st, because Daniel is the subject of a series of discourses to young men now in the course of delivery from this pulpit on

* Delivered as the opening address before the Young Men's Christian Association of New Orleans, Sunday evening, January 16, 1853. Published by the unanimous request of the Association. The occasion of this Lecture will explain how it is that there are some repetitions of ideas found in the preceding.

Sabbath evenings, and it were desirable not to interrupt wholly this series. 2dly, because, if I were at perfect liberty to select from the whole Bible, I do not know that I could find any other portion more suggestive of appropriate reflections for the opening address of this laudable Association. The first article of the constitution declares that the object of this Association "is the mental, moral, and religious improvement of young men." "We aim," say they in their address to the public, "so far as is in our power, to counteract bad example, to throw around our young men an elevating moral influence, and, by so doing, to cherish their earlier religious and moral impressions, and thus continually incite them to diligence in well-doing."

The duty, nature, and means of self-improvement and of mutual protection against the perils of a city life is, therefore, the theme which I shall attempt to illustrate from the example of Daniel and his friends in Babylon, and apply to the condition of young men in our large towns and cities, and to the design of this association. And,

I. *As to the subjects of this Association.*—They are young men, upon whom are concentrated the hopes and prayers of the good and patriotic throughout the land. No man who looks understandingly at the interests of mankind, in families, cities, churches, or states, can fail to see that the enlightened, liberal, and Christian education of the young is the fountain-head of their well-being. The testimony of many of the ablest and best men of our age and of all past ages, the sorrowful confessions of many mourning parents, as well as my own deep convictions on the subject, have made me believe that a large portion of Christian effort should be directed toward the right moral training of the young. And there are but few cities in the world where the importance of the virtuous character of young men is a subject of greater and more wide-spread interest than in this city. This is apparent at once from the greatness of their number among us, and from the commercial importance and relative position of this city to our country and the world.

Under this conviction, I may be excused in saying that I have felt it to be my duty and privilege to give my Sabbath evenings, during the winter and spring season, for more than ten years past, to the delivery of discourses to young men.

The pious Baxter says that in Kidderminster, England, where God most blessed his labors, "my first and greatest success was upon the youth. And when God, in a most marvelous way of divine mercy, had touched the hearts of young men and girls with a love of goodness and delightful obedience to the truth, the parents and grandparents, who had grown old in an ignorant, worldly state, did many of them fall into a liking and love of piety, induced by the love of their children, whom they perceived to be made by it much wiser and better, and more dutiful to them." (Works, vol. xv., p. 299.)

But aside from a merely religious view of the subject, no one that has passed through the trials of early life, especially away from home, and remembers its hopes and fears, its discouragements and success, its joys and sorrows, can think of young men coming to a strange city and entering on the same field of action, of struggle, of success or disappointment, as they did, without the deepest sympathy.

The young men, Mr. President and gentlemen of this Association, whom you seek to reach with your kind offices, are not the ordinary and common youth of the country. Those that forego the joys of home, and the cheering hearth of the paternal roof, and enter into the fierce struggles of city life, are the more excitable, the more ambitious, more able and determined youth of the country;* and their danger in a great city, where they must meet with great excitements and sensual allurements is in proportion to their own excitable and ambitious temperament. While the less enterprising are content to remain at home and grow old under the trees of their native village, or within sight of the village steeple, the more bold and ambitious seek to make their way abroad to honor and wealth. And as soon as they enter a great city, they encounter the competition of the most ambitious and hardy spirits of an enterprising country, who have got positions in the field before them. The rapacity of the avaricious, the temptations of the pleasure-offering seductions, the insolence of the proud and successful, and the indifference of the heartless, make the world they enter into very different from the one they have left at home. Removed far from parental counsels and the sweet influence of brothers and sisters, they are plunged at once into a mass of human beings who know them not, and care only to know them so far as

* See this point beautifully and strongly presented in Mr. Daniel Lord's address before the Young Men's Christian Association in New York.

their own selfish purposes may be served by their acquaintance. It is such young men your noble Association proposes to take by the hand, and point to a suitable boarding-house, and a reading-room and Christian associates, whose examples may keep alive in them the inner life they have brought from home, but which is in danger of being smothered to death by the threatening masses of a great city, where a sense of personal identity and responsibility may be so easily lost. And when your kindness has given them a table and a pillow, friends and books, and a place to worship their God, you propose to help them to honorable employment. In the fierce competition of mercantile and professional life you have the best opportunities of knowing where situations are to be had, and by your acquaintance with young men seeking employment, will be able to point out to them such situations as they are fitted to fill; and thus you may do very great service both to heads of business houses and to the young men themselves.

II. The duty of self-improvement is apparent from the faculties, gifts, and opportunities bestowed upon us by our Creator, and from the duties required of us; and the duty of mutual assistance in the work of "mental, moral, and religious improvement" is obvious from our social and dependent nature, from the constitution of society, and from the express teachings of our holy religion. This part of our theme there is not, however, time to dwell upon. The means for accomplishing the objects of this Association call for more extended remarks. The end in view by you, young gentlemen, is substantially the same that was desired and gained by Daniel and his companions, namely, honor and happiness. What, then, did they do which you may imitate?

1. They scrupulously maintained the moral and religious principles that had been imparted to them in their earlier education. They made a supreme regard for the will of God their rule of conduct, even in little things. Daniel and his three friends seem to have entered the capital and palace of the proud heathen king, who was the great Napoleon of his day, just as many young men enter our cities, with full purpose of heart to preserve their integrity, and to keep their soul undefiled from the various temptations which, in such a place as Babylon, there was every reason to fear would assail them. They probably thought on these things as they were marched over the weary sand deserts from Jerusalem to the Euphrates, and reckoned beforehand that they should have to bear hard treatment from their superiors, and the sneers, the shrugs, and taunts of their less pious companions—things that fall keenly upon the raw sensitiveness of youthful spirits; but they made up their minds that, let it cost what it might, their religion they would not abandon. And soon their trial came. They were placed in circumstances of great peril to their principles by their heathen conqueror. The strength of their attachment to the religion of their earlier youth was put to the severest test. But when tried, they were found to be pure gold; and their triumph proves that a pious education is one of the greatest blessings that can be bestowed upon youth. If you, young men, have received such an education, be profoundly thankful for it. Thank God every day of your lives for Christian and intelligent parents, who have

secured to you a liberal education, and endeavor to appreciate its advantages by using them for your own happiness, and the good of your fellow-men. You need not be told of the degradation and wretchedness of ignorance and depravity. You need not be told that the infant generation of to-day are the adult generation of to-morrow, and that what we make our children the next generation will be. The first lessons a child receives from a mother's tones and smiles are the last to fade from the memory. The lessons of divine truth taught at school may be silenced for a season, or overborne by the noise of the busy world without, yet there will come an hour when these early lessons will revive as if touched by some living influence, that makes quite distinct and fresh what was for a time invisible. The lessons Daniel had learned in his childhood home in Jerusalem were the lessons that sustained him against temptation, and guided and comforted him while a captive in Babylon.

The King of Babylon tried by all means in his power to remove all the religious impressions of these young men, and to make them adopt his religion. He did not on this occasion try to root out their principles and implant his own by persecuting them, as if the tormenting of the body could convert the soul. He tried a more rational plan. He treated them well, gave them portions from his table; he changed their names, hoping by thus erasing the name of their God, and supplying that of his own, to make them forget their early lessons and associations, but he failed. Their principles were too strongly rooted. They remained steadfast. The refusal of these young Hebrews to eat and drink of the royal portion was not grounded upon any mere fancy or whim, but on the most substantial reasons. The animals eaten were either such as were unclean according to Hebrew law, or were killed in such a way that the law of Moses forbade the Jews to eat of them; or, which alone was a sufficient reason for declining, the king's meat and wine had been dedicated to his idols, and could not, therefore, be used by these pious Hebrews without compromitting them with heathenism. Nor were they over righteous in this firm but courteous refusal. Nor were they narrow and bigoted sectarians. They were liberal Christians, but not latitudinarians. The Bible and the very nature of the human mind command us to be liberal, but forbid us to be latitudinarian. True liberality of sentiment and largeness of soul are the attributes of strength and conviction of one's own mind. But latitudinarianism gives up essential foundation principles, and says there is no difference between right and wrong—that it is equally a matter of indifference what a man believes, or whether he believes any thing at all. Dr. Cumming, of London, on this part of Daniel's life, says: "We cannot be too liberal in conceding to a brother the largest husks of his prejudices; we cannot be too strict in refusing to compromise the least living seed of vital and essential truth." (See his Lectures on Daniel.)

It is true that it was not in itself sinful to eat meat and drink wine; nor was it sinful to eat meat and drink wine with a king; but it was sinful for Hebrews to eat and drink in honor of idols. There are, however, not wanting those who say these young men were at liberty to do in Babylon as Babylon did. In London, Rome, or New

Orleans, young men must do as those around them do. Such a plea cannot be maintained with seriousuess. Duty is not a thing of latitude and longitude. It is the same thing every where. Conscience and God are the same in Paris or Constantinople, as in your New England or Scottish homes. Polar snows or tropical flowers cannot change the eternal principles of rectitude. God's laws, the will of the Supreme Creator, is the only standard of duty. This was the rule adopted by the pious Hebrew captives. To eat and drink of the royal bounty was in itself nothing; but as by so doing they would be considered as sympathizing with idolatry, and as having denied the religion of their parents, of their country, and their God, they refused, and were prepared to run all hazards rather than comply. They chose to live on pulse and water, the least nutritious of the elements of nature, rather than the dainties of the royal table; because they thought, and thought correctly, that a good conscience and the smiles of the God of heaven were of more importance than the patronage of the mightiest king that ever swayed an earthly sceptre.

It was not the mere concession of a prejudice, not the mere giving up of some little matters of denominational detail; but the surrender of principle, compromise of truth, apostacy from the true religion, that they were required to submit to. And the lesson taught us is of vast importance. It is that we must not sacrifice conscience, with its awful requirements, to any temporary or worldly convenience. We must not stifle its deep convictions to gain any temporary and evanescent advantage. We must not give up an article of our creed to gain a place. It is better to die of starvation than gain a valuable living by the sacrifice of the soul. It is a light thing to be judged of man, for He that judgeth us is God. Our Lord has said, "He that is faithful in a little is faithful also in much; and he that is unjust in a little is unjust also in much." The bearing of the history of the Hebrew youths, and of this Scripture text on our every-day life, is palpable, even among those who do not profess to be Christians. A young man of talents and business capacity may destroy all his prospects for honorable success in life by small derelictions. Dead flies will destroy the largest pot of the most precious ointment. The want of moral character will mar the prospects of the most gifted. Without stern integrity in little things, there is a want of confidence which is fatal to success. A most pernicious delusion prevails with many good people. They are waiting until they can do some great thing, and think that if a great crisis were to come, they would then have nerve to meet it, and do something triumphant. They cannot find, at present, a place large enough for the discharge of their duties. Because they cannot go as foreign missionaries, they will not labor in the Sabbath-school at home. As there is no romance in gathering in the poor and ragged to the house of God to be taught the way of virtue and godliness, they will do nothing. Instead of quietly laying one brick upon the earth, they are constantly building castles in the air; instead of discharging the plain every-day duty which they owe to God and their fellow-men, they pass life in looking for some grand occasion for the display of their virtues. They vainly think that, though they live not as useful

Christians, yet, if the crisis were to come, they would die as martyrs. They are mistaken. With them the crisis has come, and they have failed to meet it. They have failed to take the tide in human affairs that rolls on to the fortune of duties well done. The little things that are usually the turning-points of character, they have not apprehended. They have not learned that events which seem at first frivolous and unimportant, may become the "Thermopylæ of a Christian's conflict, the Marathon of a nation's being, or the turning-point of everlasting life or of everlasting death." The dazzling exploits of the great are too frequently ascribed to circumstances, and set down as something wholly beyond our reach, because we have not the same emergencies to bring us out. Although Providence may deny to you such circumstances as might concur in making you exactly like the great heroes of the world, still, in the essential elements of greatness—in purity of principle, industry and perseverance, and in life-long, fervent devotion to the welfare of their country, you may be like them. Integrity and patriotism are not patented to any sect, age, or nation. It is greatly to be regretted that young men sometimes copy the single vice of a great man, without attempting to imitate his many virtues. They are like the filthy birds of prey that fly over a whole continent of healthful beauties to light on one carcass. Their only resemblance to the great man they profess to admire is the one blemish that constituted his weakness. They can drink gin like Lord Byron, and so can an idiot or a clown; but are not worthy to unloose his shoe-latchet as to genius and intellect, energy, chivalry, and noble bearing.

The point with Daniel was to follow his conscience or his appetite; to cease to be an Israelite, or cease to be a favorite of the great King of Babylon. And his determination was soon made to make every thing give way to his religion. He would not let his religion bow to the world, but made the world bow to his religion.

2. The next lesson which the Euphrates sends to the Mississippi, and reads to us from the early life of Babylon's vizier or prime-minister and his friends is, *that a man is no loser for maintaining right principles.* The three years of training are ended. The high court of learning is held in Babylon. There are the treasures of the world. There are assembled the nobles, grandees, and sages of the kingdom. The king himself presides. And now the chief of the eunuchs introduces to the royal presence these four Hebrew youths. How fair, well formed, and intelligent they look! Minute, and searching, and repeated examination convinces the king that they are ten times wiser than his magicians and astrologers. And while only four are to be chosen out of all the captives that had been fed and instructed in knowledge and languages for the royal use, these Hebrews are the four chosen ones. An interesting story is told in Esdras, one of the Apocryphal books—which was extant before the time of Josephus, for he quotes largely from it—of the mental contests of these youths, which, as an illustration of this Oriental custom, is worthy of being read. The examination of the four Hebrews presents a noble example of the success of prudence, temperance, and a steady regard to religion. These young men did not think, because they were well born and liberally

educated, that they might therefore indulge their appetites without control. On the contrary, with heroic steadfastness they made the will of God, even in little things, their rule of conduct. And what was the result. Did Daniel lose any good thing by his firm adherence to principle? Not at all. The very reverse was the result. Daniel's faithfulness to his conscience, his allegiance to his God, his courteous but firm refusal to do what was sinful, was turned to his advantage, even in this world. Upon examination, the Hebrew youths were found, at the end of the three years, to have become more comely than they were before, and to be ten times more comely, fatter, and fairer than any of the other captive young men who had lived upon the royal bounty; and in all matters of knowledge and skill they were many times wiser than all the astrologers and magicians in the kingdom. *Them that honor God, He honors.* The result of their faithfulness to God was their promotion in the palace, and the favor of the king. What, then, is the true principle of expediency for young men? We answer, *True principle is true expediency.* Duty is the way of peace and promotion. *Seek ye first the kingdom of God and his righteousness, and all other things will be added unto you.* The success of these young men was owing to their good education, and the blessing of God upon their education and their own efforts. Josephus says of them, that "by the diet they took, they had their minds in some measure more pure and less burdened, and so fit for learning, and had their bodies in better condition for hard labor; for their bodies were not oppressed by a variety of meats, nor effeminate for the same reason, so they readily amassed all the learning of the Hebrews and the Chaldeans.' It is true, proverbially true, that he who striveth for the mastery must be temperate in all things. Temperance is highly favorable both to health and virtue, by keeping the faculties clear and strong, and in fitting men for great services, and the endurance of great sufferings.

The great commanders and the great scholars of the world have been remarkable, while young men, for temperance in eating and drinking. Nothing more effectually blasts the prospects of a young man than the soul-destroying sin of intemperance. The explanation, however, of the Jewish historian of the wonderful phenomenon does not give the whole *rationale* of the experiment made by these young Hebrews. God gave them favor with the king and his court, and God gave them skill and wisdom; yet God gave his favor to them in the most diligent use of the best means, and in the use of the best means according to His will. They were blessed in doing all they could themselves. God helps those that help themselves.

It is reasonable for young men to ask God for help in mental as well as in spiritual efforts. He is the father of the Spirit as well as the maker of the body. In the toil and business of life, and amid all its perplexing difficulties, cast yourself, therefore, upon the Lord's protection, and look to Him for counsel and guidance. It is easy for Him to "illumine what in you is dark." It is an old saying, that to pray earnestly is to study well. Many difficulties that seem insuperable would be smoothed, many blessed thoughts might be suggested, many desirable things forgotten be brought to mind again, many annoyances buried, many weak purposes strengthened, if we trusted more to God, and looked more confidently to Him for His blessing upon our earnest endeavors to know and do His will.

Josephus's solution of the wonderful improvement in his young countrymen at Babylon reminds us of many modern philosophers, who find God nowhere. In the plague, or pestilence, or epidemic, in wars or revolutions, in the facts and phenomena of science, history, creation, or providence, or even in the miracles of Holy Scripture, they see nothing but something they call laws. Their stereotyped explanation for every thing is, "such is the law of Nature." And what is Nature, and what are Nature's laws, without a Creator? The laws of Nature are nothing but the impressions of the ineffable Mind that created and governs all things made visible, or, at least, rendered palpable by their effects. I am persuaded, therefore, that the objects of this Association will be all the more readily and surely attained, as they may be sought by imitating Bible heroes, such as Joseph and Daniel; and as they may be pursued in obedience to the Divine will, as revealed to us by the prophets and apostles, holy men of old, who wrote the Scriptures as they were moved thereto by the Holy Spirit.

III. Let us, then, briefly examine in this light the objects of this Association.

One object is the social improvement and protection to those of your own age who grow up here, or come among you from a distance. The propriety of such an association for such an object is suggested at once from the acknowledged power of society and of united efforts, especially over those who are allied to one another by a similarity of enjoyments, tastes, wants, temptations, and dangers. Your object is also conservative, that is, the preservation of your more inexperienced brethren from the impositions and perils incident to a residence in a great and luxurious city. You seek to do for them here what their parents and friends have done for them in their distant homes and earlier years. Your object is also elevating. You propose to have a reading-room, and journals and books for the use of those young men who may be associated with you. You design to supply the hours of relaxation with employments that will both amuse and improve, by affording opportunities of conversation with those of your own age and pursuits, and for hearing instructive lectures from men of approved talent and sentiment.

You need not be told that public lecturings are now one of the chief means of enlightening the world. There never was a period in the history of the world when the public mind was so much occupied with printed and oral lectures as it is now. Lectures in Europe and in this country are now delivered on all sorts of subjects and by all kinds of individuals, from English lords and French peers to American husbands' better halves. Dull, trashy, flimsy, skeletonized, and superficial as many of the lectures imposed upon a patient public are, still, the great thinkers of our times, and the standard-bearers of civilization in past ages, have been, in the best sense of the term, lecturers. Not a few professional lecturers have made fortunes by their discourses. It is a strange but interesting feature of our generation, that lecturing is almost as good a profession as that of a great vocalist, and frequently far better than the law or medicine. In Europe, the men who "stand upon the forehead of the coming age are lecturers." The platform is more mighty than the University, for it is a cosmopolitan college, without test oaths, and almost without money and price. The best scholars and most influential men of the country have perfected their education in the lecture-room. The printing-press, the Protean, ubiquitous, daily newspaper press, public schools, and public lecturing from the platform and the pulpit, and from the professors of our law and medical schools, are the great educators of our age. It were, therefore, exceedingly desirable for you to secure a controlling influence in these great agencies. The Young Men's Christian Association of London have had each year, for a number of seasons, a regular course of lectures before them by some of the most distinguished men of Great Britain. The same course is pursued by the association in New York. Men of science are no longer shut up in their laboratories or observatories, or confined to their classes in the University. They now seek opportunities for imparting the knowledge of their discoveries or the results of their experiments and investigations to the public. Our age is truly remarkable for popularizing literature, science, and art. The rapidity with which winged words grow into facts, and with which the results of the profoundest theory and the most patient and thorough experiments are applied to popular use, is most astonishing. Voices that move senates, and control courts, and sway assembled masses of the "fierce democratie," are now heard imparting reason and argument, and the results of life-long study and experience, to the multitudes who, in the best days of the classic ages, were considered the "unwashed and profane," who were shut out from all sympathy with the truths of philosophy and the blessings of knowledge, and doomed forever to be hewers of wood and drawers of water. These delusions have passed away forever.

Your object is also religious—not, indeed, to proselyte or fill the mind with dead sectarian dogmas, but to encourage one another in firm adherence to religious principles, and, by your own example of a pure and holy life, preach the most powerful sermons in favor of the ways of heavenly wisdom. The object of this Association is not religious, in the cold sense of schoolmen and theologians, but religious as to the bearings of pure Christianity upon social life. It is manifestly a perversion of the Bible to make it enjoin or sanction a hermit life, as it is also a failure as to self-cultivation. The highest piety has not been found in the professed secret communion of the heart with its Maker on the tops of mountains and pillars, and in the caves and deserts of the earth. The highest piety does not consist in deserting the ordinary commerce of men, for fear of its distractions, contaminations, and dangers, but in meeting them, and maintaining one's principles immaculate.

I rejoice that you have incorporated with "mental and moral" the term "religious improvement;" for I am persuaded that every plan of social improvement, or social enjoyment and usefulness, not resting on the basis of religious principle, will be uncertain both as to its final tendencies and as to its permanency. Nothing but a sense of a personal religious accountability can give life to any scheme of human advancement. With earnestness, an aged senator (Mr. Cass,) at Washington, said, in his place, a few days since:

"I am free to confess, sir, that for myself, I rejoice at the occasion thus given to us, while pleading for the full toleration of religion, to bear our testimony on its priceless value. Independent of its connection with the human destiny hereafter, I believe the fate of republican governments is indissolubly bound up with the fate of the Christian religion, and that a people who reject its holy faith will find themselves the slaves of their own evil passions, and of arbitrary power. And I am free to acknowledge that I do not see altogether without anxiety some of the signs which are shadowed forth around us.

"A weak and sublimating imagination with some, and irregular passions with others, are producing founders and followers of strange doctrines, whose tendencies it is easier to perceive than it is to account for their origin and progress. But they will find their career and their remedy, not in legislation, but in a sound religious opinion, whether they inculcate an appeal to God by means of stocks and stones, and rappings—the latest and the most ridiculous experiment upon human credulity—or whether they seek to pervert the Scriptures to the purposes of their own libidinous passions, by destroying that safeguard of religion and social order, the institution of marriage, and, by leading lives of unrestricted intercourse, thus making proselytes to a miserable imposture, unworthy of our nature, by the temptations of unbridled lust.

"This same trial was made in Germany some three centuries ago, in a period of strange abominations, and failed. And it will fail here. Where the Word of God is free to all, no such vile doctrine can permanently establish itself."

There is no preaching like a kind and social example, no argument so effective as the exhibition of religious character in the vicissitudes of every-day life. One great reason of the failure of Christianity in not producing the effects desired upon Christendom is, that its practical nature is not acted out in the life of professed Christians. They do not constrain the world by the social contact and the free and warm intercourse of a loving heart.

True religion is not a cold, austere, forbidding, mere psalm singing, long-faced thing. It is not a mere Sunday dress, to be hung up in the vestry, as the clergyman does his gown, all the rest of the week. On the contrary, it is a thing of life, a "thing of beauty which is a joy forever." It is full of motion, grace, and unction. It holds no parley with vice. It requires severe and persevering piety, but it is intensely practical and eminently social in all its bearings. Instead of being a mere catalogue of hard names and dry propositions, it is a vital and diffusive spirit. It mingles itself not only with the inner life, but sanctifies every action of the outer life. It applies its holy teachings to all our relations, personal, domestic, and public. It is by intimate and vivid associations with men of like passions with themselves, and of like dangers, who, amid the furor of passions and the imminency of dangers, exhibit the simplicity and earnestness of Christianity, that its power is to be clearly seen.

The Bible does not tolerate a lukewarm, lopsided, segmental Christianity; but a deep, equable, and ever-flowing, circumferential, whole-bodied, whole-hearted piety, a piety that is in strong sympathy with our individuality in this up-and-down world, that seizes the soul and fastens upon it the great vitalized convictions of truth, as it flowed from the lips of the Divine Saviour, and carries them out into the parlor and the highways of life. The bearing of the examples in hand upon you, young men, is palpable. You should seek such places of residence, and such associates, and give attendance upon such ministers of the Gospel, as will most effectually assist you in maintaining correct religious principles.

You must choose for yourselves your church, and your associates, and your business; but I urge you to choose such as will be consistent with what your conscience tells you to do. Join yourselves to some Christian congregation. Be regular and punctual in your attendance upon the pulpit instruction of some servant of God. The benefits you may derive by so doing are manifold. Such a course would keep you out of the way of many temptations, and would fortify your principles and increase your respectability. Enter into no business where you are required to violate your conscience. Engage in no business where it seems to be necessary to violate the Sabbath, or to neglect the public preaching of God's Word. If the issue is made, a continuance in such and such business, and a good living, or the sacrifice of Christian duties, you must not hesitate. God is to be obeyed rather than man. Duty is ours, and God will take care of the consequences. Nothing is plainer, from the highest testimony and observation on the course of things, as well as on the philosophy of the physical constitution of men and of animals, than that by sacrificing your Sabbaths you will, in the end, be losers, even in a temporal point of view. There has yet to be produced a single instance in which true Christian principle has not been found the highest expediency.

The Bible *vade mecum* for young men is, "Fear God and keep his commandments." Make religion the great thing of your hearts and lives, and all the rest will follow in its place. "True godliness hath promise of the life that now is, as well as of that which is to come." The knowledge of our Creator is before all other things. You should study science, and observe men and things; but not science, not philosophy, not literature, not music, nor painting first, and then Christianity, but Christianity first of all. Take the knowledge of God into the school, into the University, into the learned professions, and into the encyclopedia of life, as first and last. You should not go through college, and through the world, and come to Christ last, but seek first to know him whom to know aright is eternal life.

Secular knowledge, deep and varied, we would have you all diligently seek; but we would also have you possess true piety, which will adorn, exalt, and sanctify you as students, and make you heirs of the kingdom of heaven. The first and highest study of every man is the safety of his soul. And no man ever yet gained the world by the sacrifice of his soul, though many have made this wretched experiment. Our Saviour says, "If you gain the whole world and lose your own soul, what shall it profit you?" The meaning is not that if you set out to gain the world by sacrificing your soul, you must succeed. The result is certainly, in most cases, far otherwise. Those that set out to gain the world by sacrificing the soul, in ninety-nine cases out of a hundred lose both. While, on the other hand, the man who sets out in life determined to provide first for his soul, and then pursue and enjoy the world as it may be found subservient to and consistent with his soul's salvation, finds, if not the greatest abundance of worldly things, yet far the greatest enjoyment. Pulse and water are far better with the blessing of God, than the king's meat and the king's wine without it.

Finally, let me say to you, young gentlemen of this Association, you have done nobly in beginning this enterprise. Grow not weary in your undertaking. Your high calling savors of that divine charity which is "the perfume of the blossoms of the Tree of Life." In doing good to the bodies and souls of your fellow-men—in finding situations for them, places of rest, relaxation, and improvement, and places for them to worship God, and retreats for them in sickness, and succor in temptation and want—you most nearly resemble the Son of God, who spent his life in doing good to men. And whether or not you succeed in doing all your hearts have purposed for others, still your efforts cannot fail as it regards yourself. God is a good paymaster. He gives back again with large interest, good measure, and pressed down, and shaken together, and running over. The history of Joseph and Daniel strikingly proves this. I doubt not the wise, patriotic, and good will give you their hearty co-operation. Your example and efforts will encourage a public spirit, and the exercise of social virtues, and the permanence of good laws. From your ranks a discerning public will look for statesmen, public men, and merchants of wealth, who shall be examples of social virtue and true religion. Our high places in the Church and the State must soon be filled from your numbers. And perhaps the happiest thought on your dying bed will be that you leave your mantle to some young man occupying a useful and honorable position in society, whom you took by the hand when he came a stranger to the city and helped to a situation, and led to the house of God, and by your timely aid and influence his life has become one of honor and usefulness. Such a result may well be said to be a monument in your memory that will fade last on earth, and loom up first and brightest in eternity. They that turn many to righteousness shall shine as the stars forever and ever. In the examination of the great day, may you all be found worthy to stand before the Eternal King. Amen.

LECTURE V.

THE LOST DREAM.

On Dan., ii., 1–30.

Daniel's personal Relations.—The Triangle.—Rail-road via *Orontes to India.—Josiah's Death.—Daniel's Times.—His Chronology explained.—Oriental Salutations.—Professors of occult Sciences.—Chaldeans.—Punishment of the wise Men.—Altercation with the King.—Prophetic Dreams from God.—Daniel's Answer to the King.—Resemblance to Joseph.—Inferences :* 1. *How contemptible a Tyrant in a Passion.* 2. *God is in Modern History as well as in Ancient.—Washington not a Pantheist.—Politics and Religion.—Must read the Old Testament as well as the New.—Erasmus on Reading the Bible.—Infallible, unfailing Source of Relief to all young Men in Trouble.*

To understand the history and writings of Daniel, it is necessary to remember his relation to two other prophets and to three kings, all of whom are frequently named in the Scriptures. These three kings are, Pharaoh-necholi of Egypt, Jehoiakim in Jerusalem, and Nebuchadnezzar in Babylon. It is curious that something like an equilateral triangle, whose base should be a line from the Persian Gulf, near which stood the city of Susa, also called Persepolis, running west to the Mediterranean, would comprise that portion of our globe most renowned in the history of ancient times. With this line for a base, and the Mediterranean on the west side, and the Euphrates on the east side, and the apex in the Mountains of Lebanon or of Northern Syria, we have the area of the supposed Garden of Eden, and the sites of Tyre, Sidon, Babylon, Nineveh, Edom, Petra, Mecca, and the cities of the Philistines, Egypt, and the Holy Land. Any one that will take the trouble to look at a map of Asia and Africa, will see that from Alexandria the Mediterranean shore inclines to the east, and that as one ascends the Euphrates and the Tigris, he travels west as well as north, so that the head of the valley of the Euphrates and the northeastern side of the Mediterranean come near together. You are aware that it has been proposed in England to open up a highway to India by a railroad from the Mediterranean, up the Orontes, through Celo-Syria, and then down the valley of the Euphrates to the Persian Gulf, and thence by steamship to Bombay.

Such is the relative position of Egypt, the Holy Land, and Babylon. And the prophets to whom I have alluded, whose positions, history, and writings, are nearly allied to Daniel, are Jeremiah and Ezekiel. Jeremiah prophesied first in Jerusalem and afterward in Egypt, where he probably wrote his Lamentations. Ezekiel prophesied in Babylon, by the River Chebar; and Daniel, as you know, begins his public life at the court of Nebuchadnezzar, in Babylon. He lived also in the reign of the Medo-Persian kings, and probably died at Susa, *i. e.*, Persepolis, then the capital of Persia. The Pharaoh just named marched a great army out of Egypt and made conquests as far as the River Euphrates, and took the city of Carchemish. At that time the young and pious king of Judea was named Josiah. Imprudently he was induced to march against the King of Egypt, and in the battle that followed he was slain, and his dead body was conveyed to Jerusalem, and there was great mourning for him in all the country. After the defeat of the Israelites and the death of Josiah, Pharaoh hastened to Jerusalem, and carried away captive into Egypt the young Jehoahaz, whom the people had made king in the place of Josiah. The King of Egypt made Jehoiakim, another son of Josiah, king in Jerusalem, and he reigned as a tributary to Egypt. In the mean while, God brings Nebuchadnezzar into the field. At the head of a powerful army of Assyrians, he marches against the Egyptians under Pharaoh-nechoh, and defeats him in a battle near the Euphrates, and drives him back to Egpyt, and proceeds to lay siege to Jerusalem. Jehoiakim surrenders the holy city, and becomes tributary to Babylon instead of Egypt. And among the captives taken as hostages by the King of Babylon were Daniel and his three friends. Nebuchadnezzar engages in other wars, but hearing of his father's death, returns to his capital laden with immense riches, and builds a most magnificent palace. But God, who had determined to make this great king—just as he afterward did with Alexander, Cyrus, and Napoleon—an instrument in carrying out His providences to the human race, caused him to have a dream, which filled his soul with terror. Such were the times, and such the kings whose history it is necessary to know in order to understand the writings of Daniel. The scene of the history before us is laid in the far distant country of Babylon, by the great River Euphrates, and about two thousand five hundred years ago. *And in the second year of the reign of Nebuchadnezzar.* We are aware of an alleged chronological error here, which it may be worth while to notice. It is said in ch. i., v. 1, that Nebuchadnezzar, as King of Babylon, besieged and took Jerusalem. And it is admitted that Daniel and his three friends were subjected to a three years' discipline, and then presented to the king, and all this was done before the king's dream, which is said in the text to have occurred in the second year of his reign. The explanation of the difficulty given by some is, that Nebuchadnezzar is called king in ch. i., v. 1, by anticipation, because he did actually become king before the history was written. This would be in accordance with common Hebrew usage. The solution, however, which I greatly prefer is different from this, but strictly in accordance with history. It is this—that in chap. i., v. 1, Nebuchadnezzar is called king, being then colleague with his father, and that he reigned two years *with* his father; and that the second year of verse 1 of chap. ii. means the second year of his reign after the death of his father. The dream happened, therefore, in the *fifth* year of his reign, and in the fourth year of the Jewish captivity.

One morning the King of Babylon rose from his royal couch in agitation and alarm. An indescribable dream had chilled him with horror, and yet he had forgotten all its details. All he remembered was its terrible majesty. It was unlike any thing that had ever troubled his sleep before. It had made a deep and abiding impression on his mind. He felt quite sure that it meant something more than an ordinary or common dream. He was convinced it imported an affair between Heaven and himself, which he was, of course, extremely anxious to have explained.

And as to the sneering Infidel question, How could a *forgotten* dream trouble the king? it seems quite a sufficient answer to ask whether its propounders have common sense enough to dream? For every one must know from experience that the mind is often greatly agitated by visions of the night, which vanish, leaving only a general impression. It is easy to suppose cases where the agitation would be even increased by the very fact that the particulars were no longer remembered, and the relief that might be hoped for could not, therefore, be so readily obtained. Every one knows that impressions from dreams remain after their particular details have escaped recollection. The dimness, indistinctness, mysteriousness of the subject only increases the agitation.

The king knew three things. He had had a dream. It was lost: but still it greatly troubled him. He therefore called for his wise men.

1. *The salutation* of the 4th verse is exactly according to Oriental style. There are other instances of the same kind of address in the Bible. Xenophon, Ælian, Quintus Curtius, and others confirm the correctness of the Bible account of Oriental salutations. You are not ignorant of the style of Oriental sovereigns, particularly on the Nile and the Euphrates. They are called on the monuments, "King of kings," "Lord of the world," "Light of life," and such like names. The meaning of, *O king, live forever*, in the sober every-day language of the common life of us Western Barbarians is, may your life be very long, and your reign prosperous.

2. Four classes of Babylonian professors of occult sciences, are named in the 2d verse: Magicians, Astrologers, Sorcerers, and Chaldeans. The first and last orders are supposed to have been the Magi so often referred to, in whom the priestly character was connected with the pretensions made to the interpretations of dreams and

prodigies, and the foretelling of things to come. This last order is recognized in the Assyrian Sculptures, from the peculiar dress of the functionary, and from the distinctive offices in which he is seen to be engaged. In Babylon, as also in other Oriental countries, the priests were also diviners. These priestly Magi are represented as wearing a peculiar dress, such as is also represented upon the persons of gods and deified persons. Their garb is composed of jeweled head-bands, and bracelets, and flowing skirts. They are generally represented with a gazelle upon their left arm, and a flower in their right hand. I cannot now, however, even if I were able to do so, stop to describe these several classes of philosophers and astronomers, and point out the difference between them.

It is more important and more difficult to know who are meant by the Chaldeans (v. 4,) than it is to inquire after the rest. Some suppose they were a college of learned men, where all arts and sciences were professed and taught. Dr. Clarke suggests that they were the most ancient philosophers in the world, and that they dwelt in the Babylonian Irak; and as they preserved themselves from contact or mixture with the inhabitants of the other one hundred and twenty provinces of which the empire was composed, so they appropriated to themselves exclusively the name of *Chaldeans.* They spoke to the king *in Syriac*, that is, in the language of Aram. Here begins the Chaldee part of the book of Daniel, which continues to the end of the 7th chapter. The Syriac, then, differed but little, if at all, as a language, from the Chaldee. It was written, however, in a different character. The language of the New Testament is frequently called

Syro-Chaldaic—that is, it was the Hebrew-Chaldee that was used in Syria after the conquests of Alexander the Great. The idioms and many of the words are Hebrew and Chaldee, but the characters are Greek.

It is a well-known historical fact, that the kings of the East had in ancient times a learned body of men about them, whose duty it was to entertain the king with intellectual discussions, and to explain to him all high and difficult questions. With such a corps of learned men, who professed such high degrees of knowledge, it is not surprising that the king thought they should restore to him his lost dream, if their pretensions were well founded. When summoned into his presence, they professed to be ready to interpret the dream, if the king would only tell them wnat his dream was; but to tell a dream which the dreamer had himself forgotten, was beyond their power.

3. The punishment threatened was not singular, but such as was known to the country and the times. *Cutting to pieces* was known to the Jews, for Samuel "hewed Agag to pieces." But to render the abode of the culprit a memorial of abomination occurs only in Babylonian and Persian decrees. We have the same punishment in Ezra, vi., 11; and again in Daniel, iii., 29. Xenophon tells us that such a custom existed also at Athens, for that there were many spots in that city that remained vacant, where the habitation had either been destroyed by fire, or erased by a decree of the people. "No sooner was a citizen," says De Pauw, "accused of high treason, or some such crime, than immediately his house was demolished, as a vessel is broken that has contained poisonous liquor. Neither was it lawful to rebuild there, for the very ground

was supposed to become fatal and execrable, from the crimes of its former possessors."*

You may remember that it was an ancient custom to pronounce a curse against him that should attempt to rebuild a ruined city. It is believed, says Strabo, that those who might have wished to rebuild Troy were deterred from so doing, partly by the sufferings they endured there, and partly by the curse that Agamemnon had pronounced against him that should attempt to rebuild it. The same thing is true of the attempt to rebuild Jerusalem by Heraclius. And you know that Joshua cursed the man that should rise up to rebuild Jericho. The language of the text is a strong expression, indicating that their houses would be utterly destroyed, or converted into ruinous heaps, which should become receptacles for all manner of filth. The threatening, moreover, was the more to be dreaded, as their houses were built of straw, bitumen, and unburned brick, and as the rains of their winter season were more like torrents than showers, and when once their houses should begin to give way and fall to pieces, they would soon crumble into a shapeless mass of ruin. Every traveler has a feeling and vivid impression of the masses of ruins about the ancient cities of the old world.

4. With us there is no resource by which to recover a lost dream. It was different with the King of Babylon He supposed his wise men could tell him his dream His court was crowded with men of professed learning and science. At this time Babylon was as renowned for

* A note quoted by Kitto, p. 350.

learning as Egypt had been in the days of the great Pharaohs. Indeed, from both sacred and profane history, it is doubtful whether the Babylonians were not more devoted, especially to occult sciences, than the Egyptians. The Bible and profane history agree in stating that there were several classes of persons who devoted themselves to the different branches of learning and curious arts. In the East, in ancient as well as in modern times, those who really have some science are not content with what is really known, but always connect themselves with some kind or other of necromancy or charlatanry, just as the wise men of the Indians of our own continent do. They seem to think it necessary, in order to keep up their credit as wise men, that they must at least profess some knowledge of hidden and peculiar sciences. For example, astronomy, which it is believed was first studied by the Chaldeans, was with them intimately connected with astrology, so that, in fact, the two formed but one science, of which astrology was deemed far the most important. This is still the case in the East. And English history furnishes us with a trial for *constructive* treason, in 1477, in which the accusation is stated in these words: "That the accused had imagined and compassed the death of the king and prince by calculating their nativities, to 'know when they should die;' and thus, in order to carry their traitorous intention into effect, worked and calculated by art, magic, necromancy, and astronomy, the death and final destruction of the king and prince."*

Read verses 10 to 13.

* From the Athenæum of 1832, quoted by Kitto in hoc loco.

5. Let us pause here, and for a moment listen to the ALTERCATION between the wise men and their royal master. They declare that his demand is unjust, unreasonable, and unusual. They say no other king has ever taxed the skill of his diviners to such an extent as this. The king becomes enraged, and says, your want of power to tell me my dream is a proof that if I could tell you the dream, you could not interpret it. I strongly suspect you are all a set of knaves, that pretend to great wisdom, in order that you may eat of my meat and drink of my wine. According to your professed principles and pretensions my requirements are reasonable, and if you do not tell me the dream and the interpretation, you shall all be destroyed.

6. Read verses 12 to 18.

It is strange that the king or Arioch did not apply to the Hebrews at once, as they had been found ten times wiser than the magicians and astrologers of the kingdom. Perhaps they were thought to be too young, or too recently brought to court to be consulted in such grave affairs, or perhaps the court was prejudiced against them on account of their nation or religion. Whatever may have been the cause, Providence so ordered all the circumstances as to make Daniel's discovery of the dream more remarkable.

7. The decision of the Chaldean wise men, that none could restore to the king his lost dream but *the gods, whose dwelling is not with flesh*, was eminently correct. Their decision was right, and when the living and true God, who indeed condescends to dwell with men, and who alone could reveal the dream and the secrets con-

tained in it, actually made it known to Daniel, He evinced the infinite difference there was between Jehovah and his prophets, and the idols and magicians of Babylon. Daniel's opinion was the same as that of the Chaldean diviners, namely, that none but the gods could do what the king required. And when he and his companions were called for to be put to death with the other wise men of the kingdom, he besought time to seek the aid of his God, confident that the secret would be imparted to him. The execution of the sentence was accordingly delayed. Daniel and his friends have recourse to the God of their fathers. They gave themselves up to prayer, and God heard them, and revealed the whole matter to Daniel in a night-vision. And when Daniel gave the dream and the interpretation, the wise men of Babylon were consistent in saying that *the Spirit of the holy gods was in him.*

And here we cannot but admire the Providence of God that brought Daniel and his friends forward at the time and in the way that were most conducive to their advancement of the Divine glory.

8. Read verses 24 to 30.

Dreams are not confined to the East nor to ancient times. Men dream dreams still, both when awake and when asleep. But there are no such dreams now as this of the great King of Babylon. Nor is the losing of a dream any thing very remarkable. All of us know how deeply we have been absorbed in the visions of the night, and how they have vanished as dissolving scenes when we awoke, and how vain have been all our efforts to retain the circumstances that so deeply affected us in our sleep; but they elude our grasp. It was not, then, the fact that Nebuchadnezzar had a dream that calls for remark—nor the fact that he lost his dream, but its recovery and significance. The dream was intended to make known the succession of empires and of revolutions, which in their turn were to decide the destinies of nations and of the people of God in ages to come. Every schoolboy and girl knows something of the four great monarchies represented in the king's image—the Babylonian, the Persian, the Grecian, and the Roman—and can tell more or less of their founder s, Nebuchadnezzar, Cyrus, Alex ander, and Cæsar

"*Arioch went in to the king in haste*, to tell him that he had at length found a person who could make known to him his dream. How courtier-like this man's manner. Surely he was at great pains to find an interpreter, and surely it is owing entirely to his diligent researches that Daniel is brought to give the king his dream and its interpretation; and yet the fact was, Arioch had no care nor trouble in the matter. It did not concern him that all the wise men in the kingdom were to be torn to pieces, for he did not belong to that order. All the diligence he used was to find this innocent youth Daniel, to put him to death for belonging to the learned class. "*I have found*," said he pompously, "*a man of* the captives of Judah, that will make known unto the king the interpretation." And the king seeing Daniel, a youth of some twenty years, brought forward to explain what all the wise men of Chaldea had not been able to do, said to him, evidently with astonishment and surprise, "Art thou able to make known unto me the dream which I have seen, and the interpretation thereof?"

And Daniel said, "The secret which the king hath demanded cannot the wise *men*, the astrologers, the magicians, the soothsayers, show unto the king; but there is a God in heaven that revealeth secrets, and maketh known to the king Nebuchadnezzar what shall be in the latter days. Thy dream, and the visions of thy head upon thy bed, are these: (As for thee, O king, thy thoughts came *into thy mind* upon thy bed, what should come to pass hereafter; and He that revealeth secrets maketh known to thee what shall come to pass; but as for me, this secret is not revealed to me for *any* wisdom that I have more than any living, but for *their* sakes that shall make known the interpretation to the king, and that thou mightest know the thoughts of thy heart.")

Daniel's answer is sublime and beautiful. It was exceedingly appropriate. He agrees with the wise men of the kingdom, that it was impossible for them, or for him as a mere man, to do what the king required. It was as if he had said to the king, Your wise men cannot do what you require of them. Do not, therefore, put your confidence in them as diviners; but do not treat them so cruelly. If I come to make known to you your dream, it is not because I have of myself more wisdom than they have. I have not discovered it myself. It has been revealed to me by the God of heaven, whom I serve. What is indeed impossible with you and with your wise men, and with all men, is possible with God. There is a God in heaven that revealeth secrets, and He it is that maketh known unto the king the revolutions of empires and the great things which shall be in the latter days. Mark how much he resembles Joseph in his modesty. Both, when called before the great heathen kings, were particular to ascribe their wisdom and ability to interpret dreams to the revelations made to them by the God of heaven; and they are both careful to instruct their royal masters that their dreams and the thoughts of their hearts were made known that they might give glory to the God of heaven, who is the Maker of all things, and to whom all secrets are known.

A few inferences, and I am done.

1. How poor and wretched a creature is a man left to the power of fierce and ungovernable passions! How contemptible a figure does the great King of Babylon make in demanding what was impossible! Hot-headed and furious men are generally without reason, and deaf to all remonstrances. How blessed are your privileges, that you live under constitutional laws, and are not subject to the arbitrary power of a tyrant! Magna Charta, Habeas Corpus, and trial by jury are blessings that cannot be too highly valued. As your lives and property are protected by law and courts of justice, so you, as good citizens, are bound to honor the magistrate, and uphold the institutions of your country. To fear God and honor the king, that is, the civil government, are apostolic injunctions.

2. In the rise and fall of nations, shadowed forth in prophecy, and presented in history, it is of great importance to bear in mind the fact that the Supreme Being

does rule over all the inhabitants of the world, and yet does no violence to the free agency of any rational creature. The mightiest planets in the highest heavens sweep round in their orbits at his bidding, and so arise and fall the mighty dynasties of our race, both in ancient and modern times, and in both the Old and New World. Not a few seem to think that God's providence was concerned with ancient nations, but has ceased to take notice of modern nations. This is nothing but practical atheism. God is not less vigilant and supreme now, in the midst of our inventions and improvements, than He was in the days of Jerusalem and Babylon. The historian of the times of Daniel does not say, "Jehoiakim fell into the hands of the King of Babylon;" but he does say, "The Lord gave Jehoiakim into his hand." The celebrated and pious Bogue was in the habit of saying, when he took up the papers in the time of Napoleon the Great, to read what was passing: "Let us see how God governs the world." You cannot be too often nor too earnestly reminded that God is supreme in the modern world, as he was in the ancient. Nor can you be too deeply impressed with your dependence upon God for your social, domestic, and public blessings. It is remarkable how often the Divine Providence is mentioned in the writings of Washington. You will find that in more than one hundred different places in his writings he refers to the care of Providence over him and the affairs of the American people.

3. In the history of nations there are always two classes of interests and facts very distinct, and yet exercising over each other a powerful influence. I mean

political and religious events. The first relates to kings, emperors, rulers, cabinets, and forms of government; the second relates to the moral character, religious sentiment of the people, and pertains to the salvation of their souls and the condition of the Church of the living God. These interests must necessarily exercise over each other a powerful influence. The history of nations and the history of the Church of Christ reflect mutually the state of the other. It has always been so. It will continue to be so. It cannot be otherwise. As patriots, then, you are bound to be truly pious yourselves, and to uphold by all proper means the true religion.

4. It is a solemn and imperative duty on all of you to make yourselves acquainted with the Old Testament as well as with the New Testament. Many do not read the Old Testament at all, or if at all, only that portion of it which speaks of giants and of wars. They seem to think that two or three orthodox doctrines picked out of the Scriptures are all that is necessary for them to know. This was not the view our pious fathers had of the duty of searching the Scriptures. They thought, and correctly too, that *all Scripture*, the whole Old Testament, is "given by inspiration of God, and is profitable for doctrine, for reproof, for correction, for instruction in righteousness." It was in reference to the Old Testament Scriptures that the apostle thus speaks. And it was of them the blessed Saviour speaks when He says: "Search the Scriptures, for they are they which testify of me." Nor is it enough to read the Bible occasionally or superficially, or by fits and starts. It requires care and study

to understand the Scriptures. They must be read regularly, systematically, and with such helps, as maps, dictionaries, and concordances, as are needful for the interpretation of any other ancient book. The Bible must be read with the profoundest reverence, and with the docility and humility of a little child, and with fervent prayer to the Father of our spirits to "illumine what in us is dark." It is for the want of patient, persevering, diligent study of the Holy Scriptures, that so many people are fickle, and easily carried away with every wind of doctrine that may chance to blow on their path. No wonder that such persons make little progress in the divine life. They neglect to study the Scriptures, in which are hidden the treasures of wisdom and knowledge. They do not grow in knowledge and grace, because they do not seek nourishment where it is to be found. "My people perish for the lack of knowledge, saith the Lord."

"I speak it from experience," says the celebrated Erasmus, "that there is little benefit to be derived from the Scriptures if they be read cursorily or carelessly; but if a man exercise himself therein constantly and conscientiously, he will find such efficacy in them as is not to be found in any other book whatsoever."

Finally, here you are taught where to go in all cases of difficulty. How did Daniel obtain the knowledge of the lost dream? By asking for it. He prayed to God. He sought help in the right direction. We do not, indeed, expect miracles now, yet we do expect answer to prayer. You may be far from home. You may be in distress in a foreign land. The stern, cold, inquiring gaze of strangers may be your only welcome in the populous city. But there is one ear always open to your cry—one arm always stretched out for your relief. The God that heard Daniel in Babylon, on the banks of the Euphrates, will hear your prayer on the banks of our mightier river. Make Daniel's God your friend, and you will always have a protector. Ask, and you shall receive. Amen.

LECTURE VI.

THE DREAM RECOVERED.

On Dan., ii., 31–49.

Daniel's Modesty.—Not vain or rash.—Effect of his Address to the King.—The great Image.—Its Meaning.—The Dream interpreted an Argument for the Book of Daniel.—The fifth Kingdom.—Napoleon's Testimony on the Divinity of Christ.—The four Empires.—The Book authentic.—Rise of Cyrus.—Washington.—Las Casas' Map.—Alleghany Eagle.—God supreme Sovereign in Providence and in Nature.—The Creator's physical Code.—The Religion of Astronomy.—Professor Mitchell.—The two Testaments.—Prophecy the Inspiration of the Almighty.—Newton's Eclipses.—A Comparison.—Romulus founding Rome.—History important to young Men.—Elements of a Nation.—Religion essential.—Young Men must be Politicians.—Be something.

The king's inability to recollect the dream that caused him so much anxiety gave occasion to call for Daniel, and enabled him to prove the vast superiority of his God over the gods and magicians of Babylon. By being able to restore the lost dream, he proved at once that he was able to give its true interpretation. By restoring the dream and giving its interpretation, he revealed to the king *two mysteries* at once—a mystery from the past and a mystery of the future. On hearing the *past*, the king must have felt—"that is true, it was just so; I now remember it. Surely this is from God." And thus was he prepared to hear concerning the *future*, which his dream was to reveal. It was natural, therefore, for him to reverence Daniel when he heard the interpretation of his night vision. As soon as Daniel was done speaking, the king replied. See verses 46 and 47. It has been urged, as an objection to the history before us, that Daniel is here represented as receiving improper homage from the king. We answer, Daniel does not seem to have desired it. He certainly expresses no approbation of the king's conduct. He may, indeed, have objected to it, and the objection have been omitted from the record. He was a subject—a slave; it was not for him to dictate to his master. Repeatedly, however, he assured the king that all he could do was to be ascribed to the power and wisdom of the God of heaven. He gave God all the glory. He never for a moment, by word or deed, failed to show his fixed aversion to idolatry. On all occasions, with singular modesty, firmness, and fidelity, he avowed that the God whom he served was the only real and true God. Some suppose that the text means that Nebuchadnezzar was willing to worship Daniel, but that, seeing Daniel's opposition to it, he did not do so. But, aside from these conjectures, it is a sufficient answer for you to recollect that the Hebrew, and even the English translation of it, do not determine whether the king meant to pay *divine* or merely civil honors to Daniel. Such prostration and tokens of respect were common before kings and princes, and any one whom it was intended to honor. Abraham paid such honor to the children of Heth, who gave him a burying-place for Sarah. If the king did actually fall on his face before Daniel, it does not follow that he paid him homage in the sense of religious worship. Neither do the sweet odors indicate the kind of homage intended; for these are and were as common in the East as prostration, and are in themselves merely a token of honor. It is enough for our present purpose to know that Oriental history, and coins, and monuments, and the well-known customs of the East to this day, prove that prostration and the presenting of costly perfumes was one of the ways in which honor was shown to any person deemed worthy of such homage.

The effect of Daniel's interpretation upon the king was not altogether such as was desired. The impression was, at the time, deep, but not abiding. The lesson which he had to learn, as we shall see in succeeding lectures, had to be repeated; and its repetition was harder than when given for the first time. Some suppose that Nebuchadnezzar was converted when he fell on his face and worshiped Daniel. His subsequent conduct, before his second chastisement, renders this improbable. If he ever was converted, as I hope he was, it must have been after his restoration to his mind and kingdom, and shortly before his death, when he said, "*The heavens do rule, and he blessed the Most High.*"

Let us now hear the lost dream. Read verses 31–35.

A great image. Verse 31. It appears from ancient coins and medals that both cities and nations were represented by gigantic figures of men and women. The old writer Florus, in his history of Rome, represents the Roman empire under the form of a human being, in its different states from infancy to old age. The recently-discovered monuments of the Nile, and of Nineveh, and of Babylon, show that stupendous human figures were objects and emblems familiar to the ancients. Geographers, also, have used similar representations. The Germanic empire has been represented by a map in the form of a man, different parts being pointed out by the head, breast, arms, &c., according to their geographical and political relation to the empire in general. The various metals of which Nebuchadnezzar's image was composed represented the various kingdoms which should arise subsequent to the fall of his own empire. Their position in the body of the image clearly denoted the order of their succession. The different metals and their position also expressed different degrees of strength, riches, power, and durability. Clay, earth, and dust, of course, mean weakness, instability.

The interpretation we have in verses 36 to 45, which please read with me. The image is a symbol of empire. Its different materials symbolize different dynasties arising out of, and subsequent to, the Babylonian. The extreme part of the gigantic image, which was a mixture of iron and clay, represents a very heterogeneous and mixed domination. It does not come within my present purpose to dwell upon the empires symbolized by this image. It is sufficient, while referring you to authors who have ably treated this subject, to say that the image doubtless was designed to represent four different governments, and to show their successive risings, and their comparative strength and grandeur. It was the Spirit of the God of heaven that taught his servant things which could only be known to himself; and this inspiration proves the truthfulness of the Bible. Daniel must have been an honest and truthful man; and his interpretation of the king's dream, foretelling events to transpire in distant ages, must have been, as he said it was, a *revelation* from God. It cannot be supposed that the Supreme Being, who is infinite purity, and wisdom, and goodness, would inspire a knave to predict, as Daniel did, some of the greatest political events that have ever taken place on earth. Daniel, then, must have been a good man, and he must have received his knowledge of things to come from God. He was a man of truth, and he says his understanding of the king's dreams was given to him by Jehovah. The argument here alluded to for the Divine authority of the Bible is one that grows stronger by the lapse of time.

If it be true that the argument from miracles is weakened by age, the argument from prophecy, on the contrary, gains strength by every revolution of time and of the nations of the earth.

Daniel's prophetic mind was not, however, limited to the rise, extension, glory, and fall of the four great monarchies, which he saw so distinctly in the king's great image. He speaks of a *fifth* kingdom, and his predictions concerning it have not only been true thus far, but are now in the course of fulfillment. The phrase *last days*, in the Prophets, signifies the times of the Messiah. The kingdoms of the image arose and prepared the way for the advent of the Son of God, who is the King and Head of this fifth kingdom, set up by the God of heaven. *Mountains*, you recollect, in the Bible are the emblems of mighty kingdoms, states, and empires. The *stone cut out without hands* means Jesus Christ and his kingdom; and being cut out of the mountain *without hands*, signifies without human aid or power. The hand is a common Hebrew symbol for power; and we find all these particulars remarkably fulfilled. The kingdom of the true

Messiah is spiritual, in contradistinction to the other kingdoms foreshadowed in the image, which were of the earth, earthy—founded by blood and conquest. Christ, you recollect, is represented in many Scriptures as a stone.

And in the days of these kings—that is, in the days of the Cæsars, *the God of heaven set up a kingdom*. Palestine, at the birth of Jesus, was a Roman province. Messiah was born, and his kingdom set up under the Roman government. Christ came as the messenger of free, sovereign love. God GAVE His Son. His birth was an extraordinary miracle, and His kingdom, in its origin, nature, extension, and preservation, is a miracle of miracles. Its whole nature is different from all others that have ever been established by the Nebuchadnezzars, Cæsars, and Napoleons of the world. This fact did not escape the quick and powerful mind of Napoleon himself, and you know that he considered it the most remarkable fact known in human history, and regarded it as an infallible proof of the Divinity of Jesus Christ. His empire was founded in blood, but in his own. Its policy and maxims are not according to the rules of the courts of this world. It was not by might, nor by power, but by the Spirit of Jehovah of Hosts that the kingdom of Heaven was established in our world. But let us briefly consider Daniel's interpretation. *Thou, O king, art a King of kings: thou art this head of gold.* Verses 37, 38. Under Nebuchadnezzar the Chaldean empire rose to its height, and embraced not only Chaldee, but also Assyria, Arabia, Syria, Egypt, and Lybia. The head of gold represents its immense riches. In gold Babylon far surpassed any other ancient kingdom. Next after Nebuchadnezzar's empire arose that of the Medes and Persians, whose union was denoted by the breasts and arms of silver. Cyrus captured Babylon B.C. 538, when this Medo-Persian empire may be said to have been founded.

The third kingdom was the empire of the Macedonians, or Brazen-coated Greeks, aptly represented by the belly and thighs of brass. This empire was founded by Alexander the Great, who put an end to the Persian monarchy by the defeat and overthrow of Darius Codomanus at Arbela B.C. 331.

The fourth empire was the Roman, which comprised nearly the whole known world. Its elements were discordant, and the empire was, therefore, fitly represented by iron and clay, which would not cleave one to another, even as iron is not mixed with clay.

The Roman empire was weakened by a mixture of barbarians, and by their incursions was finally overthrown, and at length divided into ten kingdoms, answering to the ten toes of the great image. It is thus the image is generally interpreted. Josephus, Tacitus, Gibbon, Herodotus, and Rollin furnish us with abundant evidence of the fulfillment of the predictions of Daniel. As to the insinuation of modern skeptics, that the book of Daniel is a mere political satire, written long after the events happened of which it speaks, it must suffice for the present for me to say, as I have shown in a previous lecture, that the evidences internal and external, are all arrayed against it, and prove, on the contrary, as clearly as such a subject admits of proof, the authenticity and genuineness of the book. We have positive proof of the existence and general knowledge of the book of Daniel *before* the rise of Antiochus Epiphanes and Alexander the Great. And all the discoveries yet brought to light by M. M. Botta, Layard, Rawlinson, and Hincks, as far as they bear on the subject at all, corroborate the general truthfulness of the commonly received opinions about the book of Daniel and the four great empires.

I have said the position of the different parts of the image and the different kinds of metal are descriptive of the *time* of the rise, and of the nature of the several empires spoken of.

A change in the metal denoted a change of the people and language; and, as there is no interval in the image between the gold and the silver, so the empire signified by the gold and silver is one. It was begun by the Chaldeans, and continued by the Persians without interruption. The gold, *i. e.*, the Babylonian empire; the silver, that is, the Persian, are succeeded by the empire of *brass*—an empire less rich and less glorious than that of Babylon, but more powerful and terrible. The chronology of these empires is indicated by the *position* of the metals in the image. The order of time is the order of the parts of the body from the head downward. Nor is the geography of these empires less clear and satisfactory than their chronology. Time does not allow me to point out this. I gave in a sort of a triangle, in the last lecture, a sort of a bird's-eye view of the geographical position of Judea, Babylon, and Egypt. From that triangle we have now to look westward for the rise of Alexander the Great, and eastward for the rise of Cyrus. As in the human body the two arms unite above the breast, so in like manner the Medes and Persians were united, and made but one empire and one people. Cyrus' father married a daughter of the King of the Medes, and this led to the union of the two kingdoms; and the rise of Cyrus and of the Medo-Persian kingdom, from an obscure province, under tribute to Babylon in the time of Daniel, is certainly very remarkable. Five years after the interpretation of the dream by Daniel—that is, 600 B.C., in the mountains east of Babylon, in a country called Elam or Persia—a child was born, whose parents gave him the name of *Cyrus*. His father and mother were heathens. They lived at least twelve hundred miles from Jerusalem. There was no travel between the two countries, except as armies were marched and counter-marched. The Jewish nation was weak and despised. The Medo-Persian parents were very far, therefore, from suspecting that the name of their child had been written down in a Hebrew book two hundred and forty years before. And yet all this was true; and not only the name but the *deeds* of their son were foretold by the Jewish seer, who wrote his name in the sacred book of his nation. Now suppose a book, relating chiefly to the religion and national concerns of the Chinese, had been written two hundred years before the birth of Washington, and deposited among the sacred books of the Chinese empire, in which it was foretold that a child should be born in the province of Virginia, belonging to the crown of Great Britain, and that his name should be called George Washington, and that he should become a great general and statesman, and that the colonies should declare their independence of the mother country, and that Washington, at the head of their armies, should capture Lord Cornwallis at Yorktown, and that the colonies should then become a nation, and Washington be the first President of the United States; and suppose copies of this book were multiplied, and that it had been translated into another widely-spread tongue, and that the original of the chief translation had been so sacredly kept that it was impossible for them ever to have been materially corrupted or interpolated—with what profound astonishment and reverence would we look upon a copy of such a book? We need not wonder, therefore, that when Cyrus became acquainted with the Hebrew Scriptures, and read the prophecies of Daniel, that he favored his nation, and issued his decree for their return to their own country.

Another observation here seems worth making in this place: that Las Casas, the friend of Napoleon, drew up a series of synoptical charts while he was with the emperor in St. Helena, in which he distinguishes both the empires and the subdivisions by different colors. I have not these charts at hand, but this is a correct description of them. Now it is not probable that Las Casas thought of Daniel while he was engaged in drawing them; yet Daniel, two thousand four hundred and forty-three years before, at the side of his friend, the Emperor Nebuchadnezzar, could have drawn them for him just as accurately as he did. Like Daniel, Las Casas divides the history of the world into four parts, and he employs *four colors* to designate the empires of the Babylonians, the Persians, the Greeks, and the Romans. The Macedonian empire he divides into four kingdoms, of which the Syrian and the Egyptian are the two most powerful; and so also does he divide the Roman empire into ten parts. And thus the friend of Napoleon and the friend of Nebuchadnezzar have given the history of the world substantially, and in many things even to the most minute particulars in the same way. The one writes from an island in the ocean, about 2400 years AFTER the events transpired which he relates, and the other writes from the banks of the Euphrates 600 B.C., and BEFORE the events themselves took place. The main and only essential difference between the historic charts of Daniel and of Las Casas is that, while the latter had no Messiah, the former speaks of a fifth kingdom to be set up by the God of heaven, which was to rule forever —the kingdom of the Messiah, Jesus.

WE SEE THE HAND OF PROVIDENCE in bringing Daniel and his friends forward at the Babylonish court at the time when it was the most proper they should be honored. He who gave the dream to the king ordered all the circumstances that took place, and gave to Daniel the honor of restoring and interpreting it, and through Daniel brought out the heathen king's acknowledgment that the God of the Hebrews was superior to the gods of Babylon. The elevation of his faithful servants, the Hebrew youths, was another result of the Divine interposition. God never forsakes those that trust in Him.

I. THE DREAM, ITS PREDICTIONS, AND THEIR FULFILLMENT PROVE THE SUPREME AND PARTICULAR PROVIDENCE OF GOD, AND THEREBY ALSO SHOW THE TRUTH OF THE BIBLE. As the eagle hovering in the clouds, above the summit of the Alleghanies, discerns from a distance the valleys of the Ohio and Mississippi, toward which he wings his flight, with their tributary streams, forests, and cities, so does

Daniel, the man of God, in the sublime revelations which God gave him, rise above time, and mount up into the heights of faith, and soar tranquilly over the vast future, and discover in the distance the kings, the empires, and events which were to agitate the world at successive periods; and in one glancing of his prophetic eye he takes in the whole series of ages, from his stand-point in the palace of Nebuchadnezzar to the second coming of the Lord Jesus Christ. Now this prediction of the future destinies of nations could not be without revelations from God, nor could it be unless God be both SOVEREIGN IN PROVIDENCE AND IN NATURE. It is God only and alone who can foretell the distant changes of time and nations; and this he can do and has done as infallibly as he knows the revolutions of the heavenly bodies. God knows as perfectly and as certainly what the commotions of the people and the thousand passions of kings and statesmen will produce, as what the thousand attractions of the stars and their most distant courses will bring about in immensity. Astronomers give us beforehand the details of eclipses, because the Creator has impressed his will upon the universe as a code of physical laws. These laws are regular, harmonious, and certain; just as much so as if we could see myriads of angels executing them in all directions throughout the universe. The globe, the orrery, and the planetarium demonstrate the existence, beauty, harmony, accuracy, and sublimity of these laws. Astronomy proves to us that the world had a beginning, and that its beginning was caused by an Infinite Mind, and that it is still governed by Supreme Intelligence. The Psalmist well understood these things when he said, "Forever, O Lord, thy word is settled in heaven. Thou hast established the earth, and it abideth." Now the God who governs the seasons and governs the stars is the same God that governs the nations of the earth. He rules mankind, who dwell *on* the earth, as well as the worlds which roll in infinite space. He stays the commotions of the people, as well as the billows of the sea. He holds in his hand the hearts of the rulers of the earth, as He counts the hosts of heaven and calls them all by name. Hence it is that Daniel, by the Spirit of God, could predict the revolutions of empires, just as Sir Isaac Newton was able to predict, centuries beforehand, the variations and revolutions of the remotest planets in the regions of space, where they travel at the rate of one million and a half miles per day. Newton, with his telescope, and his pen, and the use of mathematics, read the laws which the Creator has promulgated in the physical universe. Daniel, by the Spirit of God, read the laws which the Almighty Creator hath ordained in the intellectual and sensitive world, and saw their results. You know that such is the precision with which the motions of the heavenly bodies can be ascertained, than an astronomer in his observatory at Babylon, 2500 years ago, could have foretold every eclipse of the sun and moon that has happened from that day to this. Our countryman,* on the hill at Cincinnati, can say, "I will fix a telescope opposite that window, with two threads of spider's web placed across one another in the centre of its glass, and if one of the heavenly bodies touches on them for a thousand years, I can tell at what

* Professor Mitchell.

hour, what minute, what second, any given world shall pass the intersection of those two threads at the end of a thousand years, after having traveled millions of millions of miles in all directions of the universe. I can even tell at what distance from the earth that star will be at the expiration of three thousand years." Now how is it that astronomers are able to predict such things? It is because, *first*, they have minds trained, disciplined to thought, which are capable of perceiving objects which the Creator has made, and the laws He has given to them; and, *secondly*, because God has been pleased, by the putting forth of his omnipotence and wisdom, to ordain laws in nature which are permanent; and, *thirdly*, because it has pleased God to discover to such men, by the permanence of his laws in nature, that he is a God of order and of truth, and will certainly accomplish all that his hands begin. And is not God as truly sovereign in the Bible as he is among suns, moons, and stars? Are not the heavens and the earth one volume, and the writings of the prophets and apostles but another volume having the same author? Nature and Revelation are the Old and New Testaments of the same Creator and Redeemer, God. The first is written in huge hieroglyphs and symbols, while the second is written in human languages. The first are the inscriptions of an Omnipotent finger, flaming on the forehead of the universe, and declaring the power and ownership of the Creator; the second is the inspiration of the Almighty, uttered to us in words of our own tongue. And these two volumes—these two Testaments—are harmonious. And as the astronomer, with his pen, and paper, and telescope in his hand, can predict, ages before, the positions of the heavenly bodies, their motions, changes, eclipses, and revolutions, so the prophets of the Bible were able, by the Spirit of God, to predict, ages before, the positions of kingdoms, and the rise, prosperity, and fall of conquerors.

The dream of Nebuchadnezzar, as interpreted by Daniel, and as understood by Josephus and by most biblical scholars, agrees with the best historians of ancient and modern times. Nebuchadnezzar was himself the golden head of the image. The Medes and Persians come next. And at the time that Daniel wrote out his interpretation of the king's dream, the Persians were as insignificant a people as the inhabitants of Siberia are now, and far more unknown to the world. And, to use the suggestion of another, there is as much probability now that some Cyrus will be born just five years hence in the mountains of Siberia, who shall capture St. Petersburg, and put the Autocrat of all the Russias to death, as there was, in mere human view, in the time of Daniel, that Cyrus should be born in Persia, and conquer Babylon. The Persians dwelt in their own mountains, and were especially unknown to the Hebrews; and yet there lived at Jerusalem, about two hundred years before Daniel, a Hebrew prophet, who not only predicted the downfall of Babylon, but even told the name of its conqueror. Isaiah also foretells the birth and conquests of Cyrus about 240 years beforehand. See 44th and 45th chapters. Thus, if there had been a Bible-class or a Sabbath-school in Jerusalem, a child with the book of Isaiah in his hand, two hundred years before the Medo-Persian empire, could have foretold its rise, and the downfall of Babylon by the hand of

Cyrus, just as our astronomer at Cincinnati, with his telescope and his mathematical tables, can predict an eclipse of the sun a thousand years hence, and tell in what places such an eclipse will be visible. It is no wonder, then, that Sir Isaac Newton, one of the greatest mathematicians and astronomers that has ever lived, set himself to the study of prophecy, saying, "I have long studied the stars, and the glory of God in creation; I will now study Daniel, and the glory of God in the prophecies of His word!" And the result of his studies are, *first*, a work on the "Principles of Natural Philosophy," in which he teaches us to look far into the mysteries of creation; and, *secondly*, we have, from the same gigantic mind and laborious pen, a work on the "Prophecies" of Daniel and the book of the Revelations of St. John. It would be extremely interesting to trace out, if we could, the internal and experimental connection in the mind of this illustrious philosopher between his studies of creation and his studies of prophecy, and see how the one influenced and operated upon the other. May it not be that he said to himself, I have fixed, by discoveries and calculations, with certainty the motions, eclipses, and revolutions of the heavenly bodies. By all these I am firmly persuaded the universe is governed by an all-wise, supreme, and benevolent Creator. May it not be true that, by the revelations of His prophets, He has recorded for us the revolutions of men on the earth, as He has recorded by His laws the motions of the planets in heaven? And accordingly, we find that he set himself to work to fix the chronology of ancient times by eclipses. As he could fix the time of the eclipses mentioned by ancient writers, so could he fix the date of all contemporaneous events which they recorded. For example, when he read in Plutarch that the sun was vailed in darkness in Italy the year that Romulus founded the city of Rome, he turned to his astronomy, and it revealed to him with absolute certainty that this celestial phenomenon took place 753 years B.C., and at 4 o'clock, P.M., on the 5th of July. This, then, was the year in which the foundation of Rome was laid. And the connection of this fact with prophecy is remarkable in two ways. First, in counting back in this way, he found that the events spoken of by Daniel as to the rising of the four great monarchies, and the seventy weeks, and the appearance of the *fifth* kingdom set up by the God of heaven, were all perfectly correct as to time. And a second point brought out is very remarkable, which I give in the words of Professor Gaussen, of Geneva. Sir Isaac Newton "employed for his computations a catalogue of eclipses drawn up by a very ancient astronomer named Ptolemy. This man lived 140 years after Christ, and was a heathen. He left in his writings an account of astronomical observations made at Babylon for a long series of years. Now what must have been Newton's admiration for Daniel when he saw that the heathen Ptolemy, to mark the years of his eclipses, had divided the ages of antiquity exactly as the Hebrew prophet had done 745 years before him; that is, Ptolemy the astronomer looked back, and saw the four great monarchies, just as Daniel the prophet did in the distant future. One would suppose, in reading Daniel, that he had followed Ptolemy, or, in reading Ptolemy, that he had copied Daniel. Ptolemy, in his list of kings, which he calls a mathematical rule or canon of kings, counts the kings of Babylon just as Daniel does."* The coincidence is certainly very remarkable.

What, then, is the result which we have obtained? In a few words, it is this: GOD IS THE GOVERNOR OF NATIONS, JUST AS HE IS OF WORLDS. HE IS AS SUPREME IN PROPHECY AS IN ASTRONOMY. He rules in the rise of nations and in the fall of empires, as He does in the revolutions of heavenly bodies, which make their mighty journeys day and night in immensity. His laws are equally potent and harmonious in both. The astronomer, by the use of his intellect and the appliances of science, stands in his observatory and predicts the motions and phases of stars and planets. The Hebrew seer stood on the mount of holy vision, and predicted the developments of the predetermined counsels of the Almighty concerning the nations that were to appear upon the earth.

II. Again, young friends, the study of the prophetical history of nations is of vast importance to young men, not merely as such history is a running commentary upon mankind, and a volume of evidence in favor of Christianity, but also in this: namely, that the history of nations presents TWO ELEMENTS in themselves perfectly distinct, and yet always more or less united, and always more or less subjected to mutual and reciprocal influences. I mean the *political* and *religious* history of a country. The religious habitudes of a people do of necessity deeply affect their morals, and their social and national char-

* Gaussen's Lectures on Daniel, p. 91, 92. Presbyterian Board of Publication.

acteristics. So palpable is the influence of religion upon a nation, that it has long been received as a canon of philosophical history, that the religion of a country being known, all the rest of that country's history can be easily known. It is not essential to mere physical existence that we have comfortable houses to live in, and that they are adorned with the products of industry and filled with the comforts of commerce. We could live in tents or in *adobe* houses. But certainly those who have once tasted the elegances of refined life will not desire to go back to semi-barbarism. So it is not essential for all pious people to be politicians, yet all the members of Christ's Church are interested in the political interests of the world; and Christian young men should prepare themselves to take a part in the civil affairs of their country. If the administration of our laws and the outwork of our great institutions are left wholly in the hands of ungodly or unprincipled men, we cannot expect God's blessing to rest upon us. Noisy demagogues are not good models for Christian young men, but all Christian young men should make themselves intelligent about civil affairs, and by their votes and influence promote only good men and uphold only correct principles. We are on the eve of great events. You should prepare yourselves for acting a high and noble part in the great history of the future; you should cherish a love of country and of your fellow-men; you should habitually pray for your rulers, and throw your whole influence in favor of the laws of the land.

III. Observe how careful Daniel was to remember his friends in his prosperity. Like Joseph, when exalted, he was not ashamed of his poor kin. At his request his three friends were promoted to high employments in the department over which he presided. As his friends had shared his anxieties—as they had united with him in prayer to God for wisdom, so it was becoming for him in his advancement to secure them places of trust.

IV. Throughout Daniel's history we see in him, as in Joseph, *a disposition to humble himself and exalt his God.* Without prevarication or hesitancy, he shows his abhorrence of idolatry, and his deep and earnest conviction that the God whom he served was the only real and true God. He claims nothing for himself. When the king asks him if he is able to make known the dream and its interpretation, he reminds the king that there had been no power in the gods of his diviners which had enabled them to do this; but "there is a God in heaven that revealeth secrets, and maketh known to the king Nebuchadnezzar what shall be in the latter days." And in the whole affair we hear him ascribing every thing to God: the dream itself—the interpretation—the existence and power of the Babylonian empire—the power of the king himself, and all the historical developments which the dream prefigured—all he ascribes to the God whom he served. And his object was in part attained. The king's mind became so powerfully impressed with Daniel's arguments and demonstrations, that he made the remarkable declaration: "OF A TRUTH IT IS THAT YOUR GOD IS A GOD OF GODS, AND A LORD OF KINGS." The king, like other heathen nations in those times, supposed that every country had its local deities, and that Daniel's God was certainly one of the superior ones. His confession was remarkable, but it was far short of what he ought to have said: "There is only one living and true God, who made heaven and earth, and besides Him there is no God.

Finally, from the imperfect and hasty view presented, of the beauty and harmony with which God, as sovereign both in nature and providence, governs the universe, *is not your duty palpable?* Clearly it is your duty to study both the works and the word of God. You were created in His image and after His likeness. You have, therefore, a noble heritage. Cultivate your minds—elevate your affections—seek the knowledge of great and glorious subjects. The earth beneath you, the heavens above you, and the elements around you, and the history and achievements of your race in ages past, and the prophecies of its futurity, all demand your attentive research. Resolve to be something—to do something for your age—to serve your generation and your God. Every thing in the universe invites your intellectual exertions. Suffer not your mind and your affections to go to waste by indolence—destroy them not by excesses. Let them not rot in dissipation or selfishness. Cleave to your mother's Bible. Admire the spirit of heavenly prophecy, which laid so broad, and deep, and sure a foundation for your faith. Be thankful that the God of heaven has set up a kingdom that will endure forever, and that you are all invited to become its subjects. While you are enjoying the blessings of this kingdom, pray earnestly for its advancement, and labor diligently to bring your fellowmen into it. Strive to walk worthy of Him who hath called you, through the Gospel, to GLORY, HONOR, and IMMORTALITY. Of the God of heaven, Christ is made unto us wisdom, righteousness, sanctification, and complete redemption. Seek first the kingdom of God, and all things needful shall be added unto you. Amen.

LECTURE VII.

THE FIERY FURNACE.

On Dan., iii.

Recapitulation.—Daniel a close Student of the Holy Writings and of the Ways of Providence.—Sat in the Gate, Grand Vizier.—The Image set up in the Plain of Dura.—The King enforcing Uniformity.—Propagandism by the Sword older than Mohammed or the Pope.—Rawlinson's Reading of Assyrian Inscriptions illustrates the Text.—Size of the Golden Image.—Colossus of Nero and of Rhodes.—Burning Heretics not original with the Jesuits.—Truthfulness of Daniel's History.—Measures used by the King to produce Uniformity, seductive and minatory.—How like Popery.—Best Music.—Eunuchs.—The Furnace: Savages understand it.—The Fire that would not burn.—Young Hebrews inflexible.—Freedom of Conscience.—The old Hebrew Catechism of Jerusalem in Babylon.—WHY these young Men remained steadfast in their Faith.

LESSONS.

I. YOUNG MEN MUST PREPARE FOR FIERY TIMES.—*The King not the Head of the Church, nor Government a Conscience-keeper for the People.*

II. TRUTH IS REAL POWER, AND WILL PREVAIL.

III. TRUE PRINCIPLE IS TRUE EXPEDIENCY.—*That only is right which is according to God's Will.*

YOU recollect that the last Lecture was on *the Dream recovered*, and that its interpretation proved to us that God is indeed supreme in Providence as in Nature, and that human history, written by man's pen, is nothing but the echo of God's prophecy uttered by His prophets. The continuous fulfillment of those ancient prophecies in the times that roll past before us is one of the strongest proofs that the prophets were indeed holy men, and spake in *times past* as they were moved thereto by the Holy Ghost.

Daniel's whole career shows that he was a man of singular sincerity, humility, and piety. He was an earnest, hard-working, close-thinking man. He was a diligent student of the Holy Writings of his nation, and a close observer of the ways of Providence. In this chapter his own narrative is suspended, to tell us what happened to his friends for their fidelity to God.

Daniel was promoted to distinguished honors. Great gifts were bestowed upon him, and he was made *Rab-Mag*, that is, chief of the learned order, and the civil government of the metropolitan province of Babylon was committed to him. Probably this was necessary to enable him—being a foreigner and of an adverse religion—to maintain his authority. He held a plurality office, such as in Great Britain would comprise both that of Lord Chancellor and Minister of the Home Department. Daniel's successor now in the East is called the "Grand Vizier" of Persia or of Turkey.

Daniel sat in the gate of the king—i. e., he was the confidential adviser of the king, and chief officer in the palace. "Judgment in the gate," "Honored among the elders in the gate," and such expressions, occur frequently in the Scriptures. You know that the gate of a city, in ancient times, was the place from which justice was dispensed. It was a strong place, and well guarded. You also know that the government of the Turkish empire is frequently referred to as the "sublime Porte." Porte is from Latin—*porta*, which means a gate. This retention of an ancient Oriental custom in a modern tongue, as at Constantinople, the capital of the Turkish empire, is a link connecting the world that now is with the rites and customs of a world that is past away. One of the most curious and suggestive sights a traveler now meets with in the Levant is the struggling of the new Western World for an introduction to the aged Orient. The Frank's coat and the Fez cap are in conflict on the soldier of Stamboul. Constantinople itself is half European and half Asiatic—partly new and partly old; and while Europe is striving to enter Asia and China from the West, young America from the farthest West knocks imperatively at their eastern gates. *It is the will of God.*

Daniel's honors and the rewards of his friends were of short duration. Yesterday they were objects of royal homage, and courtly gifts were bestowed upon them; to-day the same men, and without any cause on their part for such a change of treatment, are the objects of fury and vengeance. Surely it is a vain thing to trust in princes. Vain is the help of man.

Read verses 1 to 7. *The image is set up.*

Nebuchadnezzar was the Napoleon of his age. He was a man of vast ideas and of vast undertakings. His wealth and power enabled him to gratify a most towering ambition. He consolidated a vast empire, comprising many different nations. These nations had different gods and different forms of religious service. Being supreme in the State, he determined to be supreme in the Church also. He was another Henry VIII., as to the religion of his subjects. He resolved to enforce religious conformity—to make his god supreme over the consciences of his people, as he was himself supreme over their persons and property. To bring about this obedience to and honor of his god, he set up a vast golden image of him in the plain of Dura, and required that, at a signal given by bands of music, all the persons assembled in the vast plain at the time of the dedication should fall down and worship it. All the inhabitants of his empire could not assemble at his capital, nor fall down and worship the image in the plain of Dura. The governors, therefore, of the different provinces of the empire, who where representatives of the different conquered nations at the court of Babylon, were summoned to assist at the ceremony of the dedication.

It is not necessary to dwell on the nature of the several offices and posts occupied by the several distinguished personages named in the narrative. The governors of the different provinces, no doubt, answer to the satraps of the ancient Persian empire, and to the pashaws of the Turkish empire of the present day. Then, as now, they were generally natives of the provinces they governed. Their assistance at the dedication, as representatives of their respective nations, and cities, and countries, was proof of their subjection *politically* to the King of Babylon and of their *religious conformity* to the state religion of Babylon. Provincial governors are represented in the Assyrian sculptures in the garbs of their different nations, and are easily distinguished by their bearing the model of a city as a symbol of their office. The books and drawings of these monuments sometimes represent a distinguished personage bearing two such models, one in each hand, and these are supposed to have been governors of two adjacent provinces, or of one province containing two important cities.

Other and various motives have been assigned to Nebuchadnezzar for setting up this great golden image.

But it seems clear that his object was to promote the worship of his god, in whose likeness this image was made. The Assyrian inscriptions discovered by Botta and Layard, and read by Major Rawlinson and Hincks, show that this people were very zealous in promoting the worship of their god, Assarac, among conquered nations. Contrary to what was once the prevailing opinion, it now appears, from Rawlinson's reading of the Nineveh inscriptions, that religious propagandism by the sword was known in the East long before Mohammed. The inscriptions show conclusively that the Assyrians showed little respect to the religious creeds of the nations they conquered; but wherever they went they destroyed their idols, and endeavored to force upon them the worship of their own.*

We are not without historical confirmation of the narrative as to the existence of gigantic idols of gold among the Babylonians. Herodotus writes, that in his day there was at Babylon an idol image of gold twelve cubits high; and, what is still more remarkable, another authority, obviously speaking of the same statue, mentions that every stranger was obliged to worship it before he was allowed to enter the city.† Diodorus Siculus mentions an image found in the temple of Belus *forty* feet high, which some think was the same as the golden image of Nebuchadnezzar. Other images almost parallel in magnitude are mentioned in history. The Colossus of Nero

See Kitto on the Prophets for the quotations of these inscriptions, p. 91, 92.

† Kitto quotes Philostratus, De Vita Apollon, ch. 19, for this.

was one hundred and ten feet high. The Colossus of Rhodes was seventy cubits high, and was considered one of the seven wonders of the world. According to classic story, it took thirteen years to construct this colossus; and on its being thrown down by an earthquake, so great was its weight, it plowed up the ground, and buried itself under the ground. These historical facts show that such images were not unusual, and that it was not impossible to construct such by ancient art. The Colossus of Nero and of Rhodes were not, however, of gold; nor do we suppose that the image of Nebuchadnezzar was of solid gold. It must have been either hollow, or made of wood and covered with gold. It does not appear that the ancients made any but small images of solid gold. The proportions of this image are out of order, unless we understand the height to include the thickness of the pedestal, which it seems to me we should do. The *instruments of music* in verses 5 and 7 have Greek names. This is thought to indicate that they were brought from Tyre when Nebuchadnezzar conquered that city, and that they were introduced into Tyre by Greeks. Tyre was renowned for its instruments of music.

It is thought that we have in this chapter the first instance in the Bible of the division and measurement of time by hours. We come now to the

ACCUSATION AND THE PUNISHMENT.

Read verses 8 to 25.

The penalty for not worshiping the golden image was death, by being cast into a *burning fiery furnace*. Burning alive for heresy is not, therefore, original with the

Jesuits. It was a very ancient punishment of the body, by father confessors, to save the soul. But have we any proof that such a mode of punishment was used in Babylon? In the Bible (Jer., xxix., 22) we are told that *the King of Babylon roasted Zedekiah in the fire.* Sir John Chardin tells us that it is not long since such a custom prevailed in Persia, the great repository in modern times of ancient usages. He says, "There is still a particular way of putting to death those who have transgressed in civil affairs: as by causing a dearth, or by selling above the prescribed rate by means of a false weight, or who have committed themselves in any other way. The cooks are put upon a spit, and roasted before a slow fire. During the dearth of 1688, I saw ovens heated in the royal square of Ispahan to terrify the bakers, and to deter them from deriving advantage from the general distress." The principle acted upon was to punish *crime in kind.* Cooks were to be cooked, and bakers baked.

Some of you may remember that we found in a former lecture, on the respective modes in which capital punishments are recorded in this book, an evidence of Daniel's truthfulness as a historian. While casting into a heated furnace was a cruelty practiced only by the Chaldeans, casting into a den of wild beasts was a punishment peculiar to the Medes and Persians; and this is precisely what Daniel says. Under the Chaldeans his friends are cast into a fiery furnace, while he was himself thrown into a den of lions by the Medo-Persians.

There are two things that strike us here as worthy of notice:

First, that we have a state religion *persecuting* the

people for their religious opinions, and threatening them with death if they do not comply with its decrees. It was not that their ministers should be turned out of their manses and their livings taken from them; but they themselves were to be burned alive if they did not obey the royal mandate. The *second* thing that strikes us is the measures taken to *popularize* the king's religion, and persuade the people to embrace it. These measures were two-fold. They were seductive and minatory. They were directed to the sensual tastes and natural fears of man. If the voluptuous swells of music from all kinds of instruments could not cause the people to fall down and worship Bel, why then the furnace was to do its work. And have we nothing like this in our times? Does not the devil use great adroitness and large sums of gold to monopolize the best music? Where but in the theatre are the best voices that nature, God, and culture can produce? Where but in Popish cathedrals do we find singers maimed of their vital organs, that they may have voices to imitate angelic choirs? Where do we find ceremony, pomp, and music—a gorgeous pageantry designed to strike the senses of the rude and ignorant? Where do we see processions with images, before which all men must uncover their heads and bow down, and remain prostrate till the image passes? Where is the penalty, confiscation, exile, or death, for not worshiping the God of heaven according to the decrees of ecclesiastical states? The king desired these young men to *conform* to his decree, but did not prove to them the truth of his religion. Mohammed demanded tribute or the Koran. Papal governments give no instruction to the people further than to subject them to the sway of the priesthood. All their machinery, from beginning to end, is to enslave the people to blind submission to the priesthood.

When the three young men refused to worship the golden image at the sounding of the music, and gave a faithful testimony in favor of their God, and avowed their belief that He was able to deliver them even from "the burning fiery furnace," the king was so enraged that he caused the furnace to be heated seven times more than it was wont to be heated." The phrase, *heated seven times more*, proves that this kind of punishment was frequent, and that the furnace was the usual instrument for such executions. Whether seven times is to be understood literally and exactly, or, according to a common usage of speech, seven, a definite term, is used for an indefinite one, and means many times, is a question of no importance. We have instances in ancient languages and in our day of the use of definite numerals for large numbers, without meaning to be precise. We say a hundred times as great, or a hundred times as many, meaning a great many times more. The literal meaning is not to be urged here. It signifies *intensity*. The means of giving seven-fold heat to the furnace were very easy in that country. The whole soil of Babylon to this day, according to Mr. Rich* and others, is full of naphtha and bitumen. They had only to collect the brushwood of the forests, and cast in plenty of this naphtha and bitumen, just as our steam-boat men do rosin and bacon into

* Rich's Babylon and Persepolis. London, 1839.

their furnaces, and the heat—even *seven-fold*, would soon be produced. The infidel objection about the size and shape of the furnace is scarcely worth a remark. It was not necessarily like a modern brick-kiln, a solid, inclosed building with brick or stone walls, and with only one aperture for putting in wood, and vent holes above for the emission of smoke and flame. The furnace of Babylon was probably a simple inclosure of fire, or an area of fire, surrounded by a low wall, without a covering, into which the victims were thrown, bound hand and foot. The savage Indians of the northwest could teach such skeptics how it was that the strong men who threw in the Hebrews were burned by being caught in the flames, and how the king could easily have seen the furnace, and looked into it, even from his palace windows.

But let us see who were the real victims. So fierce was the flame, we are told, that the strong men were destroyed who were employed to throw the young men, bound, into the fire. What an awful pause and shuddering must there have been as the spectators strained their eyes to see how the sea of fire would roll over and consume these victims of the king's wrath! But to the king's astonishment, he sees the young men moving safely amid the flames, which had power only to burn their bonds, but could not hurt a hair of their heads, or so much as singe their clothing. Even "the smell of fire had not passed upon them." The witticisms of Eichorn and others at the gigantic disproportions of the king's image, and at *the fire of Daniel that would not burn*, fall very naturally, of course, into the hands of those who deny all supernaturalism in the Bible. The whole difficulty about the disproportion of the image is removed, as we have seen, by including the pedestal in the height; and the whole difficulty about the fire that would not burn is explained by remembering that the flame did what infidels do not, recognized the presence of Him that made it, and bowed reverently to the authority of Him in whose hands are the winds, and waves, and all the elements and powers of nature. The flame lost its power to consume, simply because it was commanded to do so by Him that kindled it at the first.

There were many *flattering arguments* which these young men might have urged against the conviction of their earlier education, and in favor of complying with the king's command, which they did not urge, nor even seem to have allowed to have so much as a moment's consideration. They might have said—but they did not so say—that it was their duty to obey the king, and worship the image, for this was the established religion of the empire. They chose to obey God rather than man. They believed, what we enjoy, that the worship of God should be free and unfettered, according to the prescriptions of that conscience which governments and tyrants can neither bind nor free, which laughs at fire and sword, and glories only in subjection to God as its Sovereign. GOD ALONE IS LORD OF THE CONSCIENCE. These young men might have urged also—but they did not do so—that it was most expedient to bow down and worship the image. Mark their situation. They were captives in the hands of an absolute Oriental monarch, who could take off their heads at any minute, and no one ever ask why or wherefore. They were, moreover, advanced to places of power, where they were able, perhaps, to do many kind things for their suffering countrymen. The expediency-mongers of our day would have said, "It is indeed a distressing thing to bow down and worship the image; but we hold places of power; we have excellent salaries; we may lose the means of doing good to our poor captive countrymen; we will do so only once; and besides, our parents and friends in our fatherland will never know it. Had we not better bow down the body, though we will not bow down the soul, to this golden image?" But they did not parley thus. They remembered their old Hebrew Catechism, which had taught them that God had said to them, "Thou shalt not bow down to any idol gods, nor worship them." The matter touched their conscience. It lay between their souls and their Creator. They could not hesitate. Like Joseph, and like Daniel about the royal fare, they determined to do what was right, whether it seemed to be expedient or not. They could not do this great wickedness and sin against God. It is plainly taught in God's Holy Word that *right is always true expediency.* It may not seem to be so; but it will always be found so in the end. Do not, then, look before you nor behind you for a rule, nor compare yourselves with yourselves, but look to the law of God. What does He command? That you must do. Duty alone is ours; all the region beyond is God's. He will take care of the issues of duty.

Nor did these three Hebrew youths urge that they were compelled to obey the king's commandment because they were under great personal obligations to him. He had shown them much kindness, and heaped honors upon them; but their duty to God was stronger than gratitude to the king. Employers, parents, teachers, and benefactors may lay you under great personal obligations; but you must follow your conscience in the matter of religion. "He that loveth father or mother more than me cannot be my disciple." If you would be saved, you must take up your cross and follow Jesus. Do all you can to gratify your friends that is consistent with your duty to your own soul and your God, but do no more.

Nor did they urge that they would be out of fashion, and marked for their singularity, if they did not worship this golden image. Singularity assumed for the sake of being singular or famous is contemptible, and indicates a weak mind; but to be singular as a necessary result of not sinning as others do, is worthy of a Christian. This was the singularity of Noah, of Moses, and of Daniel and his friends. When duty requires us to be singular, then we must not hesitate. Do not mind that the multitude are against you, if God be with you. "If sinners entice thee," God says, "consent not." "Follow not the multitude to do evil." Nor did these young men urge the terrible penalty to which they were exposed by disobeying the king's commandment. They might have said, It is a terrible thing to be cast alive into a burning fiery furnace. But they did not falter. The heat of the furnace was not so strong as their sense of duty. Is there any young man here to-night, who is saying to himself, "I would become a Christian: I wish to save my soul; but if I do, I must give up such and such pleasures; I must shut up my shop on Sunday, and quit my lake-rides on the Lord's day?" And what if it does cost you all these pleasures to save your soul? Would it not be better to be thrown into the fiery furnace than to have both body and soul cast into hell fire forever? "What shall it profit a man if he gain the whole world and lose his own soul?" Your privileges are greater than those of Shadrach, Meshach, and Abednego. You have heard of Calvary, its cross, its agony, its bloody sweat. The Gospel has unfolded to you its grace, glory, and riches. How then can you escape if you neglect so great a salvation? What will it profit a man in eternity to have had a few years of dissipation? What will it profit a man to have kept his store open on Sabbath, and have worked late and early to acquire riches, and then—and THEN lie down and die, a poor, miserable, unpardoned sinner, and lift up his eyes in hell? Duty, conscience, responsibility, the soul, God and the Saviour will alone stand out as great, and blessed, and eternal realities in the judgment-day.

But why, think you, did these young men refuse to obey the royal decree? They could not obey it, because, *first*, of the force of their religious impressions. *Secondly*, consistency of character and of profession forbade them to worship idols. They were Hebrews. They had avowed Jehovah to be their God. They could not obey the king without denying the God of their fathers. What satisfaction would it have been, think you, to their pious parents, who in their homes at Jerusalem had taken so much pains to instruct them in the law and in the worship of the true God, could they have seen how firmly their sons adhered to the principles they had implanted with so many fears, and tears, and prayers? Remember, young men, in all the vicissitudes of the world, that you are

Americans, that you are Protestants, that you are Christians. Never allow yourselves to imbibe any creed or do any thing inconsistent with your birth, education, privileges, and destiny.

Thirdly. These Hebrew youths refused, because they were sustained by the *hope* of deliverance. They do not seem to have had any special revelation on the subject. Their faith taught them that their God was able to deliver them. They believed in God's promises. They had learned to trust in the promise of their parents' God to Isaiah: "When thou passest through the waters I will be with thee; and through the rivers, they shall not overflow thee. When thou walkest through the fire thou shalt not be burned, neither shall the flames kindle upon thee." They believed that God would make all things work together for their good.

Now let us consider

THEIR DELIVERANCE.

Read verses 22 to 30. And who was this that walked with them in the flame.

The king says: "Lo, I see four men loose, walking in the midst of the fire, and they have no hurt; and the form of the fourth is like the Son of God." No wonder that he was astonished—that he was alarmed, and filled with remorse, and called upon the young men to come out of the fire; and the whole court crowded around, and saw that the fire of the seven times heated furnace had no power upon those servants of God. It was natural that the king should conclude that Jehovah, the God of these Hebrews, was not a God that he could trifle with.

This conviction forced him to respect the religion of the Jews in future. Nay, he decreed "That every people, nation, and language, which speak any thing amiss against the God of Shadrach, Meshach, and Abednego, shall be cut in pieces, and their houses shall be made a dunghill; because there is no other God that can deliver after this sort." Who was this Son of God, and how did Nebuchadnezzar know any thing of the appearance of the Son of God? It is agreed that the manifestations of God in the Old Testament were either types of the manifestations of God in human flesh in the person of Jesus Christ, or that, in fact, it was Christ himself who appeared to the patriarchs and prophets, as a pledge of his Incarnation. But how did a heathen king come to have any notion of the second person of the Trinity? We answer, he may have asked Daniel and his three friends many questions, and received much instruction from them concerning their religion, of which no record is made. Daniel's superior wisdom, and the king's acknowledgment of Jehovah as the revealer of secrets, when Daniel told him his dream and its interpretation, must have excited his curiosity, if nothing more, to know something of their religious doctrines and practices.

But if Nebuchadnezzar had no such notions of the Messiah, he had notions of angels; and while it was Christ who walked with the Hebrews, the king may have mistaken him for an angel. The language is plural, and may be rendered *like a son of the gods.* This language indicated an angel or celestial intelligence. The proof that the inhabitants of this part of the world believed in the existence and interference of such angelic beings is manifold. The Assyrian inscriptions depict such intelligences with wings. The king explains his language when he glorified God for having sent "his angel" to deliver his servants.

The special lessons from the fiery furnace of Dura to young men of the nineteenth century are, I. *In the courteous but firm refusal of these Hebrew youths, we have a model for them in less painful circumstances.* The idea of heathen temples and of persecution unto death for religion's sake on American soil, are things that may well trouble us; but both will become realities, unless the pure Gospel of Christ prevails. History, the present aspect of the world, the prophecies yet to be fulfilled, and the promises concerning the spread of the Gospel and the establishment of Christ's kingdom over all the world, indicate to our mind times of great commotion and peril. Even now we almost dread to receive the intelligence of the steam-ships from Europe. That we are to have general peace for many years, I do not believe. It certainly is not probable. That the next general war in Europe will involve the hatred of races and the cruel asperity of opposing religions, I think is certain. Our reading of the future of the Gospel Church teaches us to expect fiery trials. The sword, the dungeon, and the stake will yet have many, many victims. Young men, therefore, who are coming forward on the stage should seek enlarged, accurate intelligence on religious subjects, and strive to know the truth, that they may support correct views and high moral principles. They should prepare themselves to endure all manner of opposition rather than sacrifice principles. It may not be proper to demand or expect of them in health and peace, when there is no opposition to their profession of Christ, the grace that would enable them to die for the Gospel. When God's providence calls for martyrs, then He will give grace sufficient for the crisis. The principle, however, must be well settled, that if the day comes when you are required to give up your liberty or religious freedom, or perish in the field of battle or at the stake, you would firmly prefer the latter. The prior point, in our times of freedom from persecution, is to become the true followers of Christ. To repent of our sins, believe in Him, and trust alone upon his most perfect righteousness, and take up our cross and follow Him by discharging all our duties toward God and man. Then, when the crisis comes to try our souls, God's grace will appear in our deliverance. There are not wanting authors and public teachers who argue that these young men should have complied with the wishes of the king, because the religion of Bel was the established religion of the empire. As loyal subjects, they should have embraced the same religion that was professed by their king. This is the old worm-eaten effête doctrine, that the government or the king is the head of the Church, and the keeper of the consciences of the people. Such is not the teaching of the Bible. The kingdom of Jesus Christ is not of this world; nor has He given to any human power the authority of enacting laws for Him. THE SCRIPTURES ARE THE ONLY RULE OF FAITH. The mere fact that a religion, or a system of dogmas, metaphysical, political, or religious, is established by law throughout a country, does not make it true or false. Mormonism prevails in Utah; if I go to the Salt Lake, must I turn Mormon? Brahminism is the established religion of certain parts of India and China, must the English and Americans that go thither become Hindoos? If you live in Constantinople, must you, therefore, become a Mohammedan? If you live in Paris, is it right for you to become an Infidel, Papist, or Socialist; or if in Germany, a Pantheist or a Protestant, simply because any one of these may be the established or prevailing creed around you? It is monstrous to suppose that a man's duty to his Creator is to be decided by any such standard as this. The only authority binding on the conscience is the authority of God. There is no real power but that of truth. Wealth is power, talent is power, and knowledge is power; but more mighty than all is truth. It is of God, and invested with His attributes of eternity, omnipotence, and

It is the most potent element of social or individual life. It may be tossed upon the billows of popular fury, or cast into the seven-fold heated furnace of persecution, or be trampled to the dust by the iron heel of despotism; but it is absolutely imperishable. "Hers are the eternal years of God." Nor can those die who fall in her great cause:

> "The earth may drink their gore; their limbs
> May sodden in the sun; their heads
> Be hung on castle walls and city gates,
> But still their spirit walks abroad."

All the resources of earth and hell cannot crush it, nor vitiate and poison it. It has never failed, and it never will. Cleave to it; it is more than your life—it is your salvation.

II. *As Christian young men you have, therefore, the great consolation of knowing that the greatest efforts of the mightiest men are utterly unavailing against the Gospel of Christ.* The most furious opposition to the Church has only served to spread its principles, and to add new attractions to those that professed them. If you will read history, you will see how insignificant are all the plans of the mightiest on earth against the Church of Christ. The gates of hell cannot prevail against it. The Hebrew youths walked amid the glowing furnace as amid groves of orange and myrtle. The fury of the king was disappointed, the party spirit of his ministers checked, and they that kindled the fire were themselves its first and only victims. All the power of earth and hell cannot burn out one single truth from God's word; nor can all the popes and assemblies, cabinets, and armies on the globe add one single doctrine or precept to the Bible necessary to salvation. It is God's great law of the universe that all things shall, directly or indirectly, build up the truth, and work together for the good of them that love him; and the greatest of all truths is the FAITHFUL SAYING, AND WORTHY OF ALL ACCEPTATION, THAT CHRIST JESUS CAME INTO THE WORLD TO SAVE SINNERS, EVEN THE CHIEF, WHO BELIEVE IN HIM.

III. Learn then, and though this lesson has been taught before, I must repeat it, that TRUE EXPEDIENCY IS TRUE PRINCIPLE. "The path of duty is the path of safety." "Honesty is the best policy." It was so with Joseph. It was so with Daniel and his three friends. It has always been so with the great and the good. Without sincerity, depth of conviction, and firmness in one's principle, there is no foundation for greatness. Let nothing, therefore, induce you to do a thing because it seems expedient unless it also seems to be right; and remember that that only is right which is according to the will of God. And remember also, that the experience of the wisest and happiest, greatest and best men, teaches us that what God declares to be right is the highest possible expediency. He that walketh uprightly walketh surely. Godliness hath the promise of the life that now is and of that which is to come.

Whatever God calls you to do or to suffer, fear not to obey. He will be with you in whatever he calls you to. If he calls you to enter the fiery furnace, hesitate not one moment. He will be with you, and either sustain you or deliver you, or make it conducive to your higher and future good. If you could go to Paradise itself upon any other rule than what is right, according to God's will, Paradise would become a Marah—a fountain of bitter waters only. The greatest prosperity, without God's blessing, is nothing but a curse—a very furnace seven times heated. God is always able and is always willing to deliver you. And remember, I beseech you, young men, in every place and under all circumstances, that if you put your trust in him he will deliver you in the way that shall be most for his glory and best for you. God never forgets his own. Nature is pliant in his hand. There is but one thing in the universe to be afraid of, and that is sin; and God is faithful and just to forgive us our sins, if we confess them to him and sincerely repent of them, FOR THE BLOOD OF HIS SON JESUS CHRIST CLEANSETH US FROM ALL SIN

LECTURE VIII.

CAVILS AT THE KING'S PROCLAMATION.

On Dan., iv., 1–33.

Auto da Fe at Babylon.—Objections to the King's Proclamation.—Insufficiency of the Argumentum a Silentio.—Daniel does not profess to write a complete History of Babylon nor of Nebuchadnezzar.—Webster.—George III.—Omissions are not Contradictions.—Nothing improbable in this Proclamation.—Necessity of considering Infidel Objections.—Nobles hunting for the King.—Who built Babylon?—Eclipse of Thales.—Wives bearing the King's Name.—Description of Babylon.—Tunnel of the Euphrates.—Nebuchadnezzar's Greatness and Weakness.—Justness and Nature of his Punishment.

LESSONS.

I. Beware of pride.
II. Insanity a great misfortune.
III. Benefits of sanctified affliction.—*Randolph's Letter.*
IV. Omniscience of God should comfort youth and old age.

In the last Lecture we saw Daniel's three friends in the fiery furnace of Babylon, and heard of their deliverance by one whose appearance was like that of the Son of God. We were carried back to an *auto da fé* celebrated on the banks of the Euphrates, in the plain of Dura, some two thousand five hundred years ago. It was just such an *act of faith* as was witnessed about two hundred years ago in various cities of Italy, France, and Germany, and especially in Spain, and even in Great Britain. This *act of faith* was persecution unto death for the sake of religion. In the one case we are in the distant East, about six hundred years before Christ, and the head of the persecution is Nebuchadnezzar, aided by his courtiers, and the victims are pious Hebrew captives. In the other case we are in Europe, about one thousand six hundred and fifty years after Christ, and the leader of the persecution is the Pope of Rome, aided by a college of Holy Inquisitors, who were priests, and the victims were hundreds of men and women, burned alive in the public market-places for no other sin than that they would not surrender their conscience to the confessor and believe as he told them. The Saint Bartholomew Massacre and the revocation of the Edict of Nantes are not yet forgotten, nor yet washed out from the history of France. All persecution for righteousness' sake—for religious opinion—is wholly irreconcilable with the Gospel of Christ. Never can we pay the debt we owe for civil and religious liberty; never should we forget to do to all others as we would that they should do to us. I refer to the *auto da fés* of the Old World to quicken our zeal for liberty of conscience and freedom to worship God, and not because I cherish any unkind feelings toward any sect or party, political or ecclesiastical. But it is our duty to keep our eyes open to the dealings of Providence with us, and to the pages of history, and learn hence what principles to support.

This chapter is a most remarkable one. It was written by Nebuchadnezzar himself, and sent as his royal proclamation unto *all people, and nations, and languages that dwell in all the earth.* It is one of the most ancient decrees on record. It was copied, no doubt, by Daniel from the state papers of Babylon.

The fashionable criticism of the day has urged several

objections to this chapter of Daniel, a few of which only seem to deserve serious consideration. 1. It is said *that it is an utter improbability that Nebuchadnezzar should have published such a decree as this, for it holds him up to the contempt of his subjects and to public disgrace.* To this it may be answered, we have the decree in the original Chaldee in our Hebrew Bible, and in the Greek translation made at Alexandria about two hundred and eighty years before Christ. The language of the decree is just such as we are led to believe prevailed at Babylon in the time of Nebuchadnezzar, and such as would in all probability have been used by him. The internal evidence for the truth of this proclamation is very strong. The proof of its genuineness and authenticity—that is, of its being the actual proclamation of the King of Babylon, and that it sets forth truth and not fiction—is as strong as, in the nature of the case, it could be. Abydenus, a historian, who probably lived in the second century B.C., relates the story of Nebuchadnezzar's madness. And although his story differs in some minor points from the account in Daniel, yet it is evident that he framed his story out of the traditions that reached him concerning the king's malady.

The *argumentum a silentio* has been well called "one of the most treacherous of all that encumber the logic of history."* No one at all acquainted with history, either ancient, Oriental, or modern, will dare to set up such a standard as the test of historical truth in contradistinction to fiction. For example, no one supposes that the his-

* Professor Stuart, page 121.

torical veracity of the writer of the book of Chronicles should be called in question because no mention is made by that writer of the adultery and murder committed by David, nor of the polygamy, sensuality, and idolatry of Solomon in his old age. It is easy to raise similar questions in regard to the New Testament. For example, how could such miracles as that of the pool of Bethesda, or the raising of Lazarus from the dead, be passed over in silence by three of the Evangelists, and be recorded only by John? As to the history of Nebuchadnezzar, at best we have nothing but fragments. The Bible does not profess to give us a full account of all the wars and works of his long reign. Daniel writes of this king only what related to himself, and his countrymen, and prophecies. Jeremiah and Ezekiel died before the close of his reign, and of course have left nothing concerning it. The Scriptural history of this great king is confined to the early part of his reign. And Herodotus, who writes so much about Babylon, never mentions Nebuchadnezzar, nor does he speak at all of his great expedition to Egypt. Josephus and Eusebius, who have brought together all they could find about Nebuchadnezzar, mention only six writings which recognized him, and in no two of these is there a perfect agreement. There is, I believe, no essential contradiction between them; but while one relates one thing and speaks of one part of his reign, another speaks of a different part of his actions in a different part of the world. The Phenician annals merely mention his attack on Phenicia. Another account speaks of his besieging Tyre. The fragments of his history in the Bible speak of his wars upon Syria, and of his connection with the

Jews. It is unreasonable to expect that all the facts mentioned in one account of a great man must be mentioned in all the other accounts of his life. Because one of the compilers and authors of a life of the sage of Marshfield, in giving to the public what he knew, heard, and saw of the late Daniel Webster, *omits* what another heard and saw, and gives in his own way to the public, it does not follow that either of them forces upon the public a pure fiction. Suppose a historian, writing the history of George III. during a long and eventful reign, and being confined to a few pages, should omit to speak of this king's madness, and the particulars of the interim regency, would it follow that his history was a fable or a fiction, and that George the Third was never afflicted with such a malady, and that there was no regency in his reign? Here, then, let us settle once for all, that *mere omissions in historians are not contradictions, nor proofs of fiction.* Acknowledged truthful history abounds with omissions. Manetho, and the great writers generally, for instance, celebrate the victory of Pharaoh-nechoh, over the Israelites at Megiddo, but they do not tell us of his defeat at Carchemish. The plain reason is that Manetho did not wish to wither the laurels of his hero. What Persian historian acknowledges the defeat of Xerxes by the Greeks, or of Darius by Alexander in Asia? Where is the English historian that acknowledges manfully the defeat of the eighth of January, or the French writer who details the disasters of Waterloo? In the gallery devoted to *all the glory of France* at Versailles, there is no picture of Waterloo. A nation's monuments, pictures, and historians preserve only its glory. For this reason Josephus says nothing of the golden calf or of the brazen serpent; and for the same reason, perhaps, no monument on the Nile tells us the particulars of the Hebrew bondage and deliverance from Egypt. As to national disasters, the rule with great and proud nations is to speak no evil of the dead.

But after all, is it indeed so improbable that Nebuchadnezzar would have been unwilling to publish such a decree? This act is in harmony with his character. If any thing could humble his pride, what he had suffered must have done so. The impression on his mind from Daniel's character and the interpretation of his dreams, and their exact fulfillment, must have been very strong. It is unreasonable, therefore, to suppose that he was willing to publish such a decree as might lead his subjects to do what he himself did—*praise the most High, and acknowledge his dominion over all things?* The very first thing to which all strong emotions of penitence lead, is ample confession of sin and reparation; and is it not probable that even Nebuchadnezzar became truly penitent? Certainly he felt deep regret for his pride and haughtiness, and a strong sense of humiliation. The state of mind in which the historian presents the king leaves no room for selfish and honor-saving devices. From the ardor and intensity of his emotions, from the energy and earnestness of his character, and from the nature of true penitence, we should have expected Nebuchadnezzar to do just as Daniel says he did do. And besides, may not the providence of God have been exerted to procure such a proclamation from such a hero and conqueror, who had advanced his country to the highest pinnacle of dominion and fame?

Would not such a proclamation have a powerful influence on the minds of the Babylonians, and induce them to treat the Hebrew exiles among them with more respect and kindness? and does not the testimony of such a man, under such circumstances, convey to us in these ends of the earth some exceedingly important lessons? It is not impossible for Major Rawlinson to find a copy of this very decree amid the ruins of the Euphrates, and identify the Nebuchadnezzar of Daniel, and confirm in every particular the Bible narrative of his reign. This appears the less impossible, since he has actually made out from the inscriptions on the great Assyrian bull the truth of the Bible account of Senacherib's campaign against Hezekiah. The learned Scaliger and other writers quote a fragment of an ancient historian of the days of the Babylonian empire, who gives some account of the wonderful things that befell this king. He was a man of impulses, of strong passions, and of a haughty spirit, but, when the storm of passion had blown over, capable of vast undertakings and susceptible of generous impulses. It is not Nebuchadnezzar as the head of a great empire, nor as a mere conquering general, who speaks in this chapter, but Nebuchadnezzar as rebuked, punished, disciplined, instructed, and made to feel that he was powerless in the hands of an all-wise and overruling Providence. His proclamation is a singular testimony of his susceptible and variable temper, and vast conquests. It must have been issued near the close of his life and reign. It is the last account we have of him in the Bible.

2. Again, it is said, *if Nebuchadnezzar ran wild with the beasts, how could his nobles seek after him, and know*

where to find him, or know when his reason returned, or know whether it returned at all? I have scarcely patience to notice such pitiful and insignificant criticisms, and the less so because they are made in ignorance of the language of the text, though made by men who profess great learning; and yet I suppose it is best to consider them, for you are aware that the tendency of our times is to extract the life out of the Bible by criticisms and sophistries. It is too late in the age of the world to deny the Bible its place as a history; therefore the mode of attack now usually made is to impeach the correctness of our *translation*, or to destroy its *spirituality* and *inspired authority*, or to tear out all of the miracles, the distinguishing works of Christ as the Son of God, and all Divine influence.

The isms out of the Church and the infidelity in the Church agree in this mode of attack. It is necessary, therefore, to strengthen our defenses by removing objections to the sacred text, and to prove the truth of the great doctrines taught in the Bible. But to return to the matter in hand. When it is said that his nobles sought for him, it is not meant that they *hunted* for him as for a *lost* animal. When Arioch, in chap. ii., v. 13, is said to have *sought after Daniel* to kill him—the term is the same in the original—the meaning is not that Daniel had either run away or concealed himself. Such was not the fact. The meaning is, that he *made inquiry* for him. And this is all that Nebuchadnezzar's nobles did, as soon as they heard of his restoration to reason. No doubt his haunts were known, and that some kind of watch-guard was placed over him, whose business it was to look to any exigency that might occur. His rank, popularity, and relations would certainly have secured for him, even in his madness, such attentions; and when his mind was re-established he would, of course, return to his home and his friends. There was no need of *hunting* him out of the forest. It often happens that persons who have fallen into a mania which lasts for years come suddenly to the consciousness of the state and circumstances they were in when attacked by the malady; the intervening period is entirely lost.

The fantastic representations of Nebuchadnezzar that are sometimes made, founded upon a forced literal interpretation of the text, do not deserve consideration. The text needs no illustration nor proof from heathen hydras, chimeras, centaurs, and the like. Stripped of its gorgeous Oriental costume, the narrative is easily explained. The meaning is not that he became an ox or an eagle, but fancied himself such, and resembled them in his habits and residence. Madmen have often acted over scenes just like those here described.

As to the objection about the length of time that the king was mad—*till seven times passed over him*—only a few words need be said. Calvin thinks that *seven* is here an indefinite number employed to denote a considerable period. The term is often so used. The idiom of the book forbids that we should regard the times of the text as *astrological periods*, as Havernich does.

But why object to the term of *seven years?* Surely a seven years' madness is not so unusual a thing, even among crowned heads, as to throw a suspicion on the record. Nor is this the only case in which men have imagined themselves to be beasts; nor, alas! it is the only case in which men have made themselves like beasts.

And the kingdom, for even seven years, could have been preserved for him, and his affairs have gone on as usual. The extent of his conquests and the durability of his power show that he was a man of promptness, decision, and discipline, and it is probable, therefore, that his state affairs were all in a prosperous condition when his madness began.

3. Again, it is said *that it is not true that Nebuchadnezzar built Babylon.* It is of very little consequence whether he did or not, so far as the integrity of the text is concerned. Daniel is not responsible for the truth of what Nebuchadnezzar said, but only for giving us a correct report of what the king did say. If it is an error, it is the king's fault, and not Daniel's. The inspiration of the Bible is not responsible for the matter and manner of the speeches of Job's friends, nor for the words of Jethro, nor for the letter of Claudius Lysias to Governor Felix, nor for the decrees of Nebuchadnezzar, nor of the Persian kings. It has pleased God to have these and other similar things spread on the pages of Revelation for our instruction; but the prophets and apostles are not fairly chargeable with the errors of the speeches which they merely report.

But let us look a little at the case in hand.

From the Bible we gather that Nineveh was standing 609 B.C., but had fallen in the year 605 B.C. It was taken and destroyed by Cyaxares, who formed an alliance with Nabopolasar, king of Babylon, about the year B.C. 606. This Nabopolasar was the father of Nebuchadnezzar. And from this time Nineveh ceased to occupy any place in prophecy or in the history of the world. With the fall of Nineveh the history of all Assyria and Media is merged into that of Babylon, and with Nebuchadnezzar as its king commences the grand era of Babylonian greatness. After the capture of Nineveh, Nitocris is named as the wife of Nebuchadnezzar and queen of Babylon by Herodotus, and mother of Nabonnadius. This passage of Herodotus agrees with the history of Daniel as to facts, and gives us in addition some of the names of the king and queen, which are omitted by him. It is to Nebuchadnezzar and to his queen, a Median princess, that ancient authors ascribe most of the great works for which Babylon was renowed.* Herodotus says that the son of Nitocris was called Labynitus, after his father. He was also called Nabonnadius. It was against him that Cyrus marched in 538 B.C. Nabonnadius or Labynitus II., of Herodotus, is therefore the Belshazzar of the Bible.

I have before alluded to the use of astronomy in ascertaining the precise year of important events. As, for example, when Plutarch tells us that Romulus founded Rome in the year of the great eclipse in Italy, we have only to reckon back on the Planetarium, and we shall find the year, month, day, and hour of that eclipse. So we can come near to the year of the rise of Nebuchadnezzar by considering the eclipse predicted by Thales. The truth of this prediction is admitted by modern astronomers, and they tell us that it took place 610 B.C. Now it happened that the great battle between Cyaxares and

* Vaux's Nineveh and Persepolis, p. 42.

his enemies, which immediately preceded the fall of Nineveh and the rise of Babylon, was fought on the day of Thales' eclipse. This eclipse caused the contending armies to separate, from fear of the vengeance of the gods, and a peace was made, and one of the mediators was Nebuchadnezzar—Labynitus I., king of Babylon.

It is true, then, that Babylon existed before the time of Nebuchadnezzar. Its foundation may be traced back to the Tower of Babel and to the time of Nimrod. But it is true, also, that nothing now remains of the old city that existed before Nebuchadnezzar. Major Rawlinson tells us that not only Babylon, but the whole region around is full of ruins having his great name; but no ruins are found prior to his reign. You recollect it was a custom in Egypt to inscribe the name and titles of the monarch and of the builder of the pyramids on the stones used in their construction; so it was a custom in Babylon, as it was no doubt with the Assyrians, to stamp the brick used in building their cities with the name and titles of the royal founder; and the hope is entertained that the bricks collected from different sites on the Tigris and Euphrates may enable us to reconstruct the chronology of that country. It is stated to be a fact, that *every ruin* in Babylon proper, in an area of about one hundred miles in length, and thirty or forty in breadth, has its bricks stamped with the name of Nebuchadnezzar. Rawlinson states that he has examined himself the bricks *in situ* belonging to about one hundred different towns, and that he has never found any other royal name than that of Nebuchadnezzar, son of Nabopolasar, king of Babylon. A vast number of these brick inscriptions is in the India

House in London, showing that Nebuchadnezzar built a great many cities. The extent and number of the cities which he built would "almost pass belief on any evidence less conclusive; and certainly the necessity of finding inhabitants for the numerous towns built by him supplies a new and interesting motive for his zeal in sweeping the population of Judah, and doubtless of other conquered nations, into this quarter."—*Kitto.*

Though Nebuchadnezzar was not the actual founder of Babylon, yet he might be said to have been the builder of the city as it was in his day. When a great prince adds new buildings to those already existing, he is said to have built it. So in the Apocryphal Judith, it is said Phraortes built a very strong city and called it Ecbatana, when it is clear the meaning is, that he only repaired, enlarged, and added to its buildings; and so the Temple of Jerusalem, built after the return from captivity, is called Solomon's Temple, when the meaning clearly is, that it was modelled, built on the site of, and in part out of the materials of the old temple. Nebuchadnezzar greatly enlarged, improved, and adorned Babylon, and rebuilt large portions of it. Josephus and other old writers say that he adorned the Temple of Bel with the spoils he took in war; that he embellished all that remained of the old city—made the triple wall of burned brick around it—erected a new and extraordinary palace, and raised stone terraces which had the appearance of mountains planted with various kinds of trees. The celebrated hanging gardens were of similar construction. These terraces and gardens were erected, it is said, to gratify his Median wife, who desired to have in the dead level country of the Euphrates some scenery resembling that of her native country. The greatest wonder of Babylon was its temple of Belus and its palaces. These edifices alone are said to have occupied a space of nearly three miles square. The hanging gardens were immense parterres formed on vaulted terraces, four hundred feet square, rising one above another to the height of the wall. These terraces were built of stone, and covered first with sheets of lead, then with a layer of bitumen and reeds, and finally with a thick coating of earth, out of which rose the different kinds of trees. On the topmost platform was a large basin filled with water, forced up by a powerful hydraulic engine from the Euphrates. But another work still, that must have given strangers visiting Babylon a very high idea of Nebuchadnezzar's genius, was the passage, constructed of brick and bitumen, under the River Euphrates. The Thames Tunnel is not so stupendous a work now as the tunnel of the Euphrates was in the days of Nebuchadnezzar. It is admitted, I believe, that the works ascribed to the fabulous Semiramis belong properly to this king.

4. *Let us now consider the humiliation of the king's punishment.* (See verses 32, 33.)

Nebuchadnezzar was without doubt a very remarkable man, a man of vast ideas and of vast undertakings, and of almost uninterrupted successes; and, on the whole, a much better man, I think, than people generally suppose. The lapse of ages is continually bringing to light new evidences, long hidden, indeed, of the eminence, of the power, and magnificence which the Scriptures ascribe to him. His misfortune was not that he was the most illustrious prince of his age, and one of the most illustrious that the world has ever seen. His sin was not that he had genius, intellect, and wealth—not that he was victorious in battle, and absolute in influence, but that he was too conscious of his greatness. His sin lay in his forgetfulness of God—in ascribing all that he had achieved to the strength of his own arm and to the vastness of his own conceptions. When he looked on the magnificence of his city and on the vastness of his empire, and the multitudes of nations he had conquered, forgetting the Supreme Power by whom kings reign, and who had given him all he had, his heart was lifted up in pride, and the just punishment of Heaven fell upon him.

We may say that his pride was natural; still it was criminal. He was the successor of the Assyrian kings, whose monarchy was ancient and mighty; and from the death of his father, Nebuchadnezzar met with unparalleled and most extraordinary success for many years.

The glory of Cyrus, of Alexander, and of the Cæsars never equaled the splendor of the kings of Babylon. Hence the head (himself) in his first dream, was of gold; and in this second dream he is a tree in the midst of the earth, whose height reached unto heaven, and the sight thereof to the end of all the earth. But as he forgot God, the heavenly watchers cried, *Hew down the tree, and cut off his branches.* (See verses 14–16.)

The mind of a man was taken from him, and the mind of a beast entered into him. He rushed out into his great park on the banks of the river and mingled with the beasts that fed there, living upon the herbs of the field, fleeing from the sight of man and remaining exposed to all the vicissitudes of weather, day and night, summer and winter.

Meanwhile, his son, Evil-merodach, governed as regent, and no doubt the king was looked after and protected as far as was necessary, or as his peculiar circumstances would allow. If he had built, in the days of his power, an insane asylum, he would no doubt have been put into it. The penalty was suited to the offense. The sin was special, so also was the punishment. Pride was the sin; degradation was the punishment. As a general rule, punishment is just the rebound of sin. Generally speaking, sin may be traced out in the light of the punishment inflicted; for God sends punishment not merely to reform the sinner, but also to reveal the odiousness of sin. Sin is the conductor that draws down the lightning of God's judgment.

The severity of the king's suffering was much greater than we can easily imagine in this climate. Think of a man whose body is relaxed by the heat, and its pores open, after being twelve hours in a blazing sun, exposed to a cold falling dew, so heavy as to saturate a tent like rain,* and you will have some idea of the king's condition.

* The day is hotter in Western Asia, and the nights colder, than with us. While traveling in Arabia and Syria, I often found the heat most distressing at noon, and yet at night I required all the covering I had—a capote, quilt, and blanket. I often thought of Jacob's words in Gen., xxxi., 40, "In the day the drought consumed me, and the frost by night." After the heat of a summer day, the cold and chilling winds and frosts of night in the neighborhood of the mountains of Asia are peculiarly severe. So well known and striking are these contrasts, that they are referred to by the Arabs in at least two proverbs which are common among them. Of an unhappy man

Observe also the *suddenness* of his punishment. One day, as he walked on the terraces or roof of his palace, in a burst of imperial pride he said, "Is not this great Babylon, that I have built for the house of the kingdom, by the might of my power, and for the honor of my majesty?" And while the word was still in his mouth, a voice from heaven said, "The kingdom is departed from thee!" Verses 31–33.

Finally, let us attend to some of the lessons which this history of this remarkable proclamation of the king teaches to young men.

FIRST. The fall of pride warms you of the sinfulness and danger of presumption and vanity. "Pride goeth before destruction." "Those that walk in pride he is able to abase." More on this point at another time.

SECONDLY. *It is a great misfortune to be deprived of reason.* It is one of the greatest calamities that can befall men in this life. A great man is wont to say in his daily prayers, "Lord, deliver me from sudden death, hydrophobia, insanity, and tetanus." The fame of Nebuchadnezzar filled the then known world, but the poorest beggar in the streets of his proud capital, or the humblest peasant in his kingdom, was better off than he was in his insanity. You should be thankful, my young friends, for the use of reason and speech, and for the flowings forth of human sympathy. These are all God's gifts to you. You should be careful not to impair your understanding by neglecting to use it, or by abusing it. The great causes of insanity are the letting of our mental faculties

they say, "The sun falls on his head by day, and the dew by night." "He is scorched by the sun, and made wet by the dew."

rust, and the abuse of them by gluttony and drunkenness, and by the indulgence of violent passions and of excessive anxieties. You should do all you can to relieve such as are afflicted with this awful calamity. One of the best remedies against it is to be actively engaged in useful and honorable employments. Homes and personal comforts should be provided for the insane, as well as for all invalids; their thoughts should be drawn away from themselves. It is a sure recipe for unhappiness to be selfish.

THIRDLY. The King of Babylon *testifies to the benefits of sanctified affliction.* This is, indeed, a lesson verified from our experience, and from the general tenor of all Bible instruction. No doubt Nebuchadnezzar found, as David did, "It is good for me that I have been afflicted." He had been warned. He had been made to confess the superiority of Daniel's God to the gods of Babylon, when Daniel restored to him his lost dream and interpreted it, and had delivered his three friends out of the fiery furnace; but still he had not submitted his proud heart to God. There are lessons in affliction that we never can learn in prosperity. When God hides the sun from us, he reveals to us a thousand suns by night. You know that on a sick-bed, or in the moment of an expected shipwreck, in the hour of bitter and sorrowful bereavement, vows and resolutions are formed, which, if kept, would lead to great zeal in behalf of religion. Though bitter in the experience, yet the results of sanctified affliction are blessed. I have before me a letter, but recently published, from the brilliant but eccentric orator of Roanoke, which bears in part on the subject in hand, and which, although many of you have doubtless read it, I will take the liberty of presenting to you. It has rarely ever been surpassed for terms of tenderness and propriety. It was written by Mr. Randolph to his half-brother on the occasion of the death of his eldest son. I earnestly commend all young men, but especially law students and honorable members of the Legislature and politicians, if there be any present, to give particular attention to the points of Christian doctrine advanced in this letter, and the trains of thought which it suggests. Mr. Randolph was without doubt one of the most brilliant and remarkable men this country has ever produced:

"The father of Lord Russell, when condoled with according to form, by the book, replied, 'I would not give my dead son for any other man's living.' May this thought come home to your bosom, too, but not as the chimera of heated brains, nor a device of artful men to frighten and cajole the credulous, but as an existence that can be as much felt and understood as the whisperings of your own heart, or the love you bore to him that you have lost—may that Spirit, which is the Comforter, shed his influence upon your soul, and incline your heart and understanding to the only right way, which is that of life eternal! Did you ever read Bishop Butler's Analogy? If not, I will send it to you. Have you read THE BOOK? What I say upon this subject I not only believe, but I know to be true, that the *Bible, studied with an humble and contrite heart, never yet failed to do its work, even with those who, from idiosyncrasy or disordered minds, have conceived that they were cut off from its promises of a life to come.*"

"'Ask, and ye shall receive; seek, and ye shall find;

knock, and it shall be opened unto you.' This was my only support and stay during years of misery and darkness; and just as I *had almost begun to despair, after more than ten years of penitence and prayer, it pleased God to enable me to see the truth, to which, until then, my eyes had been sealed.* To this vouchsafement I have made the most ungrateful returns. But I would not give up my slender portion of the price paid for our redemption—yes, my brother, *our* redemption, the ransom of sinners, of all who do not hug their chains and refuse to come out from the house of bondage—I say, that I would not exchange my little portion in the Son of David for the power and glory of the Parthian or Roman empires, as described by Milton in the temptation of our Lord and Saviour—not for all with which the Enemy tempted the Saviour of man.

"This is the secret of the change in my spirits, which all who know me must have observed within a few years past. After years spent in humble and contrite entreaty that the tremendous sacrifice on Mount Calvary might not have been made in vain for me, the chiefest of sinners, it pleased God to speak his peace into my heart, that peace of God which passeth all understanding to them that know it not, and even to them that do. And although I have now, as then, to reproach myself with time misspent and faculties misemployed—although my condition has, on more than one occasion, resembled that of him who, having one evil spirit cast out, was taken possession of by seven other spirits more wicked than the first, and the first also, yet I trust that they too, by the power and mercy of God, may be, if they are not, vanquished.

"But where am I running to? On this subject more hereafter. Meanwhile, assure yourself of what is of small value compared with that of those who are a piece of yourself—of the unchanged regard and sympathy of your mother's son. Ah! my God! I remember to have seen her die, to have followed her to the grave, to have wondered that the sun continued to rise and set, and the order of nature to go on. Ignorant of *true* religion, but not yet an atheist, I remember with horror my impious expostulations with God upon this bereavement—'but not yet an atheist!' The existence of atheism has been denied, but I was an honest one. Hume began, and Hobbes finished me. I read Spinoza and all the tribe. Surely I fell by no ignoble hand. And the very man (——) who gave me Hume's 'Essay upon Human Nature' to read, administered 'Beattie upon Truth' as the antidote; Venice treacle against arsenic and the essential oil of bitter almonds; bread and milk poultice for the bite of the cobra capello.

"Had I remained a successful political leader, I might never have been a Christian. But it pleased God that my pride should be mortified; that by death and desertion I should lose my friends; that, except in the veins of a maniac, and he too possessed 'of a child by a deaf and dumb spirit,' there should not run one drop of my father's blood in any living creature besides myself. The death of Tudor finished my humiliation. I had tried all things but the refuge to Christ, and to that, with parental stripes, was I driven. Often did I cry out with the father of that wretched boy, 'Lord! I believe—help thou mine unbelief;' and the gracious mercy of our Lord to this wavering faith, staggering under the force of the hard heart of unbelief, I humbly hoped would, in his good time, be extended to me also. Mark, vii., 17–29.

"Throw Revelation aside, and I can drive any man by irresistible induction to atheism. John Marshall could not resist me. When I say any man, I mean a man capable of logical and consequential reasoning. Deism is the refuge of those that startle at atheism, and can't believe Revelation, and my —— (may God have forgiven us both) and myself used, with Diderot & Co., to laugh at the deistical bigots who must have milk, not being able to digest meat. All theism is derived from Revelation—that of the laws confessedly. Our own is from the same source—so is the false revelation of Mohammed; and I can't much blame the Turks for considering the Franks and Greeks to be idolaters. Every other idea of *one* God that floats in the world is derived from the tradition of the sons of Noah handed down to their posterity.

"But enough, and more than enough; I can scarcely guide my pen. I will, however, add that no lukewarm seeker ever became a Christian; for 'from the days of John the Baptist until now, the kingdom of Heaven suffereth violence, and the violent take it by force'—a text which I read five hundred times before I had the slightest conception of its true application.

"Your brother,

"J. R., of Roanoke.

"To H. St. G. Tucker, Esq."

Fourthly. *You are here taught the omniscience of God.* The king was walking on his palace top, and he said to himself, "Is not this great Babylon that I have built?" And, at the end of days, he "lifted up his eyes unto heaven." In both instances God was nigh unto him. He heard the thoughts of his heart in his pride, and he heard the whispering of his soul in his penitence. Prayer is equally powerful in the cabinet and in the hovel of straw. God sees as clearly the toilings of the slave as the labors of the statesman. God's eye is just as closely riveted upon you, young man, or upon you, young woman, as you pursue your occupation in the crowded city or seek a home in a strange land, as if you were the only individual in the universe. There is not a thought that flutters in your hearts—there is not a purpose in your mind formed for to-morrow or for the future—there is not a secret spring of wickedness arising in any bosom—there is not a design that is cherished in the secrecy of any heart, either for good or evil, that you can hide from God. His eye pierces the darkness—His ear hears in silence—His laws and his presence are every where. He is the final Judge, who will bring every secret thing to light, and judge every man according to the thoughts of his heart, the words of his mouth, and the deeds of his body, whether they be good or whether they be evil. How solemn is the consideration that those thoughts which you wish to conceal from that person who sits beside you in the pew are known to God; and your schemes, plans, and imaginations, that you would not disclose to a mother or a friend for all the world, are perfectly known to Him. How solemn is the reflection that all your vows and resolutions in times of danger, and on your sick-bed, are daguerreotyped for the day of judgment. How can you meet all your sins at the bar of God? What an awful idea is this, that at the judgment-day a man's secret thoughts will be set in the light of God's countenance! What a fearful spectacle to an impenitent sinner to see all his sins rise with his body from the grave! Is the doctrine of God's omniscience a source of alarm or of comfort to you? Does the thought of God trouble you? Is there any one of you ready to say, "I am a wretch undone; how can I escape the wrath of God? I am a guilty sinner!" Then hear what the Gospel says to you: "THE BLOOD OF JESUS CHRIST CLEANSETH US FROM ALL SIN." JESUS CHRIST CAME TO SEEK AND SAVE THE LOST. Amen.

LECTURE IX.

LESSONS FROM THE KING'S DREAM.

On Dan., iv.

Moral Lessons in History do not prove that History Fiction. Sparks' Washington.—Proper End of all Government.—Prosperity is dangerous.—Scotch Fir-tree.—When Riches are safe.—Danger of Pride.—Flat Roofs in the East.—Lesson of all History is that Pride goeth before Destruction.—Luxembourg Picture of the Decadence of the Romans.—Money the Idol of the nineteenth Century.—Several Characters who walk in Pride.—Obstinacy of Pride.—It prevents Conversion to God.—Sunbeams only can melt the Icicle.—Salvation only by Grace.—Finally impenitent cannot escape.—God's Providence general and special.—Preservation of Judah.—Angels in Charge of the Universe.—God has Purposes.—Man free Agent.—God warns before He smites.—A faithful Prophet and Minister of State.

The lessons which were drawn from the defense and teachings of the king's remarkable decree in the last lecture were,

I. The sinfulness and danger of pride.

II. That madness is a great misfortune, and consequently the use of our faculties calls for gratitude and their proper improvement.

III. The benefits of sanctified affliction. This is a precious though painful lesson that all of us may learn. We all share in earth's sorrowings. The remarkable letter of John Randolph, of Roanoke, was presented, condoling with his step-brother on the death of his son. In this letter, amid much that was tender and appropriate, you recollect this brilliant man bears his bold and decided testimony to the divinity of Christ, the reality of His atonement for sin, the influence of the Holy Spirit, and to the old-fashioned doctrines of conversion to God and redemption by the blood of Christ, and to the supreme authority of the Bible, and of the necessity of personally seeking religion with persevering earnestness. It is not true, then, that great and liberal minds have outgrown these doctrines. Let our law and medical students, and the members of our University, and our literary and political men, remember that America's great men have been not only believers in the Bible, but most of them decided and firm adherents to the doctrines and principles of the Westminster Catechism.*

IV. A fourth lesson was the *Omniscience of God*, as seen in his knowledge of the king's heart, and in the hearing of the king's prayer, as well as in the hearing of Daniel's prayer.

You are aware that the fact that MORAL LESSONS are taught in the history before us is alleged as a reason for denying the historical truth of the book of Daniel, and for making it a mere romance or political satire. But it is difficult to see why or how the moral lessons of the narratives and decrees should make the whole history a romance. Nor is there a single incident or shadow of proof that the book is a pious fraud. If the object of the book was, as these critics say, to represent the character and the doom of Antiochus Epiphanes, and to encourage the Jews to persevere in their opposition to that tyrant, why is there no mention of him? How comes it that

* Many of the students of the University and of the members of the Legislature attended the delivery of these Lectures.

there is nothing in his life to correspond with the chapter before us? The points are not similar, but dissimilar. Antiochus Epiphanes was no otherwise a madman than as all tyrants are. His madness was from the vileness of his conduct and the insatiable cruelty of his heart, and not from any derangement of his intellect. Nebuchadnezzar did not persecute the Jews for their religion. Antiochus did, even to the last extremity. Nebuchadnezzar repented after his madness, and proclaimed his penitence to the world. Antiochus did neither. Both, indeed, were heathen kings, and both were zealots for idolatry; but so were hundreds of other kings. There is, therefore, no speciality in his case to make him the subject. The particulars of this fourth chapter do not suit the life and death of Antiochus. And besides all this, we have proof, as I have shown before, of the existence of the book of Daniel long before Antiochus was born. Josephus boldly declares that Daniel wrote his book many years before the things happened which came to pass in the days of Antiochus. It is readily acknowledged that the book of Daniel has a moral and religious substratum. This we had a right to expect from his character, but it certainly does not follow that the historical part of it is not a true history. There are many moral, political, and pious lessons to be learned from Sparks' Life and Writings of Washington, but surely it does not follow that Sparks' Life of Washington is a political satire, or a religious romance.

Read verses 1–19. It appears from the history that there was a class or order of men in the kingdom whose business it was to interpret dreams, especially such as were supposed to be supernatural. History and the monuments of the Nile and the Euphrates tell us that such an order of dream interpreters existed generally among Oriental nations. The interpretation of the dream is given in verses 19–28, which please read. Let us continue our Lessons; and,

I. *We see what should be the end of all government.* Verses 11, 12.

A great man is often symbolized by a tree in ancient and Oriental writers. The king's tree gave shelter to some, a home to others, and protection to all. As the shade and fruits of trees protect and support the beasts that seek shelter under them, so governments should protect and support their people.

The end of every government should be the greatest possible amount of freedom and happiness to all the people. It should protect the weak, give shelter to the oppressed, hope and employment to the poor, and provide for the diffusion of useful knowledge. By the stump of the roots remaining is meant that his kingdom should not be destroyed or alienated from him during his affliction. A regent, probably his own son, Evil-merodach, governed for him during his insanity.

II. This history teaches us another thing—*that prosperity is dangerous.* It is not always the beggar that loses his soul. The man who has just lost all his property is oftentimes not in as much danger as the man who has just gained a large fortune. It requires more care to hold a full cup than an empty one. Wealth is attended with ceaseless anxiety—anxiety to keep it, to preserve it, to increase it, to enjoy it, or to make a show of it, and anxiety, more or less, for the responsibility it imposes.

"Adversity may depress, but prosperity elevates to presumption." The accumulation of wealth for its own sake brings with it its own punishment in the drying up of every fountain of human affection within us, in the disruption of every tie with which the charities of life are bound, and in the conversion of the heart into a substance "harder than the nether millstone." The hoarding up of riches is a curse both here and hereafter. *Beware of covetousness*, saith the Bible, *which is idolatry*. It is my duty frequently to ask the prayers of the congregation for a member of the Church in deep affliction, for one who is sorely bereaved, or extremely ill, or otherwise in great distress. It is always agreeable to ask the prayers of the Church for any one that desires them, but it is often true that the members of the Church who are visited with great prosperity need prayers just as much, if not more, than those that are suffering adversity. On the lofty pinnacle, where all is sunshine, we need a special power to keep us, a special arm to sustain us. "The Scotch fir-tree," says one, "to my mind, is the best symbol of the Christian. The least of earth is required for its roots; it finds nourishment in a dry soil, and amid barren rocks, and yet, green in winter as in summer, it towers the highest of all the trees of the wood toward the sky, and, with least of earth, makes the greatest approach to heaven. So it is with the tree of God's planting: with the least of earth about its roots, it towers the nearest to heaven; deriving nourishment not from the earth below, but from the sunbeams that fall upon it and the rain-drops that sprinkle it, supported by that hidden nourishment that comes from God."—*Cumming.*

Never, perhaps, was there a time of more general prosperity than the present. In all departments of business throughout the land, industry and enterprise are attended with unwonted success. Rail-roads and steam-ships are built, and commerce is carrying our influence over the world. The gold of California and of Australia, with the abundant products of the ground, promise an auspicious future. Let me warn you, then, *to remember that prosperity is not always permanent.* Commercial disasters often come in a way and at a time least expected. The tendency of prosperity is to lead to dangerous expenditures and speculations. What now seems so promising may result in disappointment. God sometimes leaves those that forsake Him to have their portion for a season in worldly things, who find that the end is bitterness and woe. But even if your prosperity continues, riches unsanctified are exceedingly dangerous to the soul. "They that will be rich pierce themselves through with many sorrows, and fall into divers temptations." Experience has long since settled the question about the vanity of worldly honors and possessions. Happiness and the increase of wealth do not always go hand in hand. The joys of a miser's heart are not to be envied. The life, experience, joys, character, and death of the richest men of this city are not such as we wish you to possess, nor such as you yourselves can rationally desire. Beware of misusing the gifts of Providence. *If riches increase, set not your hearts upon them.* Seek daily to know what God would have you do with the good things He intrusts to your hands, and especially take care that your piety and usefulness keep pace with your prosperity. If your fervency of spirit and enlargedness of heart keep pace with your increase of worldly goods, then your riches will prove to you a rich fountain of spiritual good, and your prosperity prove to be a blessing, and not a curse.

III. As the great lesson of this chapter is, that pride is in itself and in its utterances an exceedingly dangerous thing, and odious in the sight of God, I will dwell here a little upon it. "And those that walk in pride, He is able to abase." See verses 29–35.

At the end of twelve months, he walked in the palace of the kingdom of Babylon.

You all know that the houses in Bible lands are built with flat roofs, and frequently so joined together that one may go over a large part of an Oriental city without descending into the street at all. The streets are narrow, and the houses frequently protrude on both sides of the street, so as to join each other over the head of street travelers. It was and is the custom of the East to meditate and take recreation on the house-top, to pray, and even receive company, and take tea and other meals. I have seen this done in Cairo, Damascus, and Jerusalem. Peter, you know, was on a house-top at Joppa when Cornelius' messenger arrived. And we read (1 Sam., ix.) that Saul and Samuel conversed together on the house-top, and they spread a bed for Saul on the house-top, and he slept. The verse before us, then, is easily understood by all who consider the customs of the country. The king walked *upon* the roof of his palace, or upon the terrace thereof, to enjoy the fresh air and a fine prospect, and survey the city, and he fell into a revery of pride and presumption. The view was indeed a magnificent one.

His palace was the greatest and richest then on earth. It rose above the walls of the surrounding dwellings. The atmosphere of that country 'is transparent, and the skies brilliant. His palace overlooked the city, the mistress of the world—its size and riches, and the height and breadth of its walls wonderfully prodigious. Its hanging gardens, and glittering palaces, and profusion of gold and of huge statuary, are the astonishment of all historians, both ancient and modern. The great Euphrates rolled its majestic flood through the middle of the city, and was shut in both above and below by strong bulwarks and doors of solid brass. With such a view within the field of his vision, and himself the absolute lord of all, and crowned with singular prosperity for a long life, it was natural, yet wicked for him, to be elated and arrogant in the way described.

That pride goes before a fall, is one of the great lessons of all history. The providence of God has been inculcating ever since the world began, that "those which walk in pride He is able to abase."

The first sin is supposed to have originated in pride. Man tried in paradise to soar to heaven; but his frail wings were soon dissolved. He fell, and earth received the terrible retribution. "Sin brought death into the world, and all our woe." Cain, stained with his brother's blood, went forth into the world with this legible inscription upon his scathed brow, THEM THAT WALK IN PRIDE GOD IS ABLE TO ABASE.

And in the period of human history immediately preceding the flood, we are told that the pride and wickedness of men were exceedingly great. They were corrupt, and full of all iniquity. And God opened the fountains of the great deep, and the old world was drowned, and the truth disclosed was, "Them that walk in pride God is able to abase." The confusion of tongues at the Tower of Babel proves the same thing. The destruction of Sodom and Gomorrah, and of the Canaanites, like the text, are proofs that pride leads to destruction. The history of the world's great empires is a running commentary on Nebuchadnezzar's text. They have not all fallen by some sudden stroke of Almighty power, yet the same truth is demonstrated. The very principles that influenced their great founders by a slow but sure process brought their ruin. There is a picture in the Luxembourg gallery in Paris—"The Decadence of the Romans"—which made the fame and fortune of the painter Couture. This picture is a whole history, with the moral. It represents an orgie in the court of a temple, during the last days of Rome. A swarm of revelers occupy the middle of the picture, men and women intermingled in all the elaborate intricacy of luxurious posture. Their faces, in which the old Roman fire scarcely flickers, are brutalized with excess of every kind, while from goblets of an antique grace they drain the fiery torrent which is destroying them. Around the bacchanalian feast stand, upon pedestals, statues of old Rome, looking with marble calmness and severity upon the revelers. In one part of the picture a boy is seen proffering a dripping goblet to the marble mouth of a statue; and in the corner of the picture, as if leaving court—Rome, as finally departing—is a group of Romans, with care-worn brows, and hands raised to their faces, in melancholy meditation. The causes of the decline and fall of the Roman empire were within itself. They were luxury, pride, faction, corruption, and crime. Nebuchadnezzar, Tamerlane, Alexander, and Cæsar all found that the higher they soared, the deeper and the more disastrous was their fall. Whenever and wherever great schemes and systems have arisen that have thrust out God and exalted man, the same great result has invariably followed. "Let not the wise man glory in his wisdom, neither let the mighty man glory in his might; let not the rich man glory in his riches, but let him that glorieth glory in this, that he knoweth the Lord and doeth His will." Money is the idol of the nineteenth century. The banker has far more power than ever Nebuchadnezzar had; and the greater is the responsibility of having wealth, as the means for doing good with it are increased. Power and wealth, beauty and accomplishments, are not the only causes of pride. The impenitent, careless sinner, who thinks nothing of God, and cares nothing about his soul, walks in perilous pride upon the brink of an awful precipice. The self-righteous man, who thinks his own righteousness good enough to take him to heaven, and rejects the righteousness of Christ, walks in pride; and the worldly-minded man, whose living is after the lust of the eyes, the lust of the flesh, and the pride of life, walks in pride. Pride does not belong exclusively to the rich and great. It is not patented to those that have fine houses and carriages. Pride grows in a hovel as well as in a palace. We are all proud by nature. It is a part of our corrupt disposition. It is the cause of many sorrows and of most of our misfortunes. It is through pride and stubbornness, the pride of intellect and pride of standing with their neighbors, that many men live and die unconverted. Nothing but the grace of God can subdue the pride of the human heart. All the miracles of Moses, even the death of his first-born, failed to bring down the pride of Pharaoh. All the preaching, and reasoning, and pleading of the most eloquent minister of Christ that ever spoke will fail to abase the pride of a single individual in his audience, unless the rays of the Gospel are made to fall by the Holy Spirit upon his heart. The wind may beat upon the icicle—the storm may smite it—the earthquake may split it—the avalanche may descend, and send it thundering down into the valley below, but it is the sunbeam only that can thaw and melt it. Experience of mercies and of judgments cannot subdue the pride of man's heart. How often do you see this verified. Have you not tried cistern after cistern, and found them broken cisterns that could hold no water, and yet gone on digging other cisterns as laboriously as if you had had no experience of failures? And you, that other young man, have you not found flower after flower fade and wither, the instant you touched it? and yet you are still seeking other flowers as fragile. How is it that, after joy on joy has been pursued, and has perished, the instant you thought you had grasped it, that you seek, and still seek, pleasures where they cannot be found? Why is it that you will still seek the living among the dead? It is because you do not like to be indebted even to God for salvation. You would like to save yourself—to justify, regenerate, and sanctify yourself. If by money, or commercial integrity, or domestic virtues, or if even by penances and pilgrimages you could work out your salvation, you would be content; but to submit to be saved by grace, just as the greatest criminal may be saved, is revolting to the pride of every unrenewed heart. But there is no other way to heaven than by faith in Christ. The song of the redeemed ascribes all the praise to Him who hath loved them, and washed them from their sins in his own blood.

IV. We have here one of the most striking and instructive lessons of God's *power to humble the proud* that is recorded in the Bible. Babylon's mighty monarch had made many successful campaigns, and obtained great glory. He was the head of the mightiest kingdom and ruler over the greatest city then in the world; but his riches and his fame, his treasures and his power, could not preserve his peace of mind. His well-appointed guards and numerous army could not keep him from being terrified by dreams. The majesty and all-governing influence of God are here displayed in his acknowledged, absolute, undisputed sovereignty over the world. God's victory over the mightiest and proudest conqueror was easy and complete. He is made to confess that his own strength of mind and body, and the power and splendor of all his kingdom, were nothing; and all the inhabitants of the earth are as nothing before Him: "And he doeth according to his will in the army of heaven, and among the inhabitants of the earth, and none can stay his hand, or say unto him, What doest thou? At the same time my reason returned unto me, and, for the glory of my kingdom, mine honor and brightness returned unto me, and my counsellors and my lords sought unto me, and I was established in my kingdom, and excellent majesty was added unto me. Now I, Nebuchadnezzar, praise, and extol, and honor the King of heaven, all whose works are truth, and his ways judgment; and those that walk in pride he is able to abase."

How utterly in vain, then, for the impenitent to hope to escape from the presence of God! If they dig into hell, in the language of the prophet, thence will He take them—though they climb up to heaven, thence will He bring them down. The Lord God of Hosts is his name; all the universe is in his hands. There is but one way of escape, and that is to fly to Christ, the Lamb of God.

V. The history of Nebuchadnezzar and his dreams shows that God exercises a general and special providence over all the affairs of the universe and of men

Josephus, after explaining Daniel's visions which he had at Shusha concerning the Babylonian, Median, and Persian empires, and concerning the Greeks and Romans, and his own countrymen, says, "And so it came to pass, that our nation (as well as these other nations) suffered the things foretold by Daniel under Antiochus Epiphanes —which things Daniel wrote many years before they came to pass. All these things did this man leave in writing, as God had showed them to him, insomuch that such as read his prophecies, and see how they have been fulfilled, would wonder at the honor wherewith God honored Daniel; and may thence discover how the Epicureans are in error, who cast Providence out of human life, and do not believe that God takes care of the affairs of the world, nor that the universe is governed and continued in being by that blessed and immortal nature, but say that the world is carried along of its own accord without a Ruler and a Creator; which, were it destitute of a guide to conduct it, as they imagine, would be like ships without pilots, which we see drowned by the winds, or like chariots without drivers, which are overturned; so would the world be dashed to pieces by its being carried onward without a Providence, and so perish and come to naught. So that, by the before-mentioned predictions of Daniel, those men seem to me very much to err from the truth who determine that God exercises no providence over human affairs; for if that were the case, that the world went on by mechanical necessity, we should not see that all things would come to pass according to his prophecy."—*Antiq.*, book x. chap. 11.

God has always exercised a special providence over his people. Although, for their sins, the Jews were carried away to Babylon, and deprived of their political and personal liberty, still they were not left without some tokens for good—still God had not abandoned them. They still had a prophet. Nor were they reduced to an absolute famine of the word of God. By the captivity the ten tribes either became amalgamated with their heathen conquerors, or were transported to foreign lands, and thus disappeared from the pages of history. This was foretold by their prophets; and the lapse of two thousand years has brought nothing to light concerning their fate. But it was different with Judah. They were restored by the edict of Cyrus; and the especial interferences of God in the history of Daniel were intended to preserve a remnant of the kingdom of Judah, that out of the root of Jesse might come the Messiah.

The ministration of *watchers* and *holy ones*—*i.e.*, of the angels—in the government of the world, is taught in the Bible, as well as in the religions of the East. Angels are represented in the Bible as watching over and having an interest in the affairs of men, and as being the executioners of God's will, and they seem to be spoken of here as having cognizance and control of the fate of men.

VI. We see from the king's proclamation that God has PURPOSES or DECREES as well as prescience. "He doeth according to his will in the army of heaven, and among the inhabitants of the earth." God, as a being of infinite perfection, not only *foreknows* what will come to pass, but He also *purposes* the events that take place. *He doeth according to His will.* Without this prophecy would be all nonsense. How could God inspire a man to foretell an event, unless he also worked out its fulfillment? The knowledge of an event to take place, on the part of God, comprehends all the means to bring about that event. The term *foreknowledge*, used in reference to the Divine Being, is so used wholly out of regard to our weakness. There is no such thing with God as *fore*-knowledge or *after*-knowledge. His knowledge is perfect. It can never be increased or diminished—cannot be added to or taken from. His knowledge was as accurate and complete on the day of creation as it will be at the day of final judgment.

The holy men of old, who spoke as they were moved thereto by the Holy Ghost in uttering prophecies, were amanuenses of God's truth; and history is the work of men, holy and unholy, as amanuenses of God's providence. "God writes the prophecy in Scripture, and God fulfills the prophecy in history, and yet God is not the author of sin." God, though the author of every thing that is good, is not the author of any thing that is sinful. No violence is done to the freedom of the human will. Man is not a mere automaton, but a rational, reflecting, free, responsible being, deliberately choosing his own destiny.

VII. *God often manifests both his sovereignty and benevolence in warning men of the consequences of their sins*, in order that they may avert the doom threatened, but not yet sealed, by repentance and righteousness. Daniel interpreted the king's dream, and boldly and faithfully warned him, and told him how to escape from the judgment which it portended. The king had a whole year given him to reflect on the interpretation of his dream, but the warning was in vain. The fruit sought was not obtained till after the threatened punishment had been inflicted. God was pleased to pursue the same method in the time of Noah, and toward the Jews before the captivity, and to the inhabitants of Jerusalem in the time of the Saviour, and so now by the Gospel. "Moreover, O king, let my counsel be acceptable before thee, and break off thy sins by righteousness, and thy transgressions by showing mercy to the poor." He does not tell the king to redeem his sins by penance, genuflection, and pilgrimage. He tells him to break off from his sins—to cease to do evil, and learn to do well. He was reluctant to announce calamities to his king, yet he could not turn aside from the truth. While, therefore he warns him of impending afflictions, he earnestly entreats him to bring forth fruits meet for repentance, and to be ready to show mercy to others, especially the multitudes of poor captives that were in his kingdom. O that we could imitate Daniel in his honesty and earnest faithfulness. What a lesson have we here for all ministers of state, as well as of religion! He told the king honestly the whole truth, and was not afraid. Nor did he make any apology. His duty was a painful one, but honestly and faithfully did he execute his trust. If what ministers of the Gospel preach be not true, no apology can palliate it; if it be true, no excuse is valid for not preaching it, and, consequently, no apology is required. It cannot afford them pleasure to bear evil tidings to their people; yet, as they watch for souls, they must declare the whole counsel of God, whether the people will hear or forbear. Our congregations are always composed of two classes—those that are sinners by nature, and still impenitent and disobedient; and those that are penitent and believing. This is the only division that will be known at the judgment-seat. And though we have not the spirit of Daniel, yet we must say to you who are living in sin, and disobedient to the calls of the Gospel, *O that the dream were to them that hate thee, and the interpretation thereof to thine enemies.* Long have you stood as a fair tree in the vineyard, but fruitless. "And I saw, and behold a watcher and a holy one came down from heaven, and cried, Hew down the tree." "Cut it down, why cumbereth it the ground?" But, O Lord, may it not stand another year! May not this impenitent sinner live till after the next communion season, and we will dig about the roots, and see if it will not bear fruit; we will plead, O Lord! we will agonize and urge sinners to be reconciled to Thee. O that you were wise—that you would now consider your latter end, and accept of salvation while the golden sceptre is held out. Amen.

LECTURE X.

GOD'S UNIVERSAL SCEPTRE; OR, NEBUCHADNEZZAR PREACHING TO YOUNG MEN ABOUT GOD'S ABSOLUTE DOMINION OVER THE WORLD.

On Dan., iv., 1, 3, 17, 25, 34, 35.

Nebuchadnezzar's Conversion.—Liberty of Conscience.—Heavens do rule.—Origin of Sin considered.—Bible alone not responsible.—Believer's Advantages over the Skeptic.—One Sinner God's Executioner on another.—Analogy shows that Objections to God's Government are not valid.—This World a State of Trial.—Eternity a Retribution.—The Righteous and Wicked separated.—Their distinct Destinies.—Facts which show that the Heavens do rule.

LESSONS.

I. NEVER OUT OF GOD'S JURISDICTION.

II. GOD'S ABSOLUTE SOVEREIGNTY SHOULD TEACH YOU TO TAKE A WIDE AND FAR-SEEING VIEW OF YOUR RELATIONS AND OBLIGATIONS.

III. LOOK AT YOUR EVERY-DAY CONDUCT IN THE LIGHT OF ALL ITS BEARINGS.

IV. NEVER DESPAIR OF PROGRESS, EITHER PERSONAL OR OF MANKIND.

IN the preceding discourses of this series, the language and figures of speech used in the king's proclamation have been explained, objections answered, and various important lessons drawn for the instruction, warning, and encouragement of young men. Josephus and other ancient writers have been consulted, and collateral history, and the recent discoveries and decipherings of the inscriptions of Nineveh and Babylon, have been referred to as coincidental proof of the genuineness and authenticity of the book of Daniel, and of Nebuchadnezzar's edict. In the present discourse our object is to explain, defend, and apply the doctrine set forth in the king's edict concerning THE UNIVERSAL SCEPTRE AND DOMINON OF GOD. The tree in the king's dream symbolized himself. Daniel gave him a faithful interpretation thereof, and called upon him to avert the threatened calamity, by ceasing to do evil and learning to do well; but Nebuchadnezzar would not learn his lesson till the punishment threatened was actually inflicted. Afterward, when he lifted up his eyes to heaven, and his understanding returned unto him, the king sent forth his proclamation, which contained, as we have seen, many things to us deeply interesting, appropriate, and suggestive. The points to be presented now are:

I. *The result, in the king's own mind, of the conviction that God is the absolute Sovereign of the universe.* The dream, its interpretation and fulfillment, evidently produced a great change in his mind. The evidences of his true and actual conversion, at which we have hinted before, are two: first, his deep humility, self-abasement, and gratitude to God. The punishment of Nebuchadnezzar was such as was due to his pride. It was suited to his crimes, and he acknowledges God's justice in punishing him for his sins, and gives Him the glory. This proves that he felt sin to be a grievous thing, and that he was truly sorry for his sins, and now rejoiced in the humble assurance of their forgiveness; and therefore his heart blessed God, and pronounced benedictions on all mankind. The substance of his proclamation unto all people, and nations, and languages that dwell on the earth, was "Peace be multiplied to you." And the ground of this proclamation was that he might show "the signs and the wonders that the high God"—not his idol Bel, whose praises he had sung before, but, "that the high God hath wrought toward him."

Now what are the evidences of genuine conversion to God? Are they not humility, deep penitence for sin, an acknowledgment of God's just judgment and deserved wrath for sin, an humble hope of divine forgiveness, and a heart flowing with gratitude to God and good-will toward man? These seem to have been the effects produced in the king's mind by his dream and its fulfillment. The haughty monarch seems to have been altogether changed. Instead of war, he now proclaims peace. The hand that had been stretched forth with the sword from the Indus to the Hellespont, now pours forth benedictions. The lion has become a lamb. He that blasphemed and defied God, now submits and owns his power and justice, and prays that all nations may own him as God. Another and second proof of his conversion is the *missionary feeling* of his proclamation. One of the proofs of a suitable state of mind for becoming a member of the Church is that, "feeling a strong desire for the conversion of all mankind, you promise to do all you can to sustain the institutions of the Gospel, and to aim at increasing holiness of heart and life, and that you will constantly endeavor to do all in your power for the glory of God and the good of your fellow-men." Nebuchadnezzar's proclamation breathes this spirit. He seems to say, as David had done before him, "Come, all ye that fear God, and I will make known to you what he hath done for my soul." So the King of Babylon says, "I have seen the greatness, glory, and terrible majesty of Jehovah; I have tasted of his goodness. It is now my wish that all the people in my vast realm should see, and know, and learn that the God whom I now fear is not the great golden image that I once set up in the plain of Dura; but that the God I now worship is Jehovah, the only true and living God, who made the heaven and the earth, and whose kingdom is an everlasting kingdom."

The remark has been happily made in reference to some of the able addresses recently delivered in the Congress of the United States on the liberty of conscience in foreign countries, that some of our greatest men had turned preachers, and made their desk in the Senate Chamber a pulpit. Thank God for this! And we hope the persecutions of the poor Madiai, for no other crime than that of reading the Bible, and the grievous annoyances of American travelers and residents abroad about their private books of devotion and religious opinions, will never cease to stir the hearts of our statesmen until that toleration of religious opinion in other countries is secured for American citizens that is freely granted to all religions on earth in our own country. It is, brethren, indeed wonderful to see what grace can do—wonderful to see how Saul of Tarsus became Paul the Apostle to the Gentiles. Wonderful transformations of character are made by the Spirit of God even in our day. The same grace that changed the heart of Saul of Tarsus and saved the penitent thief on the cross can save the vilest of our race. The grace of God, like the air of heaven, can enter the smallest hovel and the loftiest palace. It has, and it can, and it will still find its way into Congresses, into Divans and Cabinets, and to the thrones of empires. "It will find its way into the temples of Bramah, into the mosques of

Islam, and into the cathedrals of Romanism." There is a tradition among the Turks in the East, that as their mosques were once Christian churches, so they will again become Christian temples. May this day speedily come! The Babylonian throne was once turned into a Christian pulpit. Its mighty monarch himself became a humble and faithful missionary, and his royal edict an epistle, a sermon eloquent of the wonders of God's supremacy and sovereignty, both in providence and grace—and of righteousness and peace. O how much should we all rejoice in the apostle's great announcement! It is a faithful saying, and worthy of all acceptation, that Christ Jesus came into the world to save sinners, even the chief.

II. Let us now, in the second place, consider the king's acknowledgment that the *heavens do rule—to the intent that the living may know that the Most High ruleth in the kingdom of men, and giveth it to whomsoever he will, and setteth up over it the basest of men.* I desire the more to dwell on the absolute dominion of God over the affairs of the world, and of every creature in the world, because it is a subject of great practical importance to young men, and at the same time it is a subject about which there is much practical skepticism, even where there is no avowed disbelief. There are also some honest difficulties which I hope may be explained or removed. There seems to be in the unconverted heart a proneness at all ages, and especially a strong tendency in our times to rebel against the sovereignty of God. As unconverted men do not like to retain God in their thoughts, so they are disposed to dispute the ever-present, ever-active supremacy of a living, personal Deity. The only great first cause they acknowledge is an abstract principle, or an impersonal, apathetic, far-removed God, who now takes no notice of earthly things. Many admit that there *was* an active Creator at the beginning of the world, who seem to deny or have a very faint belief that there *is* a God, ruling still in the heavens and over the affairs of men. Divested of its poetry, its dreamy generalities, and its philosophizing essays and literature, the system of many seems to be this: that God created the world, set its vast machinery going, and wound it up a few times to see that it would all work well, and then wound it up so as to run for many years, and retired from it; and that, consequently, accidents have been continually occurring ever since, and that *second causes* are now ruling, and will finally overthrow the existing economy of all things. It is on this sort of a theory that unbelievers try to explain the origin of moral evil. In answer to which, and in explanation and defense of the doctrine set forth in the king's proclamation, our *first* remark is:

That the question of the origin of moral evil, like the existence of God, is known, absolutely known as a fact, without our being able to comprehend its mode or manner of existence. There are many things admitted to actually exist, the how or manner of whose existence and essence we are not able to explain. Gravitation, the circulation of the blood, digestion, the growth of animals and vegetables, the human soul and its connection with the body, and the existence of God, are all mysteries. These are all realities, not all indeed equally mysterious, but all involving many points which cannot be explained at present. Many of the greatest minds in the Old as well as in the New, in the Oriental as well as in the Western World, have labored hard to solve the problem of the origin of moral evil; but no satisfactory solution has been found beyond the facts revealed in the Bible. All admit that sin is now in the world. How can we reconcile its entrance here with the supreme government of God? Why should a wise, merciful, omnipotent Being allow such an intruder as sin to come into our world and produce apostasy, rebellion, and discord? But, *first*, young men, remember the Bible is not responsible for the solution of this serious question. The entrance of sin into our world, "which brought death and all our woe," is not a disclosure peculiar to the Bible. It is a disclosure of fact, of human experience and observation, of geology and of universal history. The skeptic as well as the Christian is called upon to explain why sin is in the world. The historian, the geologist, the philosopher, as well as the Christian, admit the existence and the reign of a God—admit as a fact the presence and the disturbing power of sin—that it is on account of sin that we see darkness, and degradation, and guilt, where we should see knowledge, righteousness, and holiness. If there be a difficulty, then, on this subject, it is a difficulty at the door of the skeptic himself, as broad and as palpable as at the door of a Bible Christian. By denying the truth of revelation and rejecting the Gospel of Christ, we cannot, therefore, get rid of this difficulty; it still remains in all its force. But, *secondly*, the Bible believer has an advantage over the mere geologist, historian, or skeptical philosopher. He can look at the entrance and reign of sin in such a light as to see that it is not the fault of the Divine Being that sin is in the world. His faith is a telescope that reveals to him such distant worlds, and the remote, but still closely united links of the long chain of Providence, that he sees God supreme and yet just, merciful, omnipotent, and good. His faith takes in the end with the beginning, and shows him that all God's ways are perfect. The Bible believer sees that God made man in his own image and after his own likeness, perfectly free and unfettered, with every bias to good, and with no bias to evil—with every inducement to retain his allegiance—with every possible dissuasion against apostasy—able to stand, but free to fall. He gave him a heart to love—He gave him a conscience, and placed him under law. This was essential, as man was a creature. His Creator was of course the lawgiver, and when God placed Adam under law, He might, speaking with reverence, by his omnipotence have prevented him from touching the forbidden fruit. He might have struck Eve dead the moment she ate, and have prevented her from giving the apple, or whatever it was, to Adam; but it surely does not follow, because the Almighty could have thus prevented man from sinning, that it was best for Him to have done so, or that he ought thus to have prevented him from sinning. To have done this would have been to destroy human agency, and to have annihilated human virtue. The order of the human mind would then have been changed, and man become no more than an animal or a stone. But,

Thirdly. The Bible believer has such a wide sweep before him, so magnificent is the field of his vision, that he sees grander and more magnificent results to be evolved from the wrecks of paradise than ever could have been reflected from it in its pristine glory.

> "God, in the person of his Son,
> Hath all his mightiest works outdone."

It is impossible to sustain the argument, that because God was able to have prevented the entrance of sin into the world, therefore he *ought* to have done so. You have the power to burn up this city, or to throw yourself into the sea, but you need not be told that your possession of such power does not make it right for you to do so. The Almighty, by the exercise of omnipotence, might have rendered it impossible for man to have sinned; but then this very impossibility would have made man a mere automaton—a piece of machinery, moved by extraneous impulses, without a will to determine, a conscience to feel, or a judgment to reflect. To use another's illustration of this matter: if a man goes to put his hand into the fire, God tells that man, by the experience of others, and by the exercise of his reason, "If you put your hand into the fire you will burn it, and suffer pain." This is the plan which God adopts to keep a man from burning his hand. He might, speaking with reverence, have taken some other method. He might, by the mere fiat of omnipotence, render it a physical impossibility for a man to burn his hand. But he does not do so. He shows a man that if he puts his hand into the fire, such are His laws, that his hand is sure to be burned. And it was just in this way God dealt with Adam in Paradise. He did not draw back Adam's hand from touching the forbidden fruit; but he told him that if he ate that fruit, death and woe would be the inevitable consequences. He said to him, You are a free and responsible being; it rests with yourself to abstain and live forever, or to touch it and perish. In defending, therefore, the doctrine of Nebuchadnezzar's edict, which is the doctrine of the whole Bible, "we vindicate the ways of God to man," and show that permitting sin, not the sending of it, not the becoming the author of it, is the only way that God could have treated man as a rational and responsible being; and as far as we can see, or comprehend human nature at all, there was no other way to have treated man in consistency with the dignity of his nature, which would, at the same time, have been consistent with the wisdom, the benevolence, the holiness, and the justice of Him who rules in the heavens.

III. The history of Nebuchadnezzar, as drawn by the Hebrew prophets, presents another difficulty in regard to the ruling of the heavens, and that is this: *that one sinner is often made the executioner of divine judgments upon another.* This is true. Cyrus was employed to execute judgment upon Babylon. Nebuchadnezzar himself was employed to execute judgment on Nineveh, and on Tyre, and on the other wicked nations of Syria. It is expressly said in Isaiah that God would give Egypt to Nebuchadnezzar as his wages for his services in conquering Tyre. God himself says, "O Assyrian, thou art the rod of mine anger; I will send thee against an hypocritical nation, against the people of my wrath will I give thee a charge, to take the spoil and to take the prey, and to tread them down as the mire in the streets." The prophet tells us that God put a hook in his nose and led him whithersoever he would. It is not only the teaching of the Bible, but it is a chapter in the history of every nation, and almost of every individual, that one wicked man is made the instrument of punishing another, and that often a man's own sins are the executioners of their own curses. The Roman sword, in the hands of Titus and Vespasian, punished the gross transgressions of God's own people, as the Assyrians and Babylonians had done ages before. Napoleon the Great was not a saint in all his motives and plans, yet he was an instrument in the hand of God to punish the sins of profligate Europe, just as his successor, Napoleon III., may be in our day. The moral character of the agents of Providence are not always such as God accepts. His agents are sometimes winds and flames, earthquakes and wars, pestilence and plague. The personal salvation of the men employed by divine Providence for great national or political events is not necessarily embraced in their mission; that depends altogether upon their obedience to God. The agency of wicked men in carrying on the purposes of God is undesigned, and therefore not meritorious. *He maketh the wrath of man to praise Him, and the remainder of wrath he restraineth.* And may it not be that God makes one sinful man or one wicked nation execute his judgment upon another sinful man or upon another wicked nation, rather than inflict the punishment by his own hand, in order that incorrigible sinners may know that it is vain to rely upon one another for support in their rebellion against Him, or to hope to escape his wrath by their united strength? There is not, and there cannot be any conspiracy of wicked men against God, however secret, or however great, powerful, and wide-spread may be their dominions and the ramifications of their power, without having the elements of its own disorganization, decay, and destruction within itself. If all the wicked men in the world were arrayed in a conspiracy against the cause and kingdŏm of Christ, it could not last. The elements of disorganization and ruin are essentially combined in all such unions. The leagues and covenants, and tripartite and quintuple holy alliances of the despots of Europe, cannot last; nor can all the guns and bayonets that can be manufactured in all the shops in Christendom make them enduring. They will quarrel among themselves. It is as easy for God to confound their interpretations of treaties as it was for Him to confound the tongues of the builders of Babel. It is as easy for the Almighty to bring to naught the counsels of Metternich, and annihilate the armies of Austria, as it was for him to confound the wisdom of Ahithophel, and destroy the army of Sennacherib. The same God is on the throne now. Small, obscure, and unexpected causes concurred in producing the Revolutions of 1782 and of 1848. The downfall of kingdoms has generally come from sources but little anticipated. It is easy for God to light a spark that shall cause all Europe to blaze in war from the North Pole to the Mediterranean. It is easy for Him who ruleth in the heavens, and giveth dominion to whomsoever he will, and setteth over empires sometimes the basest of men, to make one conspirator rise against another, and make the very means—the priesthood, army, and fortifications of a king—designed for his protection the very instrument of his overthrow. Haman is often hanged on his own gallows

IV. Again, it is said, If it be true, as Nebuchadnezzar asserts in his proclamation, that God doeth according to his will in the armies of heaven, and among the inhabitants of the earth, and none can stay his hand, or say unto him, "What doest thou?" *how is it that one generation suffers for the sins of former generations?* The same answer in part that has just been given may be made to this objection. It is true that one generation does suffer for the sins of former generations, and it is true that God lives and reigns. The Bible, then, is not responsible for the solution of this difficulty. The Bible Christian is not alone in this matter. The chronicles of all ages and of all lands have legible records of the fact, that children for several generations suffer the consequences of the sins of their parents. The constitution of the universe and of human nature then, and not the Bible, is responsible for this difficulty. It is one you cannot escape. Whether with or without the Gospel, you must meet it. We prefer to explain it with the help of the Word of God; and as before, so here, the believer's view of the constitution of the universe, and of human nature, is far higher, more hopeful and consoling than that of the unbeliever. The Bible view of this subject teaches us lessons of the greatest practical value. Does not the very fact that children suffer for their parents' dissipation, profligacy, and improvidence, teach us that we have an interest in the well-being of all around us, and cannot escape from the responsibility of exerting an influence on the ages that are to come after us? Are we not thus palpably taught that we are morally as well as physically related to all mankind, and bound by the laws of the great Creator himself not to live for ourselves, but for the good of our fellow-men? Does not the fact that children's children to the third and fourth generation suffer in their bodies, minds, and character, for the vices of their parents, constitute a most pressing and powerful argument to induce you to live soberly, righteously, and godly? And thus a more sober, philosophical, and correct view of this matter shows you that what at first seemed to be a hardship is really a mercy, fitted to arouse all your feelings against sin, and to lead you by the deepest instincts of your nature to guard against such sins as will not only ruin your own bodies and souls, but transmit suffering, and pain, and tribulation to the distant generations of your descendants.

And as to the removal by death of parents from their children, and of children from their parents, the whole difficulty does not rest with the Bible Christian. The facts lie as palpably at the door of the skeptic as they do at his. But here again, as before, the Bible Christian has sources of reflection, comfort, and hope that the infidel has not, and cannot have. Revelation comes in to his relief, and teaches much that reason could not disclose. The Christian sorrows not as the heathen. He finds lessons in the providential dispensations of God, that elevate his affections and make him happy here, and prepare him for glory and immortality hereafter. In the fact that infants, though free from actual transgressions, do die, the enlightened faith of the Christian says there may not only not be any thing inconsistent with the universal sceptre of God, but there is that which eminently makes his reign palpable. Does not the babe die to teach us that original sin is an actual thing, and to prove what geology and philosophy teach, that some terrible disaster has fallen upon mankind, which blights the flower that has just budded and bloomed to-day, and smites down the aged man of fourscore years? Does not Revelation teach what heathen sages have said—*those whom the gods love die early*, in order that they may escape from the evil that is in the world; and as all who die in infancy are saved, are not our little ones taken from us to become missionaries to draw us to heaven? In the day of eternity it will doubtless be found that many parents are saved through the death of their little ones.

V. There are other difficulties that might be dwelt on, but only a few words can now be said in relation to them. That sentence against an evil work is not speedily executed; that vice and fraud are sometimes prosperous, while the good and pious are poor and persecuted; and that sometimes wicked men live to be very old, while pious and eminently useful men die at an early age, are facts. The Bible tells us that it has been so, and that it will continue to be so; and the Bible tells us also that these things sometimes troubled Old Testament saints, but that when they went to the house of God, and considered all, and took into the account the awful end of wicked men, they were satisfied that God did all things well, and that even on these points the heavens not only rule, but rule in righteousness and goodness. This world is not the state of absolute justice; this world is only a place of trial and probation. The world to come is the world of retribution. In hell the wicked all suffer, and in heaven all the righteous are happy. There are degrees in both future rewards and punishments, but there is no mixture in either heaven or hell. There is in the world to come a perfect separation of the righteous from the wicked. Here the wicked and the righteous are mingled together, and participate together in the vicissitudes of earth, but in eternity they are separated and rewarded according to their works. If all good men were rewarded on earth, then we should live not by faith, but by sight, and all men would become, nominally, at least, believers in Christ, for the sake of worldly prosperity; and if all pious men suffered on earth, then to become a Christian would be to become a martyr, and this would be an objection to the profession of faith in Christ. It is far better, then, for things to be just as they are—namely, that the tares and the wheat should grow together in the same field till the harvest. And such are the necessary relations of society, and such the nature of moral goodness and of Christian virtues, that whenever the effort is made to separate them now, it ends in the injury of the wheat. The mingling together of the wicked and of the pious, and the present prosperity of the wicked and the temporary afflictions of the people of God, are calculated to fasten our faith upon God, and to show us that we are to be saved by grace. And after all, who can show us that it is not far better for the pious to be afflicted just as they are? What if Voltaire did live to be eighty years of age, and Thomas Paine to be an old man and die a drunken sot?" It is only the worse for them. If Enoch is translated to heaven, it is because he walked with God. If a pious man dies early, it is because his work on earth is finished, and is pleasing to God and accepted of him. Whatever is taken off from a good man's days on earth is added to his existence in heaven, and he is abundantly satisfied.

VI. There are some positive facts which prove that Nebuchadnezzar is correct when he says the "heavens do rule," and that the reigning of the heavens is wise and good, merciful and gracious. The *first* fact now to be stated is, that it is natural to expect God to govern the world. It would be unnatural for him to leave all his creatures orphans. The presence of fixed permanent laws in every department of nature proves that He has not so left them. The vegetable and animal kingdoms, the seasons of the year, and the revolutions of the heavenly bodies, show that He is supreme in nature.

2. The perfections of God prove that He must still govern the universe. His wisdom is infinite. All that God does is, therefore, infinitely perfect. As we have said, his laws prove his presence. By them he reigns in the atom as well as in the fixed star. He rides on the tiny breeze as upon the whirlwind. The sweet odors of the spring, as well as the thundering avalanche, are but palpable manifestations of His presence. But infinite wisdom is not the only attribute of God. His goodness also is infinite. He so loved the world, not only as to permit, but actually to send—to GIVE HIS SON TO DIE for the world. The Bible does not teach that God loves us because Christ has died for us, but that Christ died for us *because* God so loved us. And if God gave his Son for us, how much more will he give us all things else needful?

And all the more so, because He who governs the world is *omnipotent*. Whatever, therefore, His wisdom devises, or His love inspires, His power will execute. It is impossible, then, for any error, mistake, or failure to occur in God's government of the world. All history and experience confirm the Psalmist's words, where he says, "O Lord of hosts, who is a strong Lord like unto thee, or to thy faithfulness round about thee? Thou rulest the raging of the sea; when the waves thereof arise, thou stillest them. Justice and judgment are the habitation of thy throne; mercy and truth shall go before thy face."

3. A third source of argument, which I cannot now present, in favor of a particular and universal providence, is the plain teaching of the Bible on the subject. You are already familiar with many such proof-texts.

Finally. Let us attend to the lessons of this subject. I am fully persuaded there is no fact in history, or in nature, or in human experience, that can be shown fairly to be in conflict with the ruling of the heavens, but that a proper consideration of all the facts in nature, human experience, and history, establishes the doctrine set forth in the proclamation of the King of Babylon—that God's dominion is particular, and absolute, and universal over the affairs of the world, and over the affairs of every creature in the world. But what have young men to do with the absolute, general, and particular providence of God? A great deal, a very great deal.

First. Ever bear in mind that there is no such thing as an accident in the true sense of that term. You are always and every where within the jurisdiction of God. You cannot escape His presence, nor hide yourself from the search-warrant of His laws. The laws which he has given to the elements and imprinted on your own soul, will always find you out when you do violence to your conscience and sin against Him. If you were in the heart of the universe, and it in ruins piled over you, still would God's eye beam full upon you, and His almighty hand be over you. Be sure of this: your sin will find you out, and you will find that it is an evil and a bitter thing. There is but one refuge from sin, and that thing is the blood of Christ.

Let this subject, secondly, *teach you to take a wide and far-seeing view of your relation to your fellow-man, and of your obligations to your Creator and to the universe He has made, and in which He has given you your place.* As the Creator has designs of ultimate good to you, and of ultimate glory to himself through you, so you should be diligent to work out your high mission among your fellow-creatures. Your first and highest duty is to seek the salvation of your own soul. There is a personal responsibility resting upon you to do this, from which there is no possible escape. It is identical with your existence. You owe it as a debt for which nothing can be substituted—as a debt imposed upon you by the Almighty Creator, a debt to Him, to the universe, and to yourself to be pious, for it is only by being pious that you are in harmony with the higher laws of your being, and in communion with the Father of your soul; and it is only in such communion you can find the happiness that will fill your longing spirit. If, then, God suffers sin to develop itself into crimes and horrible calamities upon the earth around you, it does not prove that He hates you, but that He would have you look upon this earth as the great LESSON-GIVING BOOK of the universe, and have you show your obedience and love to him by fleeing to Christ as a Saviour from all sin. And who can tell but that the inhabitants of sister orbs and sister stars may be grouped into gazing clusters, beholding with rapture how God is bringing good out of evil on our planet, and at the same time establishing his laws by the warning that is given in the punishment of sin, and exalting his grace and glory in its forgiveness through the blood of his own Son?

Thirdly. Learn, therefore, young men, to look at your conduct in all its bearings for all coming time. A stone is thrown into the sea, but when and where do the agitations of the waters cease? A spark ignites a house, and that house communicates with other houses, and a whole city is wrapped in flames. All languages have proverbs earnestly inculcating the wisdom and duty of resisting evil at its beginning. Almost all of the objections raised against revelation are raised on narrow, obscure, and partial, if not superficial views of its doctrines. Accustom yourselves, then, to take broad, and deep, and thorough, and intelligent, and high, and manly, and honorable views of all subjects. Fetter not your soul down to any thing little, low, or superficial. Guard against a narrow, envious, jealous, fault-finding spirit. If you see only the foundation of a house, you ought not therefore and thence to judge what will be the splendor of its superstructure. If you read the title-page of a book, or even the index of a book, or even a few chapters, you are not authorized, surely, to say that it is good or bad, false or true, as a whole. In judging of men and things, and of the dispensations of Providence, never allow yourself to rest on a mere outside first view. Judge not by appearances, but judge righteous judgment. Joseph's history teaches you to wait for the end before you make up your judgment. His character, or the providence of God over him, is not to be judged of from any one part of his life separated from the rest. You cannot make up your verdict concerning him or concerning God's providence as it relates to him, from seeing him on one of the Ishmaelite camels, on his way through the desert to Egypt; nor as you see him under the temptation of Potiphar's wife, nor when thrown into Pharaoh's round-house. If you stop with your pictures of Joseph here, you will say, what a poor, unfortunate young man—a very "Murad the unlucky;" if excellent in character, he is certainly most unfortunate in life. But judge not the Lord by feeble sense. Wait for the second series. See Joseph at Pharaoh's right hand—see him receiving his brethren and father, and saving them and the Egyptian empire from destruction—see him triumphant over all his trials, and dying full of years and honors, and his name held in everlasting remembrance; and then say, Do not the heavens rule? Is there not a God who judgeth righteously in the earth? So in regard to Daniel and his three friends, you must put all their life-long events into the series after their order and kind before you can make up your judgment as to the doctrines of Nebuchadnezzar in the text. And as to yourself, whether prosperous or adverse, remember that the end is not yet. Blow after blow may have fallen upon you, wave after wave have rolled over you, one disappointment after another have pursued you; whichever way you have looked, whatever you have attempted, nothing but trials and losses have met you. Wait for the end. God hideth himself that He may be trusted. *Hope on, and look up, and hope ever.* It is only when the whole chain of Providence shall be seen in the clear light of eternity that we shall be able to see that all its links are of pure gold, and that they bind together our happiness and the Divine glory, and the greatest good of the whole universe. You must look, then, at all of God's dispensations in this world in connection with another world. Your residence here on earth is but a pilgrimage through which you are passing, and the world to come is your eternal home. This world is but a small spot, a little tiny nook and part of God's universe. What seems dark and irreconcilable with wisdom and goodness now, and in its relations to this world, when seen in eternity and in its relations to the vast domains over which God's sceptre is swayed, will be found to be perfectly consistent with Almighty power, wisdom, justice, and love. GOD IS A ROCK; ALL HIS WAYS ARE PERFECT; ALL THE WORKS OF THE KING OF HEAVEN ARE TRUTH, AND HIS WAYS JUDGMENT; AND THOSE THAT WALK IN PRIDE HE IS ABLE TO ABASE.

Finally. The fact that the heavens do rule, and that all the works of the King of Heaven are truth, and his ways judgment, *teaches you never to despair of the progress and happiness of the human race.* Truth cannot die. "The eternal years of God are hers." Principles are like the Eternal attributes; they are transcripts of Infinite excellence. Hence the earnest expectation of the creature waiteth for the manifestation of the sons of God; for we know that the whole creation groaneth and travaileth in pain together until now. In looking at the scenes of horror that took place in the French Revolution of 1782, at first, it might seem strange that God would allow such awful crimes to be perpetrated within his dominions; but time and reflection have shown that great lessons were taught by these atrocities, which would not, in all probability, have been so successfully taught in any other way, nor by any other people. How else was the profligacy of the court and aristocracy, and even of the people themselves, which had been so notorious for ages, to be punished? How else was the world to be taught, asks Dr. Cumming, of London, so effectually, what a people can do and will do who cast off God, as was taught by the French nation during the reign of atheism and terror? How else could so perfect a demonstration have been given that the world cannot be carried on without religion, and that society cannot cohere without God—that, in the words of Robespierre himself, "if there be not a God, we must make one, in order to make society hold together.

Even the athiest, in his blasphemy, here proclaims God almost as distinctly as Nebuchadnezzar, when he declares that "God reigns and the heavens do rule." The miseries, then, of one generation, and the blessings of another, are often in many ways connected; and in looking at God's dispensations to men and to nations, you must look at them as a whole, and as completed only at the judgment-day. The sufferings of our fathers prepared the soil and sowed the seeds which have ripened for us, and now it is for us to prepare precious harvests for the generations to come. God reigns, and the powers of hell cannot prevail against his government. All history proves that every false religion is a blunder, and that every atom of Truth is immortal. ALL HISTORY SHOWS THAT WHERE THE SPIRIT OF GOD IS, THERE, AND THERE ONLY IS LIBERTY. Is there, then, nothing to encourage your faith and command your exertions in the faithfulness of God's providences toward his people? Is there not palpable evidence of his sovereign dominion, in making all men, in all sorts of pursuits, consciously or unconsciously, designedly or undesignedly, contribute to spread the splendor of his name? Is it no evidence that the heavens do rule, that you have proofs of the truth of the Bible dug up from the lava of Herculaneum, from the pictures of Pompeii, and excavated from the graves of Nineveh and Babylon, and from the tombs of Egypt and Arabia? Is there no proof that God is watching over the Bible of your mother, whose every page she once bedewed with tears from eyes that now can weep no more, in the fact that he is bringing forth elucidations of its truth, and proofs of his Gospel from the graves of long-buried cities, and the wreck of nations, as well as from the depths of the earth and the heights of the heavens—till at last the most skeptical minds are constrained to own that the religion of Jesus Christ is the most astonishing fact in the world? Is there nothing in your own personal history—nothing of goodness and mercy that should lead you to repentance—nothing of judgment that warns you to flee from the wrath to come—nothing that convinces you there is a Providence above that watches over you, and calls you to seek glory, honor, and immortality? You believe in God; believe also in his Son Jesus Christ, and then in the ruling of the heavens you shall find that all things work together for good to them that love God, for that the BLOOD OF HIS SON JESUS CHRIST CLEANSETH US FROM ALL SIN. Amen.

LECTURE XI.

BELSHAZZAR'S FEAST: ITS LESSONS TO YOUNG MEN.

On Dan., v.

The Bible God's Crystal Palace.—Authors on Daniel.—Prophecy fulfilled.—The Feast, why it was sinful.—Babylonians not Turks.—Their Wives might be at their Feasts.—How the Vessels were used.—The Narrative corroborated.—Toleration.—Desecration.—Music.—The Glee spoiled.—Why learned Men could not read the Writing.—Grotefend.—Woman's Agency.—She is necessary to Man's Happiness.—The Chaldean Astrologers were not Spirit Rappers—were Magi, but not Magicians.—Daniel, President of the Babylonish Smithsonian Institute.—The Stars preaching.—One Sin often leads to another.—Great Sin not to heed Divine Warnings.—Where Responsibility rests.—Deists' Condemnation.—The Worldling's Stone of Stumbling.—Do not neglect regular Preaching of the Divine Word.—Fear the Power of Conscience.—Sin is indeed a bitter Thing.—Evil-doers only fear the Law.—Reason why Universalists and Hell-redemptionists preach Nothing but that there is no Devil and no Hell.—The Orthodox Way the more philosophical.

In the morning discourse we made a hurried visit to the Crystal Palace for the exhibition of the industry of all nations, and attempted to show that the Bible is God's Crystal Palace, built expressly for the exhibition of his attributes and glory to all nations, and for the supply of their wants. This evening we ask you to go with us far to the eastward, not to an exhibition of industrial arts, but to an Oriental feast on the banks of the Euphrates some two thousand three hundred years ago. The last lecture was on God's universal providence over men and things, as taught in Nebuchadnezzar's remarkable edict. Repeatedly have I asked your attention to three works on the book of Daniel, which I again name, and hope you will procure and read as far as you have opportunity. The first is by the late Professor Stuart, of Andover, and is designed particularly for students and theologians. The second is by Professor Gaussen, of Geneva. His lectures on Daniel have been translated, and are published by the Presbyterian Board in Philadelphia. They are addressed especially to Sabbath-school children. The other work to which I allude is by Dr. Cumming, of London. The last-named works are popular in their style. They are devoted mainly to Daniel's prophecies, and are directed particularly against Popery. It is not to be inferred that by naming these authors I endorse all the opinions they advance. I do not agree with them in many places, yet they are able writers, and worthy of being read.

In regard to the chapter before us, two things are to be remembered:

Firstly. The particulars of the taking of Babylon by Cyrus, as given by Herodotus and Xenophon, correspond with our narrative.

Secondly. In the taking of Babylon we have a remarkable fulfillment of divine prophecies. The time and manner of its fall and subsequent history all fulfills exactly what the Hebrew prophets foretold. Jeremiah had said that all nations should serve Nebuchadnezzar, and his son and his son's son, and that then his empire should cease. Belshazzar was his grandson. You know from history that Cyrus gained a victory over the King of Babylon, and shut him up in his metropolis, which was considered impregnable, and had within its walls provisions for twenty years. The siege had continued over two years, when, during the feast spoken of in this chapter, Cyrus, having drained the River Euphrates, which ran through the city, marched his army into the city along the channel, and surprised the palace guards, slew the king himself, and became absolute master of the city.

I. Our purpose now, however, is first to attend to the Feast of Belshazzar. It was a great annual festival, commemorative of some great event. Some think it was Sacae, the Saturnalia of the Babylonians. Others say it was a feast in honor of the king's birth-day, or of his coronation. Whatever feast it was, it seems to have been attended with the pomp, religious rites, and services of the empire. The Babylonians were famous above all other nations for intemperance, especially in drinking. A feast commemorative of a man's birth-day or of his marriage is not necessarily sinful. A national festival, as the Fourth of July, is not in itself sinful; nor was it the eating and drinking in moderation, but the excess, and the spirit in which it was done, that made Belshazzar's feast so impious. Their excess was a great sin, but their defiance of Jehovah and impious mockery in using the sacred vessels brought from Jerusalem was a far greater sin. The king and his lords, by using the holy vessels of the Jewish temple for their licentious and idolatrous festival, hurled defiance at the God of Abraham, and showed their contempt for the power of Him who doeth according to his will in the armies of heaven. In accounting for the presence of the king's wives and concubines and the queen-mother at this feast, you must recollect that the Babylonians were not Mussulmans, nor were they even like the Persians. Vashti, the Persian queen, we are told in Esther, did not appear at the feast-table, even when commanded by the king. Among the Greeks, none but women of depraved character sat down to feast with men. But among the Babylonians, ancient historians agree in saying, the custom was different, as it was also with the ancient Egyptians. The excess of eating and drinking, and the character of the dancing at an Oriental feast, are beyond the limits of modesty in a public discourse. The dancing of men and women in the East is far worse than the Polka, which we rejoice to know is about to be prohibited in the most respectable circles.

The king, heated with wine, commanded them to bring in the vessels of the Jerusalem temple. There was needless insult to the captive Jews, as well as impious blasphemy against their God, in this desecration of their holy vessels. It was according to the customs of the times and the fortunes of war among the Eastern nations, for the victorious party to carry away the idols or images worshiped by the vanquished, as well as their treasures and other precious things. The prevailing idea was, that every nation had its own presiding god or gods, and that the respective deities were interested in the wars of their worshipers, and that therefore the gods as well as the people of a conquered country were vanquished, and made the servants of the conquering people and gods. The prophets, before the captivity, told the people that if they continued impenitent, they and their idols should be carried away to Babylon. This was true of the kingdom of the ten tribes; and of Judah it was true that the people, and the holy vessels from the temple of God at Jerusalem, and the royal treasury were taken to Babylon.

History speaks of the outrages committed on the gods of Egypt by Cambyses, and of the profanation of the gods of Babylon by Darius and Xerxes. It was very natural that a weak, haughty, and impious monarch like Belshazzar, when heated with wine, should have sent for the splendid temple vessels as evidences of his magnificence, and proof that the God of the Jews was inferior to his own. Still, the conquest of Jerusalem, the captivity of the Hebrews, and the possession of their holy things, gave no right to King Belshazzar to insult these poor captives. No King, Synod, Council, Pope, or Sanhedrim has any warrant to prescribe my faith, or to insult the humblest rite of any man's religion. Let a man's faith be that of Hindooism, Mormonism, Mohammedanism, Romanism, or any other ism, no mortal has a right to oppress, or persecute, or insult him for his faith. It is our duty to be able to give a reason for the faith that is in us. It is a great misfortune to follow a false faith and worship a false god; it is, therefore, our duty to labor and to pray for the conversion of all men from error to truth. It is our duty to try to enlighten and convince them, and bring them to the knowledge of the true God. We may labor to convince our fellow-men of their errors, but we may not persecute them nor cast ridicule upon their sacred things. The sin consisted mainly in the desecration of that which was holy, or the application of the vessels of the temple of Israel's God to profane and licentious purposes. Nor is this sin peculiar to the ancients. Unfortunately, it has not been confined to the banks of the Euphrates nor the Nile, the Tiber nor the Thames. The same sin is found on the banks of the Mississippi. Any and every perversion of holy things is a desecration of them. When the sacrament is taken without faith to discern the Lord's body, or to cover some sinister design, or to obtain a degree in some university, or as a passport to some office or as a qualification for a political or civil sphere, as is sometimes done in Great Britain, then the sacred vessels of the Lord's house are desecrated to an unholy end. When a man professes to be a Christian for any mere worldly purpose, then, like Simon Magus, he seeks to make gain of godliness, and is guilty of awful hypocrisy. "When the facts and the expressions of the Bible, its sublime, its pure, and its holy truths are used, as they frequently are, to point a pun, add edge to a jest, or keenness to a sarcasm, to excite a laugh, or to provoke a sneer, you have God's vessels desecrated to unhallowed and profane ends." It is dangerous to construct jests from the Bible. Such a habit indulged will often destroy the salutary influence of the most solemn lessons of the Bible. It may fairly be called into question whether or not many of our musical festivals are not a desecration of holy things. The opera, concert, and oratorio, it is true, are very different things from the theatre. There is no science more noble and more befitting than music for the unfolding of the attributes of God, and making more vivid and glorious the grandeur of his truth and works. But when the awful agonies of Calvary, the deep and sorrowful experiences of the Son of God, and the sublime descriptions of the judgment to come are used and *encored* by an unthinking crowd, I fear there is then a desecration of holy things. The noble productions of Handel and the magnificent oratorios of the masters of music should be used as acts of solemn worship, and not at Belshazzar's feasts. There are so many ways in which God's vessels are desecrated, that I cannot now attempt to point them out in detail. In whatever way religion is dragged from its lofty and controlling sphere, and made to gild the claims of a party or of a sect, then and there we have a repetition of Belshazzar's profanation. When the Sabbath is made a day of pleasure, of visiting, feasting, and writing letters—when the house of God is used for any thing but the purposes of religious worship—then we have an approach to the desecration of Belshazzar's feast. It does not require all the circumstances of Belshazzar's feast to be guilty of his sin. If the heart that was made for God is made the throne of Mammon—if the affections are set on things earthly, then God is dishonored, and we are guilty of desecrating holy things.

But let us leave this disquisition about the desecration of holy things and observe the feast. It was one of the greatest splendor. The most spacious and magnificent rooms in the richest city in the world were crowded with rank and beauty; wit, learning and aristocracy, and royalty were there. Precious stones and costly perfumery filled the saloons with dazzling lustre and sweetest fragrance. Wit sparkled with the sparkling of cups, and reason flowed with the flowing of the wine. They drank toasts of enthusiastic patriotism; they sang songs of boundless loyalty, and shouted defiance to every foe. The high noon of the splendor of the feast has come. All hearts were bounding and all spirits were joyous. But what is this? The cup falls from the king's hand—his countenance has changed and his thoughts trouble him;

the joints of his loins were loosed, and his knees smote the one against the other. A thrill of terror pierces like a sword through every soul; many faint, and many shriek with alarm. And what is the cause of this strange scene? A mysterious writing appeared upon the plastering of the palace wall. No eye was seen there to guide the hand—the fingers that traced the characters belonged none knew to whom, and the inscription none could read. As the king and his lords could not read the inscription, it is said, why were they thus afraid? They were afraid because their own consciences condemned them. All men who live in sin dread what is future and unknown. But the man who is at peace with God sees all events approaching him with the assurance that they shall work together for his good.

II. It has been asked why the wise men of Babylon could not read the inscription. The words are mainly Chaldean. Why could not the Chaldee scholar read them then as well as now? To this we answer, all the learned men of Spain could make an egg stand on the table after Columbus had shown them how. There will doubtless be several claimants for the invention of a caloric ship after the Ericsson is *un fait accompli.*

Several reasons are assigned by commentators for the inability of the king's astrologers to read the writing. One is, that the words were written in the ancient Hebrew character, the knowledge of which was even then lost to all except the Jewish priests and scribes, and not in the modern Hebrew character, which differs little or nothing from the Chaldee. The characters, the forms of the letters in which the Old Testament is commonly written, is not the ancient Hebrew characters. It is supposed that the square form of the letters now used is not the primitive form. We might take three or more words having the same radical letters, and having the same significations in Hebrew, Syriac, and Arabic, and yet a scholar must be acquainted with each of these languages before he could read these words in all of them. The words are the same, but the forms of the letters are different. Latin and English letters are alike, but the Greek characters are different. So, when, for convenience' sake, the printer puts the Greek word *aionios* in English letters, the mere Greek scholar does not know his old acquaintance, nor the mere English scholar divine whence it comes nor what it means. If the inscription, then, on the wall at Belshazzar's feast was in ancient characters, it is not strange that his wise men were unable to read it. Others think that the words were inscribed in hieroglyphics, of which the astrologers had no key, and that we have not the original in our Bible, but translations of the forms of the letters, as well as of the sense; others think that the writing was intelligible only to such as were aided in reading it by the Spirit of God; and others think they were so intoxicated or so frightened that they could not read. You may adopt any or whichever of these opinions about their inability that pleases you best. It is plain, I think, that the characters were neither the usual demotic nor hieratic. Grotefend has rendered it nearly certain that the Babylonians used both, and that their magi, like the priests of Egypt, were able to read both. I only insist, however, on the fact that the king's astrologers could not read this inscription, and that Daniel could; and you will be pleased, no doubt, to observe how the interpretation was brought out. It was obtained, as is often the case with our greatest blessings, through the agency of woman, the aged grandmother of the king, the queen dowager, as our European cousins would call her. Blank terror and alarm reign in the court. The king and his courtiers are at their wit's end. No one seems to be calm and self-possessed but Nitocris, the widow of old Nebuchadnezzar. She instantly steps up and suggests that Daniel should be sent for, and gives her reason. It is strange that he was not thought of before, or that he was not at hand. His services to the state seem to have been forgotten. Empires as well as republics will sometimes be ungrateful. It often happens that a woman, whose sex is usually so easily agitated by trifles, when overtaken by some great crisis, which calls forth all the latent energies of her soul, is found to display a calmness, a magnanimity, a self-possession that puts to shame the powers of the other sex.

Our London friend goes off here into an ecstacy at the magnanimity and self-possession of this aged woman. The whole history of Christianity does indeed show that woman is made for a crisis, and happy is he who has one at his side in the day of trial. Our earthly happiness depends upon the society of an intelligent, amiable woman—the mere consciousness of the presence of a female heart is a great blessing. Who was last at the cross? Who was first at the tomb on the resurrection morn? Woman. If Eve was the first in the transgression, her daughters have ever been first in healing the sorrows of the fall. The vigils of the dead, the beds of the sick, and the chambers of the dying are witnesses of her patience and sleepless care. It is important for young men to properly estimate the position of woman. She needs no other charter of rights than the Bible. No conventions can do for her what Christianity has done. It is the ordinance of God that she should be, not the slave, but the helpmate and companion; not the head, but the friend of man. Just where woman is placed in her proper position, there society culminates in its loftiest grandeur. And her proper position is just where the Bible has placed her, as daughter, sister, wife, and mother, and every where man's best friend and counselor.

III. These astrologers were not enchanters—they were not diviners—they professed no communion with evil spirits. They were men who studied the signs of the heavenly bodies, and having no written revelations, they believed that God had written the past, the present, and also something of the future in the sky—that the stars were the letters of that revelation, and that by studying them they might interpret things to come. In allowing himself, therefore, to be placed at their head, Daniel does not violate the laws of Moses against soothsayers, witches, and the like Satan-possessed persons. These wise men of Babylon were not peeping and muttering spirit rappers, whose pretended revelations were filling the land with lunatics. They were magi, but not magicians. They were philosophers, but not sorcerers. They held communion with God's outward world, and not with the spirits of the dead or with devils. When Daniel, therefore, consented to become the head master of this learned body, he became the patron of science, the principal of a university, or, as we would say, the President of the

Smithsonian Institute. Nothing more. Daniel gave no countenance to, and had no sympathy for sorcerers, magicians, or persons professing to hold communion with evil spirits. The Chaldean astrologers and wise men possessed more science than we generally give them credit for. Even now, what is more instructive, and refining, and elevating than the study of the flowers, the earth, and the stars of the sky—things bright and glorious above, and beautiful around and below? The next best book to the written Word of God is the volume of nature. It is God's will written "all in capitals." The stars teach as well as shine. They are the Creator's throne.

> "Nature all over is consecrated ground,
> Teeming with growths immortal and sublime."

Nature's volume is inferior to Revelation, never contradictory to it. We see the wisdom, power, and glory of the ineffable Godhead in the visible things of creation. We can see his smile in the sunbeams, his mercy in providence, his footprints in the depths that are beneath us, and his glory in the vast immensity that is above us. The astrologers of the distant Euphrates, where the air is extremely transparent, the skies brilliant, and the stars glowing with tropical splendor, are not to be blamed, if, without a Bible such as we have, they took for their Bible the book of the outer world, and from it sought to understand the mind, the purposes, and the will of God.

Let us then, in bringing home the lessons of this feast,

IV. *Learn, in the next place*, THAT ONE SIN OFTEN LEADS TO ANOTHER. The king makes a feast for his thousand lords. He drinks wine before them; orders in the sacred vessels; and then they drink deeper, and become more profane, and praise their idols in defiance of Jehovah.

Sensuality is usually connected with profaneness, and both lead to ruin. The king and his lords, instead of defending their city when closely besieged by a formidable enemy, were spending the night in drinking and revelry. Such low vices are always sinful, but more so when indulged in at the time that God's judgments are heavy upon us. It is a great mistake to think that sorrow can be drowned in the intoxicating cup. It is but to add fuel to the flame to flee to sensual excesses as a remedy for grief, pain, losses, or bereavement. The records of crime abound with cases illustrating the connection between sins against the body and our fellow-men, and sins against God. Men in drunken frolics proceed to profaneness that would make them shudder at other times. It is then they throw off the fear of law and justice, and vent their unlawful passions, and make a jest of holy things, and dishonor religion, and blaspheme against God. *Take heed, says the apostle, then to yourselves, lest at any time your hearts be overcharged with gluttony and drunkenness, and that the day of calamity and judgment come upon you unawares.*

V. Learn that there is great guilt and deserved punishment in not taking warning from the judgments of God upon others, especially our own countrymen and ancestors. This matter is often referred to in the Bible. Daniel was now, it is thought, about eighty-five years of age, a wise and holy man, in whom dwelt the spirit of the Most High God. When he was called before the anxious king to interpret the writing, he first reproves and admonishes the haughty monarch for not having improved the dealings of God with his father and grandfather. *Then Daniel answered and said before the king, Let thy gifts be to thyself, and give thy rewards to another; I neither deserve nor desire them. Yet I will read the writing unto the king, and make known to him the interpretation; but before I can explain the writing, it is my solemn and painful duty, as a servant of Jehovah, to try and awaken the king's mind to serious reflection.* The time is short—the crisis is at hand. If repentance is now available, it must be done quickly. Know then, O thou King of Babylon, that the Most High God, &c.—See v. 18 and 24. As though he had said, You, O king, have either wilfully forgotten or wholly neglected to profit by the confession of Jehovah's power which your grandfather made. Thou, his grandson and successor, notwithstanding his remarkable edict, and penitence, and conversion, hast not humbled thine heart, though thou knowest all this. *Thou hast not given honor to Him who has the supreme disposal of thy affairs and thy life.* Therefore, this is thy doom, this is the writing: THOU ART WEIGHED IN THE BALANCES AND FOUND WANTING.

It is a great sin not to observe God's providences, and especially in our own families and in our own personal history. It is a fearful thing to rebel against God, when he is striving to save our souls by calling us to repent and forsake our evil ways by the voice of affliction or bereavement. Since your breath and all your ways, the avenues of life and death, are in his hands, let it be your highest care to glorify him. Daniel condemned Belshazzar, not so much for the crimes he was in the act of committing, as for his not having availed himself of the opportunities he had had of knowing and doing the will of God. The history of his grandfather and of his conversion, surely, ought to have taught him who was the true God, and how he was to be worshiped. The condemnation at the judgment-day will not be that you conscientiously believed a lie, but it will be that you neglected the opportunities of acquiring and making yourselves acquainted with the truth. The responsibility of a man for his belief is just as certain as his responsibility for his conduct. You must as certainly give an account to God for the sentiments, opinions, and principles you hold and communicate, as for the deeds done in the body. The responsibility for serious errors or for false principles, or, as the apostle calls them, "Damnable heresies," does not begin at the moment they are embraced, nor end with their avowal. The responsibility goes far aback, and may rest in part on your teachers, on your companions, on the pictures you have looked at, the books you have read, the imaginations you have indulged. The condemnation will not be that men are in darkness, but that they refused to come to the light—not that they were dead in trespasses and sins, but that they would not come to Christ that they might have life. The deist will not be condemned merely for his rejection of Revelation, but for his neglect of the means of making himself a Christian. Many a man is sincere in error, but his sincerity does not change his error into truth. If a man sincerely makes a mistake that causes him to lose his property or his life, we may pity him, but neither our pity nor his sincerity changes the result. He must bear the consequences. The damning fact at the judgment-day will not be that impenitent and unbelieving sinners were honest in their delusion, and conscientious in their belief of erroneous doctrines; but that they did not use the means they had, or could have had, to know the truth. The condemnation will be, that they spent more time in the study of shells and flowers, stars and butterflies, than in the study of Moses and the prophets—that they spent more time, and strength, and means, and exertions of intellect, in enriching themselves, feeding and adorning their bodies, increasing their commissions and rent rolls, than in the prayerful study of Christ and his apostles—that they spent more anxious moments in studying out how to satisfy their own minds that there was no necessity to repent of their sins and believe in the vicarious atonement of the Lord Jesus Christ, or to establish themselves in the belief that there is no devil, no hell, no everlasting punishment, than they ever spared for the solution of the great and yet simple question, "What shall I do to be saved?"—a question which we are ready to think should be the first and the last with every thinking man. There is fearful guilt in not doing our duty, as well as in doing what we are commanded not to do. It may be that the very Sabbath which you have resolved to spend in dissipation at home might have been that on which you would have heard the truth which would have saved your soul. It may be that the very discourse which, for some slight cause you neglected to hear, was the one of all others which would have done you good. Never, therefore, lose an opportunity of hearing the truth preached as it is in Jesus, if you can possibly avoid it. You do not know when the saving word may be spoken that will turn you from darkness unto light, and from the power of Satan unto God.

VI. and lastly. LEARN TO FEAR THE POWER OF CONSCIENCE. It was a sense of guilt which put Belshazzar into such terror, and filled his lords with astonishment. There was no thunder, no lightning, no earthquake, no assault as yet—nothing but a handwriting on the wall of his banqueting hall. For aught he knew of the meaning of the writing, it might have been some good tidings of victory, some favorable message from the gods whom he was praising in his drunken feast. Why, then, was he so alarmed? *Why did his countenance change and his thoughts trouble him, so that the joints of his loins were loosed and his knees smote one against another?* Why did he cry aloud for some one to tell him the meaning of the writing? Plainly, because he was conscious of being sensual and profane, and conscious that such things were deserving of punishment. It is conscience that "makes cowards of us all." The righteous are bold as a lion, but the wicked flee where no man pursueth. It is clear, from the history, that a man's own mind can be made the source of his greatest terror. No extraneous cause of alarm was as yet brought to bear upon the king. It was his own consciousness of guilt that tormented him. So now God can easily strike terror into the most profligate man, by letting his own thoughts loose upon him. No language can overdraw the picture of a profligate sinner left a prey to his lusts, and to an awakened conscience. It is not in the power of wine, nor of splendor and companions, to calm his spirits. Sin, however gilded or sugared over, is a misery; it is an evil and bitter thing.

It was a guilty conscience that made Adam and Eve run and hide themselves. It was conscience that made Felix tremble when Paul reasoned before him. And what was it that made Herod think that Jesus was John the Baptist risen from the dead? He probably was a Sadducee, who did not believe in a devil, nor the existence of spirits, nor the resurrection; yet so strong was his conscience, that it overpowered his cold convictions, and suggested to him that John, whom he had beheaded, was risen from the dead, and had come to punish him for his crimes.

A guilty conscience is a fearful enemy, but a good conscience is a man's best friend—it is a perpetual feast. If you would be happy, you must keep a clear conscience, void of offense toward God and man. The only certain peace is to have the heart staid upon God through Jesus Christ. The great doctrines of religion, therefore, instead of leading to licentiousness, or filling the mind with gloomy terror, are the best and the only preventives of unhappy forebodings. Who is it that lives in habitual fear of the officers of the law, and is constantly talking of the pains and penalties inflicted on convicted criminals, and trying to prove that they are too severe, and should be repealed? Is it the good citizen who is intent only to do his duty toward God and man? Your reading of men and things satisfies you that it is not among such that you find continual anxiety about the penalties of the law. It is not among such that you find unceasing efforts to prove that penalties are not penalties, or if, indeed, there be any such things, there at least ought not to be such things—efforts so unceasing that they will never, never have done with their statements of the case—never satisfied with their own defense, but ever trying to make them stronger. Your observation confirms the Bible declaration, that laws and the penalties of law are for evil doers, and not for those who live in obedience to the will of God. So a little reflection will satisfy you that the old Bible method of salvation is not only the true one, but the only one that can make you happy. It is admitted men are sinners. It is admitted sin deserves punishment. It is admitted that as sinners our consciences trouble us. How, then, can we be saved from sin? How can we be saved from the guilt and consequent terrors of a guilty conscience? Does it seem to you that the best way is to set to work to prove that there is no evil in sin—that God is too good to punish sin—that the terror of conscience is owing altogether to the prejudices of education? Certainly not. Facts, realities, every one's own experience, prove that such attempts are vain. These things are not fancies, but dreadful realities. Does it seem to you, then, that the way of escape from sin and from the wretchedness of a guilty conscience is to spend your life in trying to get arguments and facts to prove that there is no hell, no devil, and no everlasting punishment? The very fact that some men spend all their lives trying to prove that there is no hell, no devil, and no everlasting punishment, proves, after all, that they themselves are dreadfully afraid of these very things. Now there is a more excellent way—a way more philosophical, harmonious, and elevating—a way infinitely more suitable for man, and honorable to the laws of the universe and to God. This way is to acknowledge what every one must feel, that we are sinners against God and deserve his wrath, and then accept of Jesus Christ as He is offered in the Gospel, as a perfect, all-sufficient Saviour. It is true, there is such a thing as sin, and that it is an evil and bitter thing. But here is a sacrifice for sin which God accepts. *He hath made Him, His own Son, who knew no sin, to be made sin—a sin-offering—an availing sin-atonement for us, that we might be made the righteousness of God in Him.* Who, then, can condemn us? It is God that justifieth. It is true, there is a devil, and a hell, and everlasting punishment; but we have no fear of these things. Christ has delivered us. It is true, by nature and practice, we have a guilty conscience, but we are saved from its terrors through faith in Christ, whose blood cleanseth us from all sin, and whose Spirit renews our hearts, and purifies our affections, and prepares us for His glory. Sickness and death, the devil, hell, and everlasting punishment, are sad realities; but they are not to be feared by us. Death is a conquered enemy; the grave a vanquished foe. The devil is overcome and his works destroyed, and we are translated from his kingdom into that of God's dear Son. It is no wonder, then, that those who reject Christ as a world-redeeming God, and who deny the personality and influence of his Holy Spirit, and laugh at the idea of being born again, and of being saved by faith in a vicarious atonement, are so unhappy, so much annoyed by a guilty conscience, that they can never satisfy themselves with their own arguments that there is no devil, no hell, and no future and everlasting punishment. The happiest and bravest men have ever been those that, believing in the realities of their enemies, have adopted such means as enabled them to triumph over them, and not such as have spent their lives in vain expedients to try to prove that there were no such enemies. Which is best, to cheat one's self into a delusion, or to believe in disagreeable realities, and adopt the sure and certain method of escape? And the more so, since religion is a present blessing. Godliness has the promise of the life that now is, as well as of that which is to come. The blessings of piety are not all reserved for the world to come. Her ways are ways of peace in this world, and all her paths are paths of pleasantness. SEEK YE THE KINGDOM OF GOD AND HIS RIGHTEOUSNESS, AND ALL THINGS NEEDFUL SHALL BE ADDED UNTO YOU. Amen.

LECTURE XII.

WEIGHED AND WANTING.

On Dan., v., 25, 31.

"TEKEL—Thou art weighed in the balances, and art found wanting."

Belshazzar's Fidelity to his Word.—Defenseless State of the City.—Nations die Suicides.—Couture's Decadence of the Romans.—Egypt's Doom.—Our Safety.—How and why Righteousness exalteth a Nation.—National Responsibility of American young Men.—God Weighs all Men.—Art of Writing in Moses' Day.—Egyptian Book of the Dead.—Bible does not fix the Chronology of the Creation, but only the Facts of its Creation and Adaptation to Man.—Objections to the Flood.—Size of the Ark.—Top of Ararat.—Quantity of Water.—Style and Proportion of the Ark.—Sum of Proofs of a Deluge.—Wrath upon the Canaanites.—Herculaneum.—Famine in Ireland.—Spirit of the Psalms not Maledictory.—Infidelity dangerous to the State.—The Moral Man wanting.—Salvation by Grace does not lead to Sin.—True Religion eminently conducive to present Happiness.—Orthodox Creed eminently the safest for the Future.—Fearfulness of our personal Responsibility.

I. THE first thing that strikes me from the history as it opens before us in the text, is the fidelity of King Belshazzar. Though he had but an hour to live, he kept his promise to the servant of God. See v. 29. Luxurious, profane, and wicked as he was, this was one good trait in his character. This one good trait did not, however, redeem him from the consequences of other sin.

II. We are struck with the defenseless condition of the city. *We see how maddened and utterly feeble cities and nations become when ripe for destruction.* After a siege of more than two years, the king and his lords, instead of watching and resisting the attack of their sleepless besiegers, were engaged in a profane revelry, and were surprised and slain, and the city taken. And thus ended the golden empire, of which Nebuchadnezzar was the head. The heathen proverb that "Those whom the gods wish to destroy they first make mad," seems to contain the verity of actual history. In both ancient and modern times, it seems that, when God has pronounced the hour of a nation's doom, the inhabitants of that nation lose the caution, the skill, and the energy they had exhibited before, and do themselves precipitate the very result they wish so much to avert. Never, perhaps, was there a more full, palpable, and fearful illustration of this than in the destruction of Jerusalem under Titus. Some of you may remember the illustration presented in a previous lecture of the causes of a nation's decline and fall, as set forth in Couture's "Decadence of the Romans," in the Luxembourg Gallery at Paris. In his picture, life-like and true to history, luxury and corruption are represented as the causes of the fall of Rome. Nations rarely fall before a foreign aggressor. Their ruin or their glory is placed by God within themselves. Epidemics and want, and even civil wars, may overturn nations, but do not destroy them. These calamities may lessen their power, diminish their influence, narrow their limits, but they do not blot them out from the map of nations. Nations die suicides. Nothing so soon dissolves the national character as luxury. It is worse than flood or fire. It hurts not the trade or agriculture of a people so much as it hurts themselves. It produces a degenerate set of men. All history shows that it is one of the greatest national evils. It is even worse that the temporary loss of freedom to a brave and resolute people. It is corruption and vice that cut off nations by the root. It is infidelity and credulity that so far materialize men as to smother all their generous instincts, and thus destroy their nationalities and annihilate them. It was thus Egypt, once so powerful and flourishing, passed, impoverished, into the hands of the Mohammedan, and became, and continues to this day, according to the predictions of the Hebrew prophet, *the basest of kingdoms*. It was thus Babylon fell into the hands of the Mede. A nation true to God and loyal to his laws, and with such a history and such a local habitation as we have, has nothing to fear from the world in arms. But we have a great deal to fear from Jesuitism, and from corruption and ignorance. Our safety consists in the purity of the ballot-box; and to preserve this, we must employ the press in all its thousand fold avenues to the popular mind; and true religion must irradiate our high places, and cast its softening influence over the lanes, and alleys, and hovels of our cities, and over the mountains and valleys of all our States and Territories. There are two great reasons why *righteousness exalteth a nation*, and why society cannot cohere without religion. These are, first, that when a due regard to God is lost sight of in the institutions of a nation, or in the administration of its affairs, a jarring inevitably ensues between the laws and doings of that nation and the universe, of which it is a part. This want of harmony—this want of conformity to the order of God's government—must result in disaster. And as the government of God cannot be subverted, every government opposed to the divine must in time fall. A second reason is, that all constitutions and laws not in harmony with the universe are unsuited to the people placed under them; and consequently, discontent, restiveness, and insurrection will inevitably arise, sooner or later. If there be not a harmony and adaptation in the laws and institutions of a country for the wants of a people, it is impossible there should be permanence in its polity. It is, then, a matter of incalculable importance to the happiness of mankind that civil government should be conducted on religious principles. And next to the salvation of their own souls, is the responsibility of American young men to study the purity, vigor, and perpetuity of their civil institutions. It is their duty to see that men of sound religious principles and proper abilities be elevated to offices of power and trust. As the principle of immortality in man consists in his capacity of knowing, fearing, serving, and loving God, so is religion the principle of durability in social bodies. When the Ship of State is far out at sea, and amid the darkness of night, and tempests are raging, there is then nothing on which to fix the eye but the eternal lights of heaven; then the only sure compass is the Word of God. It was very reprehensible, certainly, for Belshazzar and his thousand lords to abandon the defense of the city as they did. They showed themselves to be unworthy of the government of such a city. Little, indeed, did they think what would be on the morrow. Little did they think that the last hours of Babylon had come—that the remaining sands in the glass of her destiny would be emptied ere their banquet should close. But before another rising sun, the monarch was slain, his nobles captives, and Darius the Mede was sitting on the throne of Nebuchadnezzar, in the great Babylon which he had built. And so, when the hour allotted for the downfall of an empire or of a dominion, political or ecclesiastical, has come, the wheels of Providence will move with an irresistible power, and with a fearful velocity; and then all attempts to keep back the tide of divine indignation will but increase its fury. *The upholders of a doomed system always act like doomed men.* The ill-timed, impious feasting of Belshazzar did more in one night for the downfall of Babylon than Cyrus with all his troops was able to accomplish in a siege of two years. It is an awful thing for an individual or nation to be abandoned of God.

III. The Bible represents God as WEIGHING ALL MEN, all their motives and characters. It is a common scriptural expression: "The Lord is a God of knowledge, and by Him actions are weighed." David also says: "Men of low degree are vanity, and men of high degree are a lie; to be laid in the balance they are altogether wanting." The Prophet Isaiah says: "Thou most upright dost weigh the path of the just." And, again, Solomon tells us, "All the ways of a man are clean in his own eyes; but the Lord weigheth the Spirit." These texts are sufficient to show that the idea contained in the inscription on the palace wall is one frequently found in Scripture. It is also found in heathen mythology. It is a common idea in the proverbs of the Arabs to this day. The terms of the inscription are sufficiently explained by Daniel himself, and need no extended commentary.

The idea of being weighed by the Judge of quick and dead at his judgment-seat in reference to our eternal destiny, is certainly a fearful one. Who can think of being weighed against God's law? This law says, "Thou shalt love the Lord thy God with all thy heart, and with all thy soul, and with all thy mind, and with all thy strength, and thy neighbor as thyself." And it says, "Cursed is every one that continueth not in all things written in the law to do them." The requirements of God's law are absolute, perpetual, supreme. It requires all the heart, and at all times, and allows of no cessation of its love and obedience. This law is placed in one scale, and every man's character is placed in the opposite scale, and thus every man's doom is to be fixed, and that forever. What, then, have we to place in the scales of the sanctuary? One is ready to say, "I have not kept the law of God, but I place in the opposite scale my objections to it. Indeed, I object to the law of God and the revelation of His will, and the whole subject of Bible religion; and I do so for several reasons." Well, let us hear them.

First. "The law of God so called is contained in the book called the Bible, and the first five books of the Bible are said to have been written by Moses; but I do not believe this, for in the days of Moses the art of writing was not known. Man was not then sufficiently advanced from his primitive savageism to have written any such books." This is a bold and clearly stated objection, and if it is as true and heavy as it claims to be, it will certainly weigh down its end of the scale. But let us look at it. You know that Napoleon invaded Egypt, and that a corps of scientific men accompanied his army to examine the hieroglyphics, and explore in the most thorough manner possible its far-famed antiquities; and you know that they climbed the Pyramids and entered the tombs, and visited the chambers of Egypt's embalmed kings; and you ought to know, also, that in these sepulchral chambers they found many manuscripts as old at least as the time of Moses, and one which it is believed was written *two centuries before his day*. These manuscripts were found with the mummies and funeral relics which were deposited in the tombs. They have been read and published to the world. They contain their burial service and rites for the dead. And thus the matter-of-fact discovery of the French savans have silenced the objection that infidels made for centuries against the Pentateuch. It is only with the ignorant or malicious that such objections can now do their mischievous work.

Secondly. "It is alleged that the Bible cannot be relied on as teaching the will of God, for it asserts that the world was made about six thousand years ago. This cannot be true, for the learned now tell us that this world must have existed millions of ages." In weighing this objection, let it be observed that it is not correctly stated. The Bible does not say that God created the world about six thouand years ago. Moses says nothing on this point. He only tells us that *in the beginning* God created the heavens and the earth. The beginning may have been millions of millions of ages anterior to man's creation. It is evident that Moses only designs to speak of two great facts; first, that God is the Creator of all things; and secondly, that God prepared and adapted, according to his account, the globe for the introduction of man upon it. In the second place, let it be remembered that geologists are crude, unsatisfactory, and contradictory still in their speculations about the age of the earth. They are not agreed among themselves. They are guilty of monstrous errors in much of their past reasoning, themselves being judges. There is a great want of facts among them. And, thirdly, their investigations have resulted in the conviction that the human race cannot have existed on this globe for a longer period than that asserted by Moses. And thus science, in the hands of the most eminent geologists, instead of contradicting the Mosaic account, gives whatever influences she has in its favor. "Thou art weighed in the balances, and art found wanting."

Thirdly. Another says, "There is so much about the deluge in the Pentateuch that I do not understand, that I object to the whole Bible, and to revealed religion altogether. There was not water enough to drown the world. The ark was not large enough to contain one half of the animals for which it was intended; and it was such a miserable, clumsy old hulk that it could not have floated any how, and if it did ever get to the top of Ararat, there is so much ice and snow there that old Noah could never have descended. I do not understand these things, and therefore I do not believe in evangelical religion." There is so much crowded into this objection, that only a word or two can be spared for each point.

I. You do not understand all the points involved in the history of the flood; neither do I, nor any one else. The most eminent scholars and geologists confess their ignorance on this subject. But your want of understanding is certainly no good reason for denying the truth of the history. You do not understand your own existence. There are a thousand things all around you that are unquestioned realities, and yet you do not understand them. There are mysteries in nature as well as in religion. Holy mysteries are rather a proof of the truth of the Bible than otherwise. If you will not receive as true any thing till you can comprehend every thing about its essence and laws of existence, then you will perish of starvation, for you must inevitably die before you can comprehend the analysis of your food, and how it sustains the animal economy.

II. As to the *top* of Ararat, it is admitted that the term Ararat signifies a whole chain of mountains. Noah may not, therefore, have had so far to descend. The ark probably rested on one of the lower spurs of that mountain range. It may, moreover, not have been so cold just after the flood as it is now in Armenia; and besides, could not the same God that piloted him over the seas have helped him down from the highest snowy peak of all Ararat?

III. As to the *size* of the ark, it is ascertained that it was about as large as eighteen of the largest ships of our day.

The *distinct species* of four-footed animals known amount to but about two hundred and fifty. These eighteen ships will carry twenty thousand men, with eighteen hundred pieces of cannon, and provisions for six months. Who then can for a moment doubt that the ark, built, not for a clipper race from Shanghai to London—not for speed nor for beauty, but merely for buoyancy and strength, would afford accommodations for these two hundred and fifty pairs of quadrupeds, with the specified number of birds and insects, and eight human beings, with provisions for a year? It seems almost like trifling to answer such arguments, and yet deists are scattering them about among the ignorant and the credulous as powerful objections to the credibility of the Scriptures. The fact is, as stated by Bishop Wilkins, "That of the two it is more difficult to assign a number and bulk of necessary things to answer to the capacity of the ark, than to find sufficient room for the several species of animals and their food already known to have been there."

There is one very interesting fact in this connection deserving of notice. "It can be proved to demonstration that the proportion of the length to the breadth, and of both to the height, in Noah's ark, is exactly that which renders any substance the most buoyant and the most perfectly secure even in a storm." Now it is a question really deserving of thought, how did Noah obtain such skill in architectural dimensions? It has been the result of long experience and careful observation by which architects of the present day have obtained this knowledge. It has not come to them intuitively. How then does it happen that Noah, so long ago, was so accomplished a ship-builder? The deist cannot answer—the Bible believer has no difficulty.

IV. As to the *quantity of water*, it is somewhat difficult to know what to say to a man who has such crooked ideas of Omnipotence as to think that He who made all worlds and all oceans is unable to roll a flood of waters over this little globe. But frivolous as such objections are, they are not unanswerable. Bold assertions are not arguments. *First.* It is not believed by all Bible readers that the deluge was universal. I so understand the Hebrew record; but some others read it differently. *Secondly.* Nearly three-fourths of the whole surface of the globe are now covered with water; and how much more water the Creator could pour upon the land has never yet been accurately determined. Nor has it ever been shown that the Creator could not so sink the portions of land now dry as to cover them with water—just such a process as was probably carried out in the flood. *Thirdly.* The fact of a deluge is certain. Tradition, history, and geology prove there must have been such a thing, and all agree in fixing the time about the period assigned to Noah's flood in the Bible. The rocks, caverns, and mountains of the earth must have been at some former period covered with water. How else can we account for skeletons of whales on the sides of high mountains, far from the ocean? How else can we account for the remains of animals, in the frigid regions of the North, that can live only in the torrid zone? All science testifies that some great convulsion has taken place in our planet. The fact that there has been a deluge is written in living characters upon the face of nature. If you could blot out the record from the Bible, still the evidence remains indisputable. This objection, when weighed in the balances, like the others we have had before it, is found wanting.

Fourth. Another says, "I do not believe the Bible to be the Word of God, because the Hebrews were ordered to urge an exterminating war upon the Canaanites. Men, women, and children were put to death. It is impossible to believe that God would issue such a command." In weighing this objection, our first remark is, that God may use whatever instruments he pleases for the execution of his judgments. In point of fact, He does use pestilence and famine, fire, flood, and earthquake ; why may He not also use the sword? Was it not God that sent disease into the esculent roots of Ireland; and, for the want of their accustomed food, men, women, and children died? Was it not God who poured an ocean of burning lava on Herculaneum and Pompeii? Then, neither age nor infancy, neither mother nor babe, was spared. All were overwhelmed in indiscriminate destruction. Was it not God that shook the foundation of the earth, and opened one wide grave for thousands of the inhabitants of Lisbon? What but the providence of God sent the Asiatic cholera into the cities and towns, and along the river coasts of Europe and America, sparing neither age, sex, nor color? In point of fact, then, this objection is just as powerful *against the God of nature as against the God of Revelation.* Even, therefore, if we could see no reason why God should exterminate the Canaanites, we are not at liberty to cavil at the fact, any more than at the devastations of earthquakes, floods, pestilence, and famine. But, secondly, we do see a reason. Their cup of iniquity was full. Their day of grace and of probation was ended. They were abandoned to the most polluting idolatry. Their destruction was, therefore, nothing but the execution of the divine penalty upon their sins. It will not be denied that God has a right to exterminate an abandoned nation in any way that shall seem best to him, either by flood, or pestilence, or famine, or sword. In point of fact, He has often done this. Nor will it be denied that, in so doing, God may inflict the judgment in such a way as to produce the deepest impression of the enormity of sin upon the minds of those that survive. This objection is, therefore, found wanting.

Fifthly. It is objected, again, "That the Psalms, which are conspicuous in Christian worship, and much read and admired by Christians, are nothing but the ravings of malice or of personal revenge. David, or whoever was the author of the Psalms, instead of forgiving his enemies, and praying that God would bless them, imprecates vengeance upon their heads; and yet it is said in the Bible that the Psalms are dictated by the Holy Spirit." Now in answer to this, let it be remembered,

1. That in many of those passages in which David uses strong language against his enemies, he refers not to personal or political enemies—not to his fellow-men as enemies of his body, of his family, or of his kingdom, but to the enemies of his soul, those that were seeking to deprive him of his salvation. He speaks of the devil, and evil spirits, and wicked men as instruments of the devil.

2. The words which are rendered in our version in the imperative mood and present tense are, in the Hebrew, in the indicative mood and future tense. The passages, then, simply declare what will befall the incorrigibly wicked and finally impenitent. David was a prophet, and foresaw the end of the wicked and of all that forget God.

3. Let us suppose a horrid murder was committed at our very door. The axe and the knife of robbers have covered the floor of our friend's dwelling with the mangled bodies of the family. A Christian man, appalled by such a horrid spectacle, prayed, in the fervor of his morning prayer, "O God, bring these guilty men to justice! O let

them not escape! let swift retribution overtake them; let them suffer just punishment for their crime, that the honor of our laws may be preserved, and that terror may fill the hearts of the wicked." And does the infidel cry out, "What a revengeful, malicious wretch this man must be! Instead of praying that these murderers may escape and be prospered, he prays that they may be brought to justice?" And is this really the issue? Does the infidel mean that a good man ought not to pray that the laws should be honored, magistrates obeyed, the innocent protected, and the guilty brought to punishment, in order that peace and justice may reign over society?" Is it out at last that infidelity is dangerous to the state, and at war with established public morals, order, and law? Does the caviller really think that it is wicked to pray that those who are scattering fire-brands, arrows, and death through the community, may be shut up in prison, and punished according to law and justice? If so, then all law, all established order, is malignant and to be put down. But mankind have determined to the contrary. Their experience is, that established laws, enforced by penalties, are absolutely necessary for the happiness of mankind. The same is distinctly taught in the Bible. And observation teaches us, moreover, that those who receive the Bible, and live under the conviction of a judgment to come, and a belief in future rewards and punishments, are the best citizens, bravest soldiers, and purest patriots; while, on the other hand, those that have the impudence and arrogance to assert that God is too good to punish men for their sins by shutting them up in the prison of hell, are dangerous men in society. He that fears God, regards his fellow man. Both worlds are best cared for when they are taken care of together, and the present life is made a preparation for the life to come.

Sixthly. Another says, "I have nothing to do with these absurd infidel cavils you have named. I would not consider them worthy of any serious notice. I am just in all my dealings with my fellow-men. I owe no man any thing. I try to do my duty as a good citizen." And we will add, that such an one is all he claims to be, and even more; he is high-minded, honorable, generous, and characterized by every social, personal, national, and domestic excellence. But what is the result, when all these social virtues, and all this public spirit, and all this commercial integrity (and would to God that such things were more common,) are placed in the scale opposite to the holy, unchanging, everlasting law of God? The experiment will inevitably show that "by the deeds of the law no man living can be justified." Then will the Judge say, It is true you have done well, but you have not done all your duty. You have done justly toward man, but how stands the account in reference to your Creator? You have acted generously toward society, but how have you acted toward God? You have kept the last six commandments, but what have you done with the four first? If you have kept the second table of the law, why have you broken the first? Have you loved your neighbor as yourself? Have you loved God all your life-long, every moment, with ALL YOUR HEART, MIND, AND STRENGTH? If not, then you are found wanting. But is not the case better with this man's neighbor, who, in addition to such amiable instincts, and social virtues, and business traits, is a regular baptized member of the Church? He is strict in all his religious duties; he always bows at the name of Jesus—wears black on Good Friday, and dresses in white upon Easter Sunday—is never absent from confession, or vespers, or communion; he is at the prayer-meeting, the Bible class, the Sabbath-school, and can repeat the Creed, the Ten Commandments, and the Lord's Prayer. Surely, such an one will weigh well in the scales of the sanctuary. Alas! it is nowhere written in the law that such things as these will be taken as substitutes for obedience to the will of God, and for the want of the devotion of the heart to Him. The law of God is not satisfied with forms and ceremonies; the rubrics do not silence the thundering sound of the Judge's solemn voice, saying, Who hath required this at your hand? He hath required LOVE. You reply, I have done penance; I have performed this good work; and you are weighed and found altogether wanting. Nor will it at all alter your case to say, I am *sincere* in my views. Sincerity added to heresy does not make it true. No doubt there are sincere unbelievers, as there are sincere Moslems and sincere madmen. Saul of Tarsus said, "I verily thought that I ought to do many things contrary to the name of Jesus." He was as sincere in his persecution of Christians before his conversion as he was sincere in his preaching the Gospel and suffering for it afterward. Sincerity deserves to be treated with respect and pity; but it is impossible that sincerity can make error truth, or save us from the consequences of our errors. Our accountability rests in the use of the means given us for the discovery of the truth. The matter is brought down to a very definite point. The Bible considers all under sin. The Bible says, "There is none good, no, not one." "If we say that we have no sin, we deceive ourselves and the truth is not in us." There is no one that seriously looks at his heart and life, and the requirements of God's holy law, who does not feel, "If thou, O Lord, shouldst mark iniquity, who would stand?" If all have sinned and come short of the glory of God, how, then, can we meet his law? Are we all found wanting, and brought under the fearful inscription TEKEL? Blessed be God, there is a more excellent way. "God is just, and yet the justifier of them that believe in Jesus." "For of God Christ is made unto us wisdom, righteousness, sanctification, and complete redemption."

"Christ is the end of the law for righteousness to every one that believeth."

"God hath made him who knew no sin to be sin for us," &c.

Against the law, therefore, is weighed the magnifier of the law. Against the law, with its infinite demands, is weighed the infinite righteousness of him that made it honorable. Against the sin of disobeying God's law is placed the blood of His own Son, which cleanseth from all sin. Against Mount Sinai, in one end of the scale, is placed Calvary, in the opposite scale, and the voice of pardon from the latter prevails over the thundering and terrors of the former. When we look on the law, the inscription impressed upon every soul is, "Weighed and found wanting." But when we look at Christ, who is our righteousness, then the inscription, "Tekel," is washed away in his precious blood, and the following glorious and illuminated characters are inscribed in their stead·

"Therefore, being justified by faith, we have peace with God through our Lord Jesus Christ." We are "complete in Christ, without spot or blemish, or any such thing."

WHO, THEN, ARE WEIGHED AND FOUND WANTING? The atheist, the pagan, the unbeliever, the profane, the evil-doer, and the vicious. "Whoremongers and idolaters God will judge." "Drunkards cannot inherit the kingdom of God." "All liars shall have their part in the lake that burneth with fire and brimstone." And also all the impenitent and unbelieving; for it is written, "Except ye repent, ye shall all likewise perish." "Except a man be born again, he cannot see the kingdom of God." This being born again is not mere baptism, nor is it a mere outward reformation. It is a total transformation of character. It is a change from darkness and sin to a state of light and holiness. It is to become a new creature. Do not allow yourselves, my young friends, to be deceived on this matter. It is declared to be an essential point by our Lord himself. Men may laugh at regeneration, but to be saved we must be converted. And what is conversion? It is not seriousness—it is not conviction—it is not conformity to any mere outward requirement, but a thorough, inner, radical revolution of mind. It is not a change of the features of the face. It is not a revolution of the intellect, but of our views, preferences, wishes, and hopes. It is not an ecstasy, an emotion, or a passion. It is not an outcry—it is not religious excitement—it is not ecclesiastical zeal. It is life from the dead; it is a new heart and a right spirit within us, created by the Holy Spirit. The doctrine of justification by faith is sometimes greatly misrepresented. Even in the days of the Apostle Paul, as now, it was charged with leading to licentiousness; but nothing is further from the truth. The whole Gospel method of salvation comprises holiness as essential. Without holiness no man can see God; without holiness no one can be happy. Christ is called Jesus, because he SAVES HIS PEOPLE FROM THEIR SINS. Good works are not the procuring cause, but the evidences of our salvation. Penitence, faith, and charity, and holy living, are essential to happiness. Just in proportion that men are vicious, so are they subjects of misery. All men, therefore, who are living in the practice of any known, deliberate, and voluntary sin are "weighed and found wanting." Creeds, and baptisms, and confessions of faith avail nothing without a living faith in Christ, which, while it justifies, also WORKS by love. It is solemn mockery for a man to profess his faith in Christ, and yet live in disobedience to his commands. Whoever takes the name of Christ upon him, must be careful to maintain good works, and to depart from all iniquity. Do not imagine that you are a Christian, if you harbor deliberately pride, avarice, ambition, vain-glory, covetousness, which is idolatry, murdering, discontent, bitterness, lying, evil-speaking, and slandering. All who knowingly indulge in such things will be found wanting when weighed by the Searcher of all hearts.

Never forget that you need the work and righteousness of Christ, and the work of the Spirit of God in you to fit you for heaven. Amiable instincts, commercial virtues, and social excellences are praiseworthy. These things are lovely and of good report, and are earnestly to be coveted, but they cannot procure the pardon of sin. They give no title to heaven, nor do they produce any fitness for its services. Constitutional morality and amiableness of temper often exist without faith and penitence. If constitutional morality and amiableness of natural disposition entitle us to heaven and prepare us for its glory, then two things are palpable. First, that many people cannot in any way or on any account ever be happy; for, without inquiring into the cause, or stopping to show why it is so, it is a fact that many people are born with indifferent moral constitutions, and with positively bad dispositions. Secondly, in regard to those that are more fortunate by birth and education, there was no necessity for Christianity at all. Mere heathen morals are sufficient, if such things entitle us to, or prepare us for, heaven. Then Christ died in vain; the Holy Spirit is useless. But it is not thus you read the Holy Scriptures.

What are called evangelical sentiments on this subject recommend themselves to you by two plain and powerful considerations. *First.* Such sentiments are not only true and clearly according to the teachings of the Bible, and supported by a large majority of the great, the learned, and the pious, in all ages of the world, but they are EMINENTLY CONDUCIVE TO PRESENT HAPPINESS. Evangelical views of religion are pre-eminently the views that produce happiness in the present life. The reasons of this are palpable. Such views take hold of present realities, and embrace a sufficient remedy for present evils. This is true of an individual man and of the human race. Such views supply an antidote for earth's sorrows. They fix the mind on high and ever-enduring sources of consolation; they stay the heart upon God; they appease the crying of the human soul for reconciliation with its Maker. The altars and victims of all ages and of all races are satisfied in the sacrifice of the Lamb of God. All things are ours in Christ. Peace of conscience and the abundant fruits of the Spirit cannot fail to make a happy man. In keeping God's laws there is great reward. Godliness with contentment is great gain in the present world, as well as in the world to come.

But, again, our views of religion claim your attention, BECAUSE THEY ARE NOT ONLY PRE-EMINENTLY CONDUCIVE TO HAPPINESS EVEN NOW, BUT THEY ARE THE SAFEST FOR THE FUTURE.

With the conviction on our mind that they are true, and according to the Scriptures, this is an exceedingly low point of view. But for the sake of illustrating our argument, suppose the opponent of evangelical sentiments is correct, what does he gain? He gains nothing, either in this world or the world to come. The evangelical believer fares as well as he does. He loses nothing. But suppose the rejecter of evangelical religion is mistaken, that he is in error, as he most certainly is, then what is the result? He loses every thing. If it were possible for you to be in error by believing the Scriptures and receiving the atonement, and striving for a new heart, even then you lose nothing; but if such things are true, then he who rejects them is weighed in the balance and found wanting.

Finally. Live under the habitual conviction that all your actions must be weighed in the just balances of the eternal God. "It is appointed unto all men once to die, and after death the judgment."

"We must all appear before the judgment-seat of

Christ." An awful scrutiny, therefore, awaits every one of us at the bar of God. Well then might we say with the late sage of Marshfield, that the greatest idea that could ever enter a man's mind is his personal accountability to God. The very nature of the constitution of the universe requires that there should be a final judgment, and that there should be a difference between those that serve God and those that serve him not. As there is good and evil, so there is a God and there is a devil; and common sense, as well as reason and revelation, teaches that there must be a separation of the righteous and the wicked. Accordingly, our Lord has told us that the righteous shall go away into life everlasting, and the wicked into everlasting punishment. The duration of the happiness of the righteous is in this place and in other Scriptures explained by the very same Greek term that is used to express the duration of the punishment of the wicked. It is impossible for language to be plainer, and for the teachings of the Bible to be more positive than they are as to the characters and destinies of the righteous and the wicked. Since, then, these things are so, *What shall we do to be saved?* The way of salvation is through faith in Christ. All of our race, when weighed in the balances of God, are found wanting. It is Christ, and Christ only, who can turn the scale in favor of any of Adam's race. But He is an almighty, and everlasting, and gracious Saviour. He casts out none that come to Him. *He that believeth shall be saved; he that believeth not shall be damned.*

LECTURE XIII.

DANIEL THREATENED WITH THE LION'S DEN.

On Dan., vi., 1–11.

A Tragedy in four Acts on the last Night of the Babylonian Empire.—Feast described.—Herodotus and Xenophon detail the Fulfillment of Daniel's Predictions.—Cyrus' grand Review.—Cyaxares.—Darius.—Men for Places, not Places for Partisans.—Division of Labor.—As good Patriots, pray for your Rulers.—Six Satraps not too many.—Daniel a model Statesman.—Statesmen should be pious as well as capable.—Daniel envied.—His Promotion not confirmed by the State: why.—Cunning Politicians.—Daniel's Danger.—No Impeachment can lie except in the matter of his Religion.—The Conspiracy arranged.—The TYRANNY of the Edict against Prayer.—Daniel's Oratoire.—His Mother's Principles deeply rooted. "Toward Jerusalem" does not authorize high Altars looking to the East.—Daniel was not a mere heart Christian, but a CONFESSOR—a Man for a Crisis.

LESSONS.

I. Trials burn away the dross.

II. Learn patience and prudence under trials. Foundation of all law is the will of God.

III. Surrender yourselves in youth cheerfully and unreservedly to the service of God.

I. The two last lectures comprised a visit to the city and court of Babylon under most extraordinary circumstances. We were at a royal feast, on the last night of the existence of the Babylonian empire, which began in great splendor, proceeded with unexampled mirth, and became impious, and ended in fearful disasters. In this most imposing tragedy were four acts.

First Act.—A magnificent banquet—joy, splendor, bewitching beauty, sparkling wines, rich dresses, glittering jewelry, enchanting music—an assemblage of wit, rank, and beauty, such as could be seen only in the metropolis of the world.

The Second Act opens like a flash of lightning. A hand, silent and terrible, comes out on the plastering of the palace wall, and writes, MENE, MENE, TEKEL, UPHARSIN. The king is seized with terror—utters a piercing cry—his limbs tremble—his countenance is changed—his eyes are fixed—his joints are loosed and his knees smite together—he calls for his wise men; and the whole assembly is thrown into the same inexpressible anguish.

Third Act.—The queen dowager enters—she is received with marks of profound respect—she comes not as the wife of the king, but with the authority of the queen-mother. But does she come to read herself the mysterious writing? Can she explain this appalling prodigy? All is silent. Let us hear her speak: "O king," says she, "live forever! There is a man in thy kingdom in whom is the Spirit of the holy God. In the days of thy father, light, and understanding, and wisdom, like the wisdom of the gods, was found in him; he interpreted dreams, and showed hard sayings, and resolved doubts. Let him be sent for; he is the only man in your kingdom who can explain these awful mysteries."

Fourth Act.—Daniel arrives. What a moment! Here are the thousand lords—the women of the harem, in their extravagant and licentious attire—here are the festive tables—the unhallowed remains of a royal debauch—the golden vessels of Jehovah's temple of Jerusalem, still full of the wine of their impure libations. The lamps, amid all the splendors of the palace, still beam upon a thousand countenances on which terror is depicted—the king himself, lately so joyous and so proud, is now trembling, dejected, gasping for breath. But while such were the scenes going on beneath the porticoes of the palace, and on the terraces, and in the hanging gardens of Babylon, night reigned over the Eastern World. The stars, in silence, were filling their offices in the heavens; and in the camp of the Medes and Persians, without the walls of Babylon, not a sound was heard. The besieging army appears more silent and more tranquil than ever. And now the Hebrew prophet enters the royal presence. He is an old man, grown gray with years; his venerable countenance beams with devotional intelligence. The monarch reminds him, by his salutation, that though he has sent for him, yet he was only a captive and a slave. "Art thou that Daniel, which art of the children of the captivity, whom the king my father brought out of the Jewry? I have heard of thee, that thou canst make interpretations. Now if thou canst read this writing, thou shalt be clothed with scarlet, and have a chain of gold about thy neck, and thou shalt be third ruler in the kingdom." Whereupon Daniel reads the interpretation and is rewarded as the king promised. But, according to Daniel's words, that very night "was Belshazzar, the king of the Chaldeans, slain; and Darius, the Median, took the kingdom, being about threescore and two years old." Read here chap. vi., 1–11.

You are aware that all that the prophets predicted concerning the fall of Babylon was fulfilled to the letter, even to the minutest details. The accounts of Herodotus and Xenophon, who lived two hundred years after Cyrus, are in perfect accordance with the great scenes of this wonderful transaction, as recorded in Daniel, and foretold by other prophets. The confederate armies of Media and Persia were entrusted to the command of young Cyrus, who, without his or their knowledge, was to be the conqueror of Babylon, according to Isaiah and Jeremiah. Cyrus, having taken the city, held a review of his cavalry in the streets and squares. Four thousand horsemen, as the royal body-guard, were stationed before the gates of the palace, and two thousand more on either side. Whenever he went out, these marched before him, and two thousand lancers followed. Next followed four great divisions of the army of ten thousand horse in each; and lastly, two thousand war chariots, armed with scythes, four abreast, closed the order of march. The army reviewed by Cyrus in Babylon is estimated to have consisted of one hundred and twenty thousand horse and six hundred thousand foot, numbers not at all improbable in the armies of the East.

Darius the Mede was not present when Babylon was taken. Although Cyrus was the conqueror of the Babylonians, he did not reign ostensibly over the Medes and Persians, for both his father and mother were still alive. After his great victory, he went to visit his parents in Persia, and his uncle, the Darius of Daniel, called also Cyaxares, who was also the father-in-law of Cyrus, returned with him to regulate the affairs of the empire. It was to him that Cyrus yielded the first place. And after such a grand review as that which I have just spoken of, Cyrus left Babylon to lead an army to the shores of the Red Sea. It was during his absence that the events of the sixth chapter took place. Darius reigned only two years over the Babylonian empire, and under his reign Daniel was cast into the den of lions. According to verses 1 and 3, Darius, finding Daniel in favor, continued him in office. All classes were, no doubt, occupied with his predictions. He had read the mysterious words on the wall, and foretold the destruction of the king and the loss of his empire. It was no doubt also now called to mind how that for half a century he had served the great Nebuchadnezzar. The conquerors were no doubt made well acquainted with his wisdom, his probity, his presence of mind, and elevation of character. His incomparable excellence of spirit and talent for government recommended him to the chief bureau of the presidencies. Men should be selected for places, and not places made for friends. Men should be appointed to office who have shown themselves to possess capacity and integrity in the situations they have already occupied; and one proof of their requisite qualifications for office is, that they have the good sense and modesty to stay at home and diligently attend to their business until their services are called for by a discerning public. History and experience have shown that it is better for individuals and for society that there should be a division of labor, and different grades in society, and different avocations; and that society is best which allows to all the free pursuits of life and happiness in such avocations as may be individually selected, and guarantees to them security and enjoyment in the awards of their several pursuits. Without such division, freedom, and guarantee, the arts and sciences can never be carried on to perfection. It has ever been one of the greatest tests of character and of talent, as well as one of the most delicate and difficult trusts of government, to select suitable men for public services. Moses, Joshua, David, and Solomon; Nebuchadnezzar, Cyrus, Alexander, and, greater than all—except the Bible heroes—Cromwell and Napoleon, were remarkable for ther ability in this. And as you and all Christians should pray daily for all in authority, so you should never forget to implore Him who is the fountain of wisdom to give a discerning of spirits and sound understanding to all rulers, that they may be able to find men that fear God and are anxious for his glory, to fill the various offices of government. When God would punish a people for their sins, he says, "I will give their children to be their princes, and babes shall reign over them."—Isaiah iii., 4.

II. For an answer to the objection made to the very beginning of this chapter, that there was no such king as Darius the Median, I refer you to history, and to what I have just said about Cyaxares. And as to a similar objection about the number of provinces and satraps, the following remarks may suffice: The term satrap is said to be Median or Persian, and to mean simply a superintendent of revenue. In process of time, the satraps took also the office of military governor of the provinces over which they were appointed as revenue officers. The extent and number of such provinces depended wholly upon the will and convenience of the sovereign. *Sub-satraps* may be included also under the same term. It may be true, then (Cyrop., viii., 6, 1, and viii, 5, 19,) that

Cyrus did appoint *six* satraps over his kingdom. It is true that his empire was larger than that of Darius. It may be true, also, according to Herodotus (iii., 89,) that, after Thrace and hither India were added to the empire by Darius Hystaspis, only *twenty* satraps were appointed. And Xerxes appointed 127; why, then, could not Darius the Mede appoint 120?

III. As soon as Darius became lord of the then civilized world, he began to feel the cares of office and the perplexities of the power of patronage. An increase of care is the first consequence of an increase of power. The newly-conquered provinces, as well as the older parts of his vast dominions, were now to be provided with military governors and tax collectors. Over the one hundred and twenty rulers of the provinces he appointed three presidents, of whom Daniel was chief. The preference for Daniel was well founded. He was a model statesman—a prime minister that should be imitated. He was, 1, well known for his probity and talents for government under the Babylonian empire. He was a tried man.

2. He was preferred above the presidents, because an excellent spirit was in him, and the king thought to have set him over the whole realm. Kings and presidents are now often mistaken in the estimate which they form of men. But Darius was correct. Daniel was one of the most excellent of the earth. If in particular talents and services he was excelled by other Bible heroes, certainly, in the union and assemblage of gifts and graces, and in life-long devotion and uniform adherence to principles, he was surpassed by none. From his youth he honored God, by an intelligent, consistent, and exemplary piety; and

God so honored him, that even heathen kings did *him* reverence, while they contemned his religion. Great talents and high station with him were not inconsistent with inviolable purity and inflexible integrity. His badge of office was not the badge of ignominy. He did not owe his elevation to any fawning, cringing, flattering submission; nor was his high position owing to blind favoritism or party zeal. He had no patron but his God; no certificate but his character; no recommendation but his excellent spirit, and incomparable talent and experience.

Honorable as Daniel's appointment was to himself, it was no less so to his royal master. To govern a country well, rulers must not only be great men, but good men—men of public spirit and courage, who will neither seek to please themselves nor the people by sinister purposes, but endeavor, in all honesty of heart, to promote the people's welfare and the glory of God. Happy was it for the Persian empire that such a man as Daniel was chief of its prefects. But no appointment to office ever was satisfactory to all. Somebody is dissatisfied. Excellent as Daniel's character was, his appointment to the first place in the kingdom gave great offense to the dignitaries of the realm. They were filled with envy to see a foreigner, a captive, a professor of the hated Jewish religion, exalted above the ancient and hereditary nobles of the land. Probably, also, Daniel's inflexible integrity in the administration of affairs was another cause of their hatred. A man of such strict purity was in their way; he was a running commentary of rebuke; his character awed them, reproved them, restrained, and therefore irritated them. He would not join in their peculations, nor overlook their oppression. It was impossible for them to aggrandize themselves, with such a man to represent the interests of the nation always calling them to an account. As collectors of the ports and directors of the revenue deposits of those days, they could not loan to one another, upon their own pledged stock, or otherwise, the moneys of the empire, while a man so sagacious, so penetrating, so scrutinizing, was at their head to check their rapacity. They could not deceive him by the pretext that it was for the accommodation of the public they were so liberal in helping themselves to the dividends of the royal exchequer. They were, however, far-seeing politicians. They did not attack outright the justice or wisdom of the king's appointment. They set about effecting Daniel's removal. No doubt they were anxious to find some public act which they might challenge—some instance of partiality, of oppression, or injustice—some harsh expression—some instance of prejudice against the national religion, or of bigotry toward his own—some overlooking of the king's interest—something or other which, by being exaggerated or highly colored, might be so presented to the monarch as to produce Daniel's downfall, and possibly his death. And how easily they might have effected this, if there had only been found some plausible pretext, you will easily perceive, when you reflect that Daniel was prime minister in an empire where the will of the monarch was law absolute, unquestioned, irrevocable; where there was no constitutional liberty, no trial by jury, no regular impeachment and investigation; but where upon a charge, or at the pleasure of the monarch, the head of any subject rolled trunkless at his feet in a moment. These courtiers, however, find no occasion against Daniel in any matter that pertained to his official duties, or to his loyalty to the king. If keen-eyed malignity had brought some charge against Daniel, he would have fared as most public men do; but so well was his character balanced, and so great were his wisdom and prudence, that he avoided even the appearance of evil. His enemies were obliged to confess that his public conduct was unimpeachable. Did they then cease their purpose of destroying him? When did the enemies of a godly man ever cease to hunt for occasions to accuse him? When they cannot find causes, they will invent them; they will endeavor to turn his very virtues into crimes. There is no more hateful, no more unhappy disposition than one that gloats in discovering another's faults. It is a most godless and reprobate state of mind. To be gratified in discovering the sins of our fellow-men, is to partake of the fiendish disposition of the great enemy of all good. I had rather forget and forgive ten thousand times ten thousand errors in my neighbor than discover one of his faults. Our religion is love; our God is love. And though Christians are not saints, though they are imperfect, yet their principles compel them to be benevolent, forgiving, and kind. Drunkards, thieves, fornicators, and liars are nearer the kingdom of God than those persons who are full of enmity against their neighbor. He that hateth his brother is of the wicked one, the father of Cain. "He that hateth his brother is a murderer, and ye know that no murderer hath eternal life abiding in him."

I apprehend that verses 4 and 5 do not mean that there was any thing in Daniel's conduct toward his God that justly laid him liable to a charge on that ground. No, the meaning is the very opposite of this. He was not remiss in the duties he owed to his God. They meant to say, Our only hope is to find something in his religious creed or practice that can be construed into an offense against the king or the empire. There is no other way of getting up a charge against him that will have even the appearance of plausibility. And was there ever a more splendid eulogium than this upon Daniel's character? Nothing can be charged against him but what is, in fact, his highest honor.

IV. The conspirators, having arranged their arguments, approach the throne with the loudest professions of devotion and disinterested loyalty. Read verses 6, 7, and 8.

Tho *tyranny* of this law consisted in its penalty, and in its interdiction of all intercourse between God and his creatures. It was an impious attempt to banish God from the Persian empire for thirty days. It exalted the king into the place of the Creator. The decree claimed more for Darius than the Maker of the universe claims for himself. God forbids us to pray to saints, or angels, or any other creature or God but himself, but does not, as Darius did, forbid our making requests of our fellow-men. It was a most unreasonable and cruel law. If the beggar in the streets of Babylon or Persepolis asked alms for thirty days, he was to be food for lions. If the child, in the overflowings of affectionate desires, should make a request to his father, he was to be thrown straightway into the lions' den. This decree was the carrying out of the absurd, tyrannical, superstitious, atheistical principle, that rulers may legislate for the consciences of their subjects.

It is the pressure of this principle that makes Europe to-day groan under such intolerable burdens. Priests and soldiers eat up the substance of the people. The priests keep the conscience, and, by the terrors of the world to come, wrest the hard earnings of the people from them for the support of courts and armies, and the government upholds the hierarchy for their service to the state. The establishment of a religion by law, and the intolerance that forbids any other, is an assumption on the part of human lawgivers that they have the right to tell men what to believe, and to compel them to believe, and consequently have a right to debar them from all correspondence with God—to lay an embargo upon all intercourse with heaven.

The dishonest and treacherous method by which these men obtained the passing of this cruel and unrighteous decree is characteristic of zealots and political partisans to this day. The device is still the king's honor, while in reality it is their own miserable selfish purposes they are seeking, and seeking by encompassing the ruin of Daniel. So it is the good of the country—the country, the people, the public welfare, that we hear of; while it is too often party or sectarian interests, or personal aggrandizement, that lies at the bottom of all their zeal. Though the patriotism of many is like a chameleon, it cannot live on air; it has a strong passion for loaves and fishes.

V. But what did Daniel do? Verses 10, 11.

And his windows were open in his chamber—an apartment probably built on the top of the house, with a roof of its own, and designed for retirement. Such an upper room is frequently mentioned in the Bible. This upper room was the usual place for prayer: see Acts, i., 13, 9. In the Septuagint translation of Daniel, which you may remember was made from the original Hebrew and Chaldee into Greek, about three hundred years before the birth of Christ, by Alexandrian Jews, at the command of Ptolemy Philadelphus, the word that is used for Daniel's chamber, is the very same that is used in the Acts to denote the place in which the Christians met at Pentecost. This room is called the "upper room," because it was built upon the flat roof of the house, and sequestered from the noise and interruption of the other rooms. It was into this room the pious Jew retired to read the law, and pray, and hold communion with God. It was in such a room the first Christians were wont to assemble for prayer, and for the observance of the Lord's Supper. It was to such a room Daniel was in the habit of withdrawing himself from the cares of state to hold communion with the God of his fathers, and still the covenant-keeping God of his suffering countrymen. There is not to my mind any thing strange, improbable, or proud and ostentatious, in the fact that Daniel prayed with his windows open, and toward Jerusalem. It was not for the mere purpose of display, or to defy the conspirators against his life, that he did so. It had always been his custom thus to worship God. He knew that the decree was made, and that it was unchangeable; but in his hour of trial he had no thought of forsaking his God. It was the more proper for him now to seek his blessing and presence. Daniel had no difficulty or hesitancy in determining what he should do. His early education had fortunately been pious; he had studied well with his mother and father, in his quiet Jerusalem home, the laws of Moses and the Catechism of his Church. His principles were, therefore, not only sound, but deeply-rooted; and his conscience had been so faithfully trained and developed by his habits of duty, that it intuitively pronounced an instant and final sentence on the matter. What if his fortune, his life, was at stake? How could he sin against God? No sooner, therefore, did he hear that "the writing was signed than he went into his house; and his windows being open in his chamber toward Jerusalem, he kneeled upon his knees three times a day, and prayed, and gave thanks before his God, as he did aforetime."

Toward Jerusalem, because that was the place where the special presence of God was supposed to be. Thus David says in Psalm v., 7, "And in thy fear will I worship toward thy holy temple." And again, xvii., 2, "Hear the voice of my supplications, when I say unto thee, when I lift up my hands toward the holy oracle;" or, as it is in the margin, "the oracle of thy sanctuary." And again, in Psalm xx., where we have the ground of this practice, "Jehovah hear thee in the day of trouble. Send thee help from the sanctuary, and strengthen thee out of Zion." The sublime prayer of Solomon contains several repetitions of the idea that their prayers were to be directed to the temple in Jerusalem. 1 Kings, viii., 35, 38, 44, 48, 49; 2 Chron., vi., 34.

We learn from Ezekiel, viii., 16, that the worshipers of Ormuzd, the god of the Persians, looked to the rising sun, the symbol of Ormuzd, when engaged in worship. The ancient Christians used to pray with their faces toward the East. In like manner, the Mohammedans pray with their faces toward Mecca. As Daniel was east of Jerusalem, *his face was turned toward the west.* Nor can we suppose for a moment that we have here, or any where else, any authority prescribing it as the duty of Christians to look toward any of the cardinal points when they pray. It is not in this mountain, not at Babylon nor Persepolis, not in Rome, nor Jerusalem, that God requires us to worship him; but every where, in all places. God is a Spirit. and seeketh such to worship him as do it in spirit and in truth. The reason why pious Jews directed their face toward Jerusalem in prayer was, that there was the temple and its furniture which was to them the type of the Mediator, by whom their worship was to be made acceptable to God. The spiritually-minded Jew fixes his eye on the temple service as a figure representing the mediation and intercession of the Messiah. It is no argument, but a vain plea of superstition, to tell us that because the Jews prayed in ancient times with their faces toward Jerusalem, we ought to do so likewise. Of precisely the same nature is the idea that we should build our churches in the form of a cross, or with their chancels, which are ignorantly called by some "altars," and "high altars," looking toward the East. Our houses of worship should be tasteful, elegant, commodious, and fitted for the worship of God; but to burden ourselves with forms and rules such as these, is to do just what Paul tells the Galatians not to do: "The letting go the liberty wherewith Christ has made us free." This were to go back to Judaism; this were to conform to heathen and Mohammedan forms. And what is infinitely more, this is to displace Christ, the only Mediator, and to "substitute an exhausted type, a shriveled symbol, in the room of Him who is its substance, its reality, and its end." If the great law of Solomon to the Jews was, "Pray with your face toward Jerusalem," the great law of the Gospel is, "Pray every where in the name of Jesus." The Jewish Church consisted of a temple built of stones, a grand altar, overshadowing cherubims, with bright beams of ineffable glory, and the ministration of the priests with sacrifices—all of which was a type of good things to come. The Christian Church is composed not of dead stones, but of living ones. The glory is not visible and palpable, but spiritual; the worship is spiritual; its completeness is the fullness of Christ, who is all in all, and over all, God, blessed for evermore. And hence there is a true Christian Church without priest or bishop, wherever there is faith in Christ and obedience to his commandments. On the ocean shore, on the deep-sounding sea, on the mountain top, in the deep secluded glen, in the mountain gorge, hidden from persecuting tyrants; in the deep caves and catacombs of the earth; in the field, in the wilderness, in the city; wherever there are two or three met in the name of Jesus, there is a temple more glorious than Solomon's; there is the temple of the Holy Ghost, in which God dwells, and manifests his excellent glory.

It is sometimes said, Daniel could have been just as pious, and have prayed to God in his heart, and God would have heard him just as well, if he had shut his windows and prayed in secret, and not have let his enemies know that he violated the king's decree.

It is true that bodily exercise profiteth little, but the Bible does not say it profiteth nothing. On the contrary, we are commanded to glorify God in our bodies as well as in our spirits, which are His. The form of godliness is a part of religion, as well as the power. When God calls upon us to believe *with the heart unto righteousness*, no outward action, such as fasting, or praying with a loud voice, or pilgrimages, or penances, or the giving of youı goods to feed the poor, of your bodies to be burned, will be accepted by God as a *substitute for faith*. So, on the other hand, when God calls you to make confession of Christ with the mouth unto salvation—to acknowledge him before men—then no inward frame of spirit, neitheı faith, nor love, nor self-denial, will be accepted by him as a substitute for that open and visible adherence to His truth and identification with His people which He has been pleased to require as a test of your obedience to Him, and a means of salvation. In a time of trial, it is not mere inward feeling of devotion, but the outward manifestation of it, that God requires. It is not so much the image of God in the heart, as his "name upon the forehead," that proves that we are "the called, and chosen, and faithful." In the case of Daniel, the point on which the authority of God and of the king came into collision, was about the external acts of divine worship. Praying to God in the Spirit was not prohibited, but rendering him outward acts of homage was forbidden. This was the point on trial. God said, on the one hand, "In all thy ways acknowledge me, and I will direct thy steps." "In the day of trouble, call upon me, and I will answer." Darius said, "Thou shalt not ask a petition of God for thirty days." In this case, the inward state of the heart could be ascertained only by the outward act. It was not enough that the heart believed; the mouth must make confession also. If Daniel had shut his windows, if he had ceased to kneel, or ceased to speak unto God with his lips, and rested content with the mere utterances of the heart, he would have denied his God before men; but by praying as he had done aforetime, he gave his testimony, and God honored and delivered him. Daniel's high station at the head of the Persian empire, instead of excusing him from fidelity to his religion, enhanced the peculiar responsibility attached to him in this emergency. He was a city set upon a hill; he was the head of all the professors of the true religion then in the world, as well as chief of the presidents of the empire. He was the "observed of all observers." The eyes of friends and enemies were upon him. Any indecision, any appearance of hesitance, any compromiting of his principles, or seeming compliance with the decree, would have been productive of the most painful results; but happily he was the man for the crisis; the cause in his hands was safe. Closing his eyes on danger, he thought only of his duty. The fear of lions could not make him disown his God. At the perilous post, his attitude clearly defined his position; and as his faith was shown by his conduct, the Bible records only his magnanimous outward act. The Bible does not tell us how he felt or what he said, but what he did. It refers not to the frame of his soul, but to the posture of his body and the utterances of his lips. It was by his outward actions that he was to show that he was willing to lay his body down as a living sacrifice on the divine altar.

First, then, this case teaches you that God sometimes

allows his people to be placed in situations in which they are shut up by His providence either to suffer or to sin. It was not any fault of Daniel's three friends that placed them in the dilemma of worshiping the great image on the plains of Dura, or of being cast into the fiery furnace. And so here it was for no fault of Daniel that he is shut up to the necessity of deciding whether he would obey God or man, whether he would disown God or be cast into the lions' den. Joseph had similar seasons of trial. Caleb and Joshua also. They had another spirit, and followed the Lord fully. Them the Lord brought into the promised land. Moses chose to suffer affliction with the people of God, rather than to enjoy the pleasures of sin for a season. And so there are now, in the lives of most men, seasons of peril, critical periods, when they must either sin or suffer; when they must decide, and take their position on the Lord's side or against him. Such trials answer holy and wise purposes. They benefit God's true people, by burning away the dross of selfishness and worldly-mindedness. But,

Secondly. Learn from Daniel to possess your soul in patience and prudence in the days of severe trial.

Daniel adds nothing, by way of insult, to his persecutors, nor of defiance toward his sovereign, nor yet does he omit any thing from fear of danger. He worships God just as he had been accustomed to do. He goes to his own house, into his private chamber, and with his windows open, looking toward Jerusalem, he kneels down and prays to God, just as if no decree had been issued against prayer. We see here no fool-hardiness; we see no vain courting of martyrdom! nor do we see any pre caution to escape the doom that awaited him. We see him praying three times a day, as he had done aforetime. The place, and manner, and substance of his prayers were now just as before. He had been accustomed to mingle thanksgiving with prayer, and though he is now exposed to the hungry lions, he still sees abundant cause of thankfulness. He felt honored in being counted worthy to suffer for his God. He remembered how he had been hitherto sustained, and now that he was old and grayheaded, he thanked God that he would not leave him nor forsake him.

It is sometimes said Daniel did wrong in disobeying a law which had been passed by the highest legislative power in the country. First, I have no sympathy with the "higher law" faction of our times; but it is certainly clear that the foundation of all law is the will of God. Governments are ordained of God. The will of God is aback of and above all social compacts or civil enactments. Secondly, as all the authority which man possesses over man is derived from God, so that authority is limited by the Divine law, and therefore the laws of man only bind when they are not inconsistent with the law of God. The moment any decrees of man require what God has forbidden, or forbids what God has commanded, they cease to be binding upon the conscience, and in such cases it is our solemn duty to protest against them, and to disobey them. Resistance and passive obedience may be pressed to a point when they become sinful. The edict of Darius, thirdly, was tyrannical, and opposed to the plainest commands of God. It would have been, therefore, sinful in Daniel to obey it.

Thirdly. Learn then, young men, I beseech you, *the duty of surrendering yourselves at once cordially and with a whole-hearted magnanimity to the service of God.* Daniel kept back nothing. He did not waver or hesitate. But as soon as his hour of prayer comes, though he knows the decree is signed, he goes to his chamber, there to offer his protest against this impious decree, and to give his testimony for the supremacy of his God. Daniel was not dragged to duty, nor to suffering. No doubt there were those who were ready to say he was over-righteous, some that were ready to say, Why do you peril your life, Daniel, for a mere form? why will you make yourself a martyr for the little matters of keeping your windows open, kneeling down, and speaking your prayers aloud? Surely, you are not going to sacrifice your splendid emoluments and high station by refusing to obey the king for the short space of thirty days. Consider too, O mighty man! chief of the presidents, how valuable your life is to others. Consider how much you owe to your countrymen, whose cause is in your hands, and to the Church of the Living God. Surely, you will not put in peril all these great matters by such obstinacy. How many, or which, or whether any of these pleas were suggested to Daniel, I know not. There are always plausible apologies at hand for treachery to the immortal soul, and treason to God; but no one can doubt how Daniel replied to such cowardly proposals, if indeed any one ventured to name them to him. His reply, no doubt, was, "Talk not to me of prudence, nor of the value of my life; it belongs to Him who gave it to me. He can preserve me, or He can raise up others better than I am. I cannot refrain from avowing that I dare to do. I would rather refrain from praying altogether, than *pretend* to neglect it while I was secretly engaged in it. I must be honest; and, as to the time of thirty days, I do not know that I shall live thirty hours. Life, reputation, influence, is nothing without the blessing of God. I will pray, therefore, just as I have been accustomed to do. He shall hear my voice morning, noon, and evening, as heretofore. The result I cheerfully leave in His hands." And, my young friends, when you are called upon to take up your cross, deny yourselves and confess Christ before men, remember Daniel. It is no honor to be brave on the drill ground, but it is an honor to act bravely in the day of battle. It is no faint, or feeble, or fickle effort that will secure your salvation. If you would be saved, you must press into the kingdom of God. He that putteth his hand to the plow, and looketh back, is not fit for the kingdom of heaven. It is not enough to be a Christian in heart, you must be one in life. It is not enough to read sermons at home; which is not often done, after all. You must honor God's word, and house, and Sabbath, by witnessing with the solemn assemblies of his people your faith in His Son and your attachment to Him. You cannot be a secret Christian, and steal along to heaven without any body knowing it. If you would be saved, you must avouch the Lord as your God. Choose ye, then, this day, whom you will serve. And God give you grace to make such a choice as shall make you forever happy. Amen.

LECTURE XIV.

DANIEL CAST INTO THE LIONS' DEN.

On Dan., vi., 13–17, and 24.

Summary.—Interdict of Prayer not so cruel as to be improbable.—Collateral History.—Xenophon.—De Sacy.—Grotefend.—Daniel not a Defaulter.—How the Decree was obtained.—Nero, Haynau, Duke of Tuscany.—God worked Miracles.—Professor Stuart.—Cunning and Meanness of Daniel's Accusers.—Their Success.—The King's Character.—Difference between Babylon and Persia.—King's Heart with Daniel.—Church Members rebuked.—Every Atom has its Place and Laws.—Your Diamond.—Was Darius Converted, or were his Words an unconscious Prophecy?—Young Men must take a bold and open Stand for God.—Daniel was a Man pre-eminent for Prayer.—Praying Statesmen.—Congressional Prayer-meeting.

I. In previous Lectures we have seen that Daniel was a public man—a model statesman—a prime minister of extraordinary talent for government, and distinguished for diligence, honesty, and piety. Being a plain, unostentatious, tried man, to whom all persons in official stations under him had access, it was easy for his enemies, who were now conspiring against his life, to acquaint themselves with his religious faith and pious habits. Daniel was not one of those who vainly think they can be religious without letting any body know it. He professed what he felt. He acted out openly what he believed. He was a man of regular and known habits. He had at least three stated hours for prayer in his private chamber, with *windows open toward Jerusalem;* but in thus con tinually serving his God he violated the king's decree, and exposed himself to death by ravenous beasts.

Read here verses 13–17, and 24.

II. But it is said, This decree of Darius, that no prayer or request for thirty days should be made of God or man, except of himself—a decree that could proceed only from a madman—is a thing incredible. To this I answer, 1. It may be said truly that the author of such a decree deserved a *madhouse* rather than a palace; but even kings do not always receive their just deserts at once.

2. It is not, however, so *improbable a thing* as that its record should throw disbelief over the whole narrative. You know that when Themistocles fled from Athens to Persia, and wished to be presented to the king, the courtier Artabanus said to him, "It is our custom to honor the king, and worship the image of God, who preserves all things." And you know, also, that Xenophon blames the Persians because "they thought themselves worthy of enjoying the honors of the gods." They worship a mortal man, and call him a divinity, and had rather treat the gods with neglect than their fellow-men."* The king was considered among the Persians as worthy of homage, being the symbol or personification of Ormusd. Alexander the Great, in imitation of the Persian kings, required divine honors to be paid him on his entrance into Babylon. The great scholar De Sacy says "that the Persian kings call themselves the celestial germ of the race of the gods." On the ruins of Persepolis recently brought to light, kings are evidently presented as objects of adora-

* See the original references in Stuart, *in loco.*

tion.* It can no longer be a matter of doubt that the Persians did require men to pay supreme homage to their king as the representative of their god Ormusd. There are, then, no special marks of improbability in the narrative of the importunity of the king's courtiers and nobles. The king was a weak, vain, ambitious man.

Daniel's enemies knew well the weak points of their sovereign. They knew that it would gratify his vanity to have such a decree made as they proposed. They knew, also, the character of Daniel. They knew that he was distinguished for ardent piety and decision of character. They were satisfied nothing could be found against him save in the matter of his religion. He was not a defaulter to the government. He could not be charged with neglecting the king's interests in any way. As Darius, moreover, was addicted to an excessive use of wine, it is not improbable that the affair was transacted near the close of a banquet, and proposed and carried with many loud professions of reverence, loyalty, and honor toward the king. Is there, then, such a want of probability in the narrative as to throw discredit over the history of the whole matter? Have drunken despots never committed as outrageous and absurd acts as this? The king designed to gratify his own vanity. He did not think of the consequences. Nor is history without parallels. Nero, Caligula, Herod the Great, Genghis Khan, the authors of the Saint Bartholomew massacre, Haynau, and even the *amiable* Duke of Tuscany, could perpetrate such things

* Grotefend says on one of these ruins is the inscription, *Stirps mundi*

without at all throwing their histories into fables. Nor is the charge of *intolerance* against the king's decree, in the last part of the chapter, worthy of extended remark. It is probable that such a king as Darius, under such circumstances, would have acted just as our narrative says he did act. It was a Persian custom to inflict capital punishment on criminals by throwing them into a den of lions. The covering of the pit was not necessarily so tight, though sealed, as to exclude air. There may have been sufficient side avenues for light and air, without at all interfering with the closing up of the mouth. It was also usual in the East to destroy whole families for the offense of the head. In England, to this day, treason taints the blood and confiscates the property otherwise inalienable. In what, then, was the persecution or intolerance of the king's decree so remarkable, as to throw such an air of suspicion over the history? The king, under the excitement of Daniel's miraculous deliverance, as Nebuchadnezzar had, under similar feelings, done before, calls upon his subjects to do homage to the God of Daniel. He does not forbid them to continue their own worship, nor compel them to become Jews, nor even annex a penalty for disobedience to his mandate.

And as to the argument against the narrative, because it implies and affirms, indeed, as the king's edict does, *that God did work miracles*, it is only necessary now to say, that it rests entirely upon the assumption that miracles are impossible and absurd. This assumption, I am persuaded, you are not willing to take. Such an assumption is certainly no legitimate argument. Nor is it within my present scope to enter the field of miracles. It is certainly clear from the Scriptures that God has, for important ends, and with special designs, such as appear in the history of Daniel, wrought signs and wonders. Nor has it ever been shown that such miraculous interpositions are contrary to reason or inconsistent with the Divine economy. I am strongly inclined to adopt the language of the late lamented Professor Stuart on this subject, and say "that one must needs feel himself hard pressed who resorts to such objections. It is a confession which imports that he who makes it, is conscious of weakness in his cause. Simple candor and consciousness of a good cause are not apt to lead men to employ argumentation so captious."—P. 173.

III. *The duplicity, and cunning, and meanness of Daniel's accusers are seen in their pretexts.* Unable to find fault with Daniel's official conduct, they set about ensnaring him in the matter of his religion. They pretended to be actuated solely by their anxiety for the honor of the king in urging him to pass the decree against prayer to God, while in reality their sole design was to entrap Daniel; and, having obtained the king's signature to the decree, they go to Daniel's house at the hour when they knew he was accustomed to perform his devotions. They may have professed to come on business, while their real design was to get proof against him to take away his life. The enemies of truth and righteousness are always characterized for duplicity and cunning. Satan, as the grand enemy of God and man, is said in the Bible to have a face like a lamb, and yet speaks as a dragon. *The Greeks bringing gifts are always to be feared.* The outward aspect of the agents of evil is generally smooth, and harmless, and benignant, as if they were a compound of gentleness and innocence, while, in reality, their spirit is fierce, and their designs murderous to the soul. The malignant enemies of godliness usually mask their treacherous purposes underneath a smooth and often polished exterior. They seldom go straight to their purpose; they look one way and move another; they come down upon the Lord's hosts, not with the sword, and the shield, and the spear, but with the gin, and the snare, and the net. Like beasts of prey, they crouch, and conceal themselves, until they can make an advantageous spring upon their unsuspecting foe. It is thus the sons of Belial in olden time, and now the Jesuit and the Puseyite, and the enemy of civil liberty and popular education in our times, endeavor to effect their designs. As the Bible says, "He lieth in wait secretly, as a lion in his den; he lieth in wait to catch the poor, when he draweth him into his net. He croucheth and humbleth himself, that the poor may fall by his strong ones."

IV. The charge against Daniel is stated in verses 12 and 13. They recited the decree without saying a word about Daniel. They obtained the king's assent that such was the decree, and that, according to the law of the Medes and Persians, it could not be altered. This was just what they desired.

Doubtless they proceeded thus cautiously, because they knew that the king was attached to Daniel. It was not till they had gotten the king to commit himself to the correctness of the decree, and as to the unchangeableness of a Persian edict, that they ventured to inform him who it was that violated it, and, in defiance of it, continued to pray, as aforetime, three times a day to his God. This information they made known to the king in the most ensnaring and insidious terms. They tell him that Daniel, *which is of the children of the captivity of Judah, regardeth not thee, O king, nor the decree that thou hast signed, but maketh his petition three times a day.* They pretend that Daniel's disobedience arose from want of respect to the king, and disaffection toward his government. By this statement they sought to rouse the king's personal feelings, and to awaken his political jealousy; and, under all, to heighten the enormity of Daniel's disobedience, by reminding the king of his base ingratitude. He was a Jew, a captive, a professor of a hated foreign religion. He had been highly honored; and yet this is his gratitude: "He regardeth not thee, O king, nor the decree that thou hast signed." The charge was, however, palpably false. It was not from any want of respect to the king's person, nor any disposition to set at naught the king's laws as such and in themselves considered, apart from his higher duty to God, nor was it for the want of gratitude. Daniel's whole conduct was the legitimate result of his pious education. He acted from a solemn sense of duty to his God, the Judge of all men, kings as well as others. He could not elevate any creature above his Creator; he could not erect the palace of loyalty on the grave of the religion of Jehovah. The principles, also, involved in the charge of these men against Daniel were utterly false. They not only sapped the foundations of morality, but they were fraught with danger to the state.

It was not correct to say that the man who dared not to

disobey his God was, on that account, an enemy to the state. It is not true that conscientious men and pious men are traitors to the state; and yet this is the stereotyped charge against them. In distant and widely different countries and ages, the people of God have been assailed again and again with this false accusation. It is the custom of their enemies to asperse and blacken their characters, just as these men attempted to destroy Daniel. Their loyalty was but a pretense. Their regard for the majesty of the laws of Persia, and their respect for the king, were entirely hypocritical. They cared nothing for either. Their object was to gratify their envy, and advance their own selfish views. Our blessed Lord (Luke, xviii.) connects a want of fear for God with a want of regard to man; and history shows that, so far from being antagonistic, they are essentially and organically related. Intelligent piety and the highest civil virtues have ever been consistent. The best statesmen, priests, and civilians, and the ablest and most successful military leaders, have been Christian men. The maxim advanced by the conspirators against Daniel was blasphemous and atheistical. The decree which they induced the king to make exalted the king to the throne of the Deity. And Daniel's continuing to pray to his God, they said, was proof that he disregarded both the king and his government; as if they had said, "The man who regards thee, O king, will not regard his God, if thou shalt forbid him to do so. Thou hast a right to forbid any of thy subjects to pray to the God of heaven. Thou canst absolve thy subjects from their allegiance to the Creator; and as Daniel persists in praying to his God, therefore he is thy personal enemy, and should be put to death." False and groundless as the charge was, such was the weakness of the king, and such the customs of the Persians, that, notwithstanding the king's personal friendship for Daniel, the decree is executed, and he is cast into the lion's den.—V. 14.

The king labored hard to save Daniel, even "till the going down of the sun, to deliver him," but in vain. His conduct was very different from that of Nebuchadnezzar on a similar occasion. When the young Hebrews refused to fall down and worship the great golden image he had set up in the plains of Dura, he was "full of rage and fury," and commanded them to be cast at once into the furnace. Proud, imperious, self-willed, and passionate, he could not bear disobedience for a moment. However cruel and unreasonable his commands were, he would have them obeyed without a word or a moment's delay. Not so with Darius. He was a different sort of a man. Vain, rather than proud, he wished to be loved rather than to be feared. Easily flattered, and of a compliant disposition, with some generousness of heart, he was misled by his nobles. But now that the truth has flashed upon his mind, and he sees their artifice, "he was sore displeased with himself, and set his heart on Daniel to deliver him." He was not enraged with Daniel for having dared to disobey his edict. His displeasure took the right direction. It went inward upon his own heart. He sees at once the folly of which he has made himself guilty. As yet he says nothing of the deceitful, base, and insulting conduct of his nobles. He stops not to tell them how he regarded their attempt to make him the blind and degraded tool of their own malignity. He does not say as Adam did, "The woman which thou gavest to be with me, she gave me of the tree, and I did eat." He did not say as Eve did, "The serpent beguiled me, and I did eat." Darius reads no homily on the frauds of his courtiers. He urges no plea to justify himself, but sets about effecting Daniel's deliverance. He is sore displeased with himself, and desires to arrest the evil as far as he can. He exerts his ingenuity to discover, if possible, some method of evading the law. He tries to persuade the Persian nobles not to insist upon the execution of the edict. He calls upon them in private. They seem to relent. He assembles the Divan. It is a remarkable contest between the king and his parliament, between the president and his cabinet; but, encouraging one another, they become bolder and more cruel when assembled than when seen separately by the king in their own houses. The princes sternly refuse to let Daniel escape. All their boasted loyalty has suddenly vanished. They will not grant a single petition to him whom they had made the only god in Persia for thirty days. What a struggle must this have been! How unfortunate the position of the monarch! encompassed by an assembly of designing, unprincipled villains, and bound hand and foot by his own rash decree. This should teach us to turn our eyes inward—to guard well our own hearts; for out of them are the issues of evil. We should ponder well all our footsteps. One rash act may do what we shall never be able to retrieve.

V. Read here verse 15.

Such an assembly around the throne of Nebuchadnezzar or of Napoleon, or before Cromwell or Andrew Jackson, would have met with a very different reception. But the case before us is one of those remarkable and undesigned coincidences that prove the truthfulness of the history. It illustrates the character of Darius, and the peculiarity of Persian law. The incidents of this sixth chapter could not have been true of Nebuchadnezzar and of the Chaldean empire; but history informs us they might be, and actually were, true of Darius and of the Persian empire. The Chaldean emperor would have ordered these courtiers to instant execution. His power was supreme and arbitrary. In Babylon it was *Rex Lex*—the king was law, just as it is now in France with her autocrat. In Persia it was different. They had a constitution. There it was *Lex Rex*—the law was king. A law once enacted by the proper authority was not only supreme, but unchangeable. This was both ridiculous and impious in the case of Daniel. It was wrong ever to have made such a fundamental law, and now that it had been made, and was found to be against reason, morality, and religion, it should have been instantly repealed. As all human power springs from God, so the obligation to obey ceases when the obedience required comes into collision with our duty to God. In preserving his conscience, and disobeying the edict, Daniel was right; his conduct was noble, heroic, and sublime. And so when Darius found the folly and egregious iniquity of his decree, and saw the artifice of his nobles, he ought to have put his own life and the existence of his empire into peril, rather than to ha executed it. If nothing else would do, he ought to have gone to the lion's den himself, rather than have signed the warrant for casting Daniel into it. The claims of expediency, however, prevail, as they did in the case of

Herod against John the Baptist, and with Pilate against Jesus Christ; and impelled, like Jephtha, by a rash decree, *the king commanded, and they brought Daniel, and cast him into the den of lions.*

What a sight is this! Cruel policy prevails over friendship and over the most eminent worth. A venerable servant of God is given to the wild beasts. Daniel, the aged prime minister of the Persian empire, and the head of all the professors of the true religion then in the world, is cast into the lions' den; but for what? Simply for continuing to pray to God, as he had been accustomed to do all his life. "Now the king spake and said unto Daniel, Thy God, whom thou servest continually, He will deliver thee. And a stone was brought, and laid upon the mouth of the den; and the king sealed it with his own signet, and with the signet of his lords, that the purpose might not be changed concerning Daniel."

These words of the king to Daniel are remarkable on several accounts. The king seems to say, "My heart, as a man, goes with thee, O thou incomparable man of God, in opposition to my act as a king. I have done all I could to deliver thee, but I have failed. I commit thee in hope to Him whom thou servest continually. Thy God will deliver thee." Was this the king's hope? was it his fervent prayer? or had the king been made acquainted with the history of Daniel and his three friends in Babylon, and with the history of the Jewish nation, so far as to believe in the reality of Divine interposition by angels and miracles for the deliverance of the worshipers of Jehovah? Had Darius ever heard of the Jewish Scripture, which says, "Fear not, for I am with thee; be not dismayed, for I am thy God. I will strengthen thee ; yea, I will help thee ; yea, I will uphold thee with the right hand of my righteousness. I will give mine angels charge concerning thee, to keep thee in all thy ways. Thou shalt tread upon the lion and adder ; the young lion and dragon shalt thou trample under foot."

Or are we to understand these memorable words of King Darius to Daniel as a true prophecy? Was he led *unconsciously* to utter them by a divine impulse for the encouragement of Daniel? Some understand these words, together with the decree in the last of the chapter, as evidence of Darius' true conversion—so Dr. Cumming. If so, then the king, by means of Daniel's instruction and example, was brought to the knowledge of the true God. And why should this be thought a thing incredible? Were not the integrity, the meekness, the magnanimity, the gentleness, the patience, the submission of Daniel such an exponent of his religion as to make the king ask after its doctrines? and were there no lessons in Daniel's prayers that spoke to the king's inner man? Is not the grace of God quite sufficient for the conversion of kings and statesmen? and should we not pray fervently for the conversion and eminent piety of all our leading men? They need the grace of God for themselves and for our sakes. We have here, moreover, a striking illustration of the variety of means which it pleases God to use in producing the conversion of men. It is not only the truth as believed, but the lives that Christians lead, and the deaths that Christians die, that produce conviction in the minds of men in behalf of Christianity. The sick-beds of some of the humblest followers of Christ have exceeded the most learned pulpits in persuasive eloquence, and dying martyrs have made conversions that living apostles were never honored with. When soliciting, the other day, a friend, who is not a member of the Church, for his influence and contribution to advance the cause of the Saviour in the city, he said, "Go to the members of the Church; many of them are more wealthy than I am. They have not given any thing. Get them all to do what they can, and then I, as an *outsider*, will help you." These are his exact words. He is a liberal, high-minded man. His excuse was not a good one; but I shall never forget it. It was humiliating and mortifying to be compelled to feel that such accusations are just against our professed followers of Christ. I name the case now simply to illustrate the fact that it is impossible for any man, much less a Christian, to live to himself; nor can a Christian die to himself. Every atom and every planet has its place and orbit—a place and orbit that no other atom or planet can fill. The Creator has given to every particle of matter, and every globe and system in the vast universe, its own proper place, and impressed upon it certain laws; and so every human being has his or her place, and his or her duties assigned by the Creator, from the performance of which there can be no exemption. INDIVIDUAL ACCOUNTABILITY to God is as inseparable from every one of you as your identity and immortality. What if God, my young friend, should place in your hand a diamond, and tell you to inscribe on it a sentence which should be read on the last day, and shown there as an index of your own thoughts and feelings? What caution and anxiety would you feel about the selection of that sentence! Now God has given you something more imperishable and precious than a diamond. He has placed before you immortal minds, on which, by your example, your principles, and influence, you inscribe every day and every hour something which will remain and be exhibited, for or against you, at the judgment-day. He has commissioned all the elements of nature to take your daguerreotype likeness—the likeness of your inmost soul through life, and the true nature and extent of all your influence upon your fellow-men—and these pictures will all be exhibited for your acquittal or condemnation at the trial of the last day.

Happy as I should be to dwell on the conversion of King Darius, I cannot insist upon it, for the text does not fully establish it. The lessons I have just pointed out are, however, true. His words may be understood as expressive of his regret and pity, and as a sort of apology for his severity toward such an aged and eminent servant, whom he really loved. It is possible, also, that God made the king utter an unconscious prophecy of Daniel's deliverance. Balaam and Saul were prophets, though not saints. God has made men that were not pious predict truths of which they themselves knew not the glory. Caiaphas, being high-priest, gave counsel to the Jews, saying, "It was expedient that some one should die for the people." In this Caiaphas was the trumpet of a glorious prophecy. God made the Chaldean empire his *hammer*, and Cyrus his *battle-axe*, to execute his judgments upon the earth, and especially against the enemies of his people. So the Bible expressly says. God makes the wrath of man to praise him, and the remainder thereof

20

He restraineth, that his people may learn to trust in Him always, and that all men may see that all things are under the power and control of Him who holds the reins, and sways the sceptre of the universe.

With two lessons briefly stated, I close this lecture.

First. Young men are taught here to expect that God's providence will sometimes place them in such circumstances, that an open, bold, avowed performance of religious duty and adherence to principle will be the test of their fidelity to Him. It is not profession, nor equivocation, that will do; but a steadfast adherence to principle, and an open, straightforward performance of duty. The king's edict was against prayer. It was prayer aloud that exposed Daniel to the lions' den. The performance of prayer in his usual way was, therefore, the test of his fidelity to God. It is useless for us to imagine how Daniel could have employed the thirty days. There were doubtless many things which in themselves and at other times would have been proper, but which, as *substitutes* for prayer were not available. He might have shut himself up to study the books of Moses, or to read Jeremiah, and see when the captivity was to come to an end. He might have spent his time weeping and singing by the willows beside the rivers of Babylon. He might have set about some great scheme to induce his monarch to release his countrymen, and have offered this as an excuse to his conscience for neglecting his prayers; but all or any of these things would have been unacceptable to God. He remained faithful, and prayed as he had done aforetime. It is certainly no availing plea with our Maker that the performance of our duty exposes us to danger. No degree of danger can justify us in concealing our attachment to God; it is not for us to choose the circumstances in which we shall be called to the performance of duty. It is not for us to ask questions, but to obey. DUTY IS OURS, CON SEQUENCES ARE GOD'S.

Finally, this page of the inner life of the prime minister of King Darius contains a *most earnest recommendation of prayer*. You see what Daniel's habits were. He was evidently known to be a praying man. He did not begin to pray now that he was in danger. It was no family bereavement, it was not severe sickness or the fear of death that made him retire into his chamber for prayer. He prayed and gave thanks before his God, as he did *aforetime*. He was the chief of the prefects or presidents, the first man next to the king in the empire; yet he was a man of prayer. Rank and station, official duties, power and influence, do not, therefore, furnish sufficient reasons for neglecting secret and family prayer. It is impossible to be a genuine Christian and live a prayerless life. There is no reality in our profession of religion if we have not communion with God.

Daniel had set times for prayer; and if we would derive the full advantage which may be obtained from prayer, we must have stated times for engaging in it. Without set times of prayer, there is imminent danger of its being omitted or crowded out. Mere forms in religion are to be avoided; but regularity ought to be cultivated. Without order in our affairs, we shall always be liable to interruptions and confusion. Regularity will in due time ripen into a habit; and that which at first seemed a grievous burden, by practice will become light. If Daniel, with all the affairs of an empire to manage, found time, three stated times a day, for calling on the name of God, surely none of you can plead the want of time for this purpose. "Prayer and provender hinder not the journey." "To have prayed well, is to study well." "In all thy ways acknowledge thou Him, and He will direct thy steps." Daniel's inner life was fed by prayer, and hence his outer life was characterized by integrity, justice, heroism, magnanimity, and faithfulness. His home habits made his court habits so beautiful, and just, and true. His private intercourse with God made his public character so consistent. An hour in the "upper chamber" in communion with God is worth many hours in the cabinet. I have said before that I believe God has not given to any nation for so long a time rulers so able, pure, and patriotic as we have had; and I am not aware that any thing like our Congressional prayer-meeting has ever been known in the courts of Europe. Our leading men, thank God, have been and are religious men, men of religious education, and many of them of religious habits and avowed faith in Jesus Christ. This we hope will always be the case. It is impossible for statesmen to govern the world without God. We cannot expect his blessing on politicians that are godless in their principles and prayerless in their lives. It should be written on our council chambers, our halls of commerce, and the doors of our capitols, BY ME KINGS REIGN AND PRINCES DECREE JUSTICE. RIGHTEOUSNESS EXALTETH A NATION, BUT SIN IS A REPROACH TO ANY PEOPLE.

LECTURE XV.

FAITH TRIUMPHANT.

On Dan., vi., 16–24.

State of Parties.—King's Conscience.—Listen to yours.—King's Visit to the Den.—Daniel's Night with the Lions.—Servant of God, highest Appellation.—God the Vindicator of His People.—The King's Cruelty not a thing improbable.—Josephus' Account of the Destruction of Daniel's Enemies.—God's Power over Lions.—God is not to be dethroned from Nature and Providence.—Lieutenant Maury and the Sovereign of the Seas.—What are the Laws of Nature?—Cuvier.—Daniel's Flesh as sweet to the Lions' Taste as that of his Enemies.—God has the Reins of all Animals still.—The Pious every where under God's Care.—Miser and Slave.—You are NOW in God's Presence.—Newton only followed where his Creator had been before him.—Science does not overreach the Creator.—Faith triumphs over Death.

In the last lecture we saw Daniel, the servant of God and prime minister of Persia, cast into the lions' den because he would obey his God rather than his king. We come now to see how faith stopped the mouths of lions, and wrought his deliverance. It would seem from the narrative that Daniel was dropped as unfeelingly into the lions' den as a pebble is cast into the silent sea, to be forgotten forever. The moon and stars held on their joyous way over the Eastern World. Our little globe kept on its course, as if nothing had happened; the wicked seemed to have succeeded to their hearts' content; the aged servant of God was cast into the den of lions. Now, thought his enemies, he will trouble us no more. They supposed, when that heavy stone was placed over the mouth of the den, and sealed with the signet of the king and of his lords, that all was safe. They thought that, as no cry from the suffering man could be heard to excite sympathy—as the sufferings of the martyred prophet, while he was being devoured by the hungry lions, were hidden from the people, so there would be nothing to arouse popular indignation, and nothing more would ever be heard of him. But God's thoughts are not as man's thoughts, nor His ways as man's ways. Let us look a moment at the condition of the three parties. How did they respectively pass this memorable night? The conspirators returned to their homes; they drank deeply, they sang merrily; they congratulated each other that the old Jewish favorite was now out of the way—that he who feared God, and, rather than compromise his allegiance to his God, was willing to live poor, and to die a martyr, would testify no more against their rapacity.

And the poor king—he went home also. *Then the king went to his palace, and passed the night fasting; neither were instruments of music brought before him; and his sleep went from him.* How sad was that night for royalty! Filled with remorse for having signed the fatal decree, and not knowing how to retrace his steps or to retrieve the effects of his rash act, the king passed the night in agony. Ah! it is true that most crowns have thorns. It is true that palaces are magnificent piles —an Oriental court was peculiarly luxurious; but what are most palaces but splendid misery? What was the crown of France, the crown of Louis le Grand, of Francis the First, and of Clovis, a few years since? What is the throne of Naples, and the head of the house of Hapsburg, but a mark for the assassin? The one wounded, and the other maimed, within a few weeks, by subjects who sought to encompass their deaths. The sleepless king of Persia is a demonstration that conscience can shake the stoutest hearts. It is not nerve, but a conscience full of peace, that makes the bravest men. There can be no peace, no presence of mind, no true heroism, where the conscience is lashed with the scorpions of guilt. Armed battalions and thick palace walls cannot keep the sting of a guilty conscience from the chambers of the mighty. All the opiates of the physicians to his majesty—all the drugs of "Araby the Blest" and from the "distant Ind," cannot woo sweet sleep to the imperial pillow. No sounds of music are heard, all books are closed, all testimonies are silenced, not a voice is lifted up: *Why sleeps not my lord, the king?* It is on account of the presence of a visitor he cannot shut out from his bed-chamber. His own conscience, grieved, wronged, offended—God's vicegerent reasoning with him, rolling over and over with him, and agitating his royal bosom, and making him tremble; this is the disturber of his slumbers. The laborious poor through his vast dominions slept sweetly. With them the night passed as a swift hour. Refreshed with "Nature's sweet restorer, balmy sleep," they are prepared for another day's toil. But not so with the conscience-tormented master of the world. He seems to have given full scope to his inward monitor. *His sleep went from him.* He communed with his heart in the night season. He did not strive by pleasure, by company, or by dissipation, to lull his conscience asleep. And in this matter the king set you a good example. When conscience speaks, attend to her lessons; she is thy friend. Give ear to her faintest whispers; be not afraid to listen to her loudest accusations; they may be necessary to your soul's welfare. There are times in every man's history when conscience is quickened, and is faithful and tender. Whether this awakening of conscience is owing to some severe personal illness, or to some bereavement, or to the reading of some book, or to the preaching of the Word, such times are eras of immense importance in the history of immortal beings. Such a turning period in your life may be just now passing over you. Every moment is precious. While conscience pleads, and God calls, it is for you to obey. Habits of sin may be so indulged as to debilitate and exhaust the power of conscience. The impenitent sinner may be left for years without hearing her accusing voice. God can, however, at any moment quicken it by one single beam of light, and so kindle and inflame it, that the most hardened sinner will be troubled, as Belshazzar was at the writing on the wall. There is no torment like an accusing conscience. Wherever a guilty sinner goes, he carries his accuser in his own bosom. There is but one way for a guilty conscience to find peace; and that is, to have it sprinkled by the atoning blood of Jesus Christ, and purified by the sanctifying influences of the Holy Spirit.

But there is a third party in the transactions of this night we have not yet visited. The courtiers are more gleesome than usual. The king is more sad. The night is awfully tedious to him. How often did he look for the streaks of the morning light! It seemed to him as if the day would never come. But how was it with the servant of God? What tidings from the lions' den? Let us go with the king and see what has become of Daniel. *Then the king arose very early in the morning, and went in haste unto the den of lions.* Does he find it the grave of the murdered prophet of Jehovah? The king, doubtless, feared to speak; he was afraid there would be no other answer from the gloomy depths of the pit than the echo of his own voice, and the growling roar of his royal executioners. But he must speak: so, *when he came to the den, he cried with a lamentable voice unto Daniel, and said, O Daniel, servant of the living God, is thy God, whom thou servest continually, able to deliver thee from the lions?* The king was probably not altogether without hope. He had no doubt heard of the marvelous interpositions made in behalf of Jehovah's servants in times past. The records of the empire were then in his possession, and from these he may have learned how Daniel's God had preserved his friends amid the flames of the seven-fold heated furnace; and, knowing the purity of Daniel's character, he may have concluded that God would deliver him. But while he, thus half hoping, half despairing, is afraid to learn the result of his own inquiry—is afraid to look into the pit, let us look in. There is the old Hebrew prophet and grand vizier of Persia; he is on his knees, with hands uplifted and face toward heaven, beaming with calm benignity. On either side of him, and before and behind him, and all around him and almost touching him, stand, or lie, or crouch, the lions of the desert. Daniel's countenance is calm, self-possessed, buoyant with hope. We see no blood, no scratch from the teeth or claws of the fierce kings of the forest; we see no crushed bones, no signs of violence, no marks of uneasiness. This night among the lions has been the happiest night of his whole life. Free from all cares of state, and from every other anxiety, he had nothing to do but to let his heart commune with his God. But Daniel is ready to speak; and his voice that morning was sweeter to the king's ears than the music of his court had ever been. He had spent the night sick at heart, but now he is filled with gladness. *Then was the king exceeding glad for him. Then said Daniel unto the king, O king, live forever.** *My God hath sent his angel, and hath shut the lions' mouths, that they have not hurt me; forasmuch as before him innocency was found in me; and also before thee, O king, have I done no hurt.*

As Daniel's first words were to the king, so his second utterances are for the glory of his God. He explains at once the means of his deliverance.

I. The king's denomination of Daniel is worthy of remark. He does not address him as first of the presidents; but says, "*O Daniel, servant of the living God.*" This was an honor above any official station—angels and archangels can occupy no higher position. It was better for Daniel to have been a servant of the living God than to have been the first president of Persia. His official rank in the empire could not prevent him from being cast among the lions; but his being the servant of the living God protected him from their fury. His piety was not a

* The salutation of Daniel, "O king, live forever!" does not mean that he wished him literally to live forever. It was equivalent to the English "God save the Queen." It was the common court salutation, and meant nothing more than a wish of long life and prosperity.

sickly, fitful, feverish, fashionable thing; his devotion was deeply rooted; he served God *continually*, not occasionally; his mind was thoroughly pervaded and imbued with sound religious sentiments and feelings. The king had not failed to observe his punctuality in his religious duties, the uniformity, spirituality, and heavenliness of his mind in all his conduct. His religion was so natural to him that he could not hide it; every thing he did proved him to be a man that feared and loved God. O, what a living power there would be in religion if it were acted out in our social walks and public conduct, and not shut up to mould all week within the walls of our churches! Why should your labor and talents, influence and time, be principally devoted to the world which is passing away? The surest way to peace, and honor, and usefulness, is in the service of God. It is not by professing to be religious, but by consistency of conduct, that you will vindicate religion in the eyes of worldly men, and lodge a testimony to its reality in their consciences. And as you would not be a partaker in other men's sins, so you must be careful to exert a good influence, both by your example and by the sentiments you hold, upon all around you.

II. The reason for God's interference in Daniel's behalf was not that his conduct really merited such an interposition. The meaning is, that God, being a witness of his innocence, indicated it by this interposition. As Daniel was not guilty of disobedience to his God, so neither was he guilty of any treasonable designs. He harbored no disloyalty in his bosom. His conduct was not the result of any pique, or from any factious or discontented spirit, but purely from a conscientious regard to the divine au thority and glory; and God, by this interference, showed that He had taken notice of Daniel's conduct and was pleased with it, and thus declared that it was worthy of imitation in all similar cases.

You may learn, therefore, from this case, that God is the vindicator of his people. This truth is strikingly exemplified in the history of the pious who in past ages have stood in the front rank of the Redeemer's host. He has never forsaken his people. "Trust in the Lord, and do good, and verily thou shalt be fed. Commit thy way unto the Lord; trust also in him, and he shall bring forth the righteousness as thy light, and thy judgment as the noonday."

III. The *personal property in God*, referred to both in the king's words and in Daniel's reply, is remarkable. The king said to Daniel, "Is *thy* God, whom thou servest continually, able to deliver thee from the lions?" And Daniel replies, "*My* God hath sent his angel and shut the lion's mouths, that they have not hurt me." Mark the difference. Darius had heard of God by the hearing of the ear, Daniel was acquainted with him as a friend and a father. Daniel had chosen him as his portion, and devoted himself to his service. To believe there is a God is cheering compared with blank, heartless atheism. Surely it is good news that the universe is not an orphan. Surely all well-disposed minds will rejoice in the tidings that the world is governed by its Creator. How much more comfortable to be able to feel that He who is the ineffable Creator is our Father!

IV. Read here verses 23, 24.

I have already, in the preceding Lecture, shown, 1st.

That such a rash and passionate, sinful, improper, and unworthy act as this, was not so improbable a thing in the life of an Eastern monarch, or even of a Western tyrant, as to render the history of it incredible. He who could order the Saint Bartholomew Massacre, or the murder of the Mamelukes in Cairo, or murder the children of Bethlehem, or set Rome on fire for mere pastime, and then put Christians to death on the pretense that they had done what he knew he had himself done, would have been capable of doing all, and even more than it ascribed to Darius. It has been shown that it was a Persian custom to execute convicts by casting them into a den of lions, and it has also been shown that the families of those who fell under royal displeasure, were often destroyed with them. Such a custom is spoken of in the Bible as well as in profane history. The narrative, then, that mentions such things is not on that account to be thrown, at the mere caprice of a cloudy-headed critic, into fable-land. But, 2dly. The Bible does not say that the decree of Darius against prayer was right; nor does the Bible justify the cruelty of the king against Daniel's persecutors. Our history simply states the facts. These men were guilty of many crimes. Whether their punishment exceeded their guilt is not decided by the text. The Bible is responsible only for the record of the facts.

The great Jewish historian, in recording this fact, says, that when Daniel was delivered, the princes said it was because the lions had been previously surfeited with food, and on that account it was that they refused to touch Daniel. This so enraged the king that he ordered a great quantity of flesh to be given to the lions, and then com manded that these princes, Daniel's enemies, should be cast into the den, and they were all destroyed. Whether this account of Josephus be true in all its details or not, I am not able to say. The main points are true. And the history of Daniel's deliverance illustrates God's *power over the beasts of the field.* No doubt these Persian princes were anxious to explain away the miraculous interposition of Daniel's God. Like many *pretended* friends of the Bible in our day, they were so careful of the divine power, that they could not think of any useless expenditure of Omnipotence. There are those that talk of laws and nature, and yet find God nowhere. If a pestilence comes, it is not the hand of God that sent it, but the want of ozone, or it is some volcanic action that occasioned it. If the epidemic is removed, it was a change of the atmosphere, or of the wind, that removed it. If the soil yields beneficently, and rewards the toil of the husbandman, it is not the Creator, but the frosts and snows of last winter, that have occasioned the fruitfulness of the earth. If our astronomer, in his studio at Washington, predicts, from the observance of certain sailing directions, which he himself lays down, and gives to the captain of one of our vessels, the passage of that vessel from New York to San Francisco, a voyage of more than seventeen thousand miles, it is nothing but science and natural causes. God, whose works and laws are the substance of all science, is forgotten. This last illustration is a fact, and is one of the most remarkable instances of the triumphs of science that has ever been recorded. Lieutenant Maury, in his instructions and predictions of the voyage of the vessel "The Sovereign of the Seas," occupying one hundred and three days from New York to San Francisco, it is said, did not err two hours in his calculation of the time the voyage would take. And yet, strange as it is, many, practically if not professedly, make the thermometer, the state of the weather, the quadrant, the compass, the laws of vegetation, their god. But what are the laws of nature but the will of the Creator impressed upon nature? Whence these laws? What is the thermometer, the compass, the telescope, or the sprouting of seed, without the upholding power of the Creator? Nature is nothing without the active presence of her Maker; the laws of matter are nothing but expressions of the will of the Creator. Cuvier did not originate the four great plans on which the animal kingdom is constructed; he only discovered what the Creator had done. Kepler and Laplace have not made any of the laws of the universe; they have only discovered them. Of the miracle, then, before us, what think you? Was not the flesh of Daniel as sweet to the taste of the lions as the flesh of his enemies? Why did the lions leave Daniel untouched, and yet devour his persecutors as soon as they were cast into their den? The Bible answers this question. Daniel was not hurt by the lions, BECAUSE HE BELIEVED IN HIS GOD. Daniel gives himself the true explanation. "My God hath sent his angel, and hath shut the lions' mouths that they have not hurt me." It was faith, as the Apostle Paul tells us, that stopped the lions' mouths. It was in consequence of Daniel's faith in God that the angel quelled the fury of the hungry lions. Their ferocious disposition is proverbial; but they surround Daniel gently as lambs. We are not told how the angel shut their mouths; whether they were awed by the majesty and brightness of the angelic nature, or whether their physical powers were for the time paralyzed, or whether some powerful influence operated on their nature, we cannot determine. The result we know, but not the mode of producing it. The agent of Daniel's protection was an angel—probably the angel of Jehovah's presence, who appeared to Abraham and to the three Hebrews in the fiery furnace.

The Scriptures give us many examples of the agency of angels in ministering to God's people. We may not comprehend *how or in what way God exerts his power over the instincts and fierce propensities of the beasts of the earth*, and yet the fact is beyond doubt. The Creator gave man dominion over the earth and its animals, and placed his fear upon the beasts of the field. The fire of the human eye proclaims man's supremacy over the fierce monsters of the forest. Man's ingenuity in making instruments of defense is more than a counterbalance to brute agility and strength. It is supposed by some that the fierce passions of animals are consequences of Adam's fall, and that the Millennium, or the triumph of the Gospel, will restore the animals to their primeval state; that then the lion and tiger, and the fish of the sea and birds of the air, will recognize man as their lord, and do him homage as God's vicar on earth. This theory I regard more in the light of poetry than of sober truth—as more beautiful in theory than probable in reality. Still, it is true that God has power over the destructive propensities of animals. If man has lost the reins of absolute dominion over the beasts of the field and birds of the air, God has not; He still holds them. There are numerous instances scattered throughout the Bible. The ravens bring food to the prophet; the dumb ass, at God's bidding, preaches a most effective and direct sermon to the disobedient and self-willed prophet. A fish of the sea swallows Jonah, and another brings tribute-money to our Lord. And in the example before us, the fiercest of all the animal kingdom sit or stand, and crouch around the man of God, and dare not touch him; the hand of God was upon them. The power of God over the fury of the lions is seen not only in shutting their mouths, but also in opening them—in shutting them against Daniel, but in opening them upon the princes; they cannot hurt Daniel, but devour his persecutors.

God had wrought many "signs and wonders" before Pharoah, when his court was the dominant power in the world. He had given miraculous proofs of his supreme Divinity before the Chaldean court, when it was at the zenith of its power and glory. The deliverance of Daniel and the destruction of his enemies was a demonstration of the same to the court of Persia. The miracles wrought before Pharoah and Nebuchadnezzar were intended to call the attention of these monarchs toward the Jewish religion, and secure favor for the Jewish captives. The same thing was designed and secured by the deliverance of Daniel. See verses 25–27.

V. The history in hand teaches us, again, *that the power of God is not only over all the beasts of the field, and all the elements of nature*, BUT THAT HE IS EVERY WHERE, TO PROTECT AND BLESS ALL THOSE THAT TRUST IN HIM. Daniel was not hurt by the lions, "because he believed in his God." His God sent his angel to shut the lions' mouths.

because before him Daniel was found innocent of any fault either toward him or toward the king. A believer cannot be shut out from the presence of his God. He may be banished from his country and his home; he may be cast into the depths of the angry sea; he may be thrown into caves of the earth—sealed up in the lions' den; but he cannot be banished from his God. On the top of Ararat and of Mount Sinai—in the silent catacombs of Rome—amid the parching sands of the desert—on the great waves of the sea—wherever there is a Christian heart, there is the Christian's God, to bless and deliver him. How blessed is the thought that God is not confined to temples made with hands. What a blessed privilege that we are not obliged to have a consecrated altar, a priest, a wafer, holy water, and the oil of extreme unction before we can obtain the forgiveness of our sins. The Christian, whether in the depths of the forest, or in the mines of California, or toiling as a slave under the burning sun of Louisiana, or on the loftiest pinnacle of the Andes, every where finds a temple, a sacrifice, and an altar, even Jesus. "If he ascend into heaven, He is there; if he descend into the grave, He is there; if he take the wings of the morning and go down into the *depths* of the sea, even there is his Lord and Saviour too. God's eye can pierce all darkness; God's heart can pity his captive any where; and God's hand can help him in spite of all obstacles. So Daniel felt, and so thousands of God's saints have felt it too."—*Cumming.*

VI. In view, then, of Daniel's deliverance, learn, ALWAYS AND EVERY WHERE, TO PUT YOUR TRUST IN GOD Under all circumstances, at home or abroad, in health or in sickness, with friends or under the stern gaze of inquiring strangers, never cease to put your confidence in God. Do not look at things, but look at the Creator and Governor of all things. If you are an enemy to God, then all the universe is arrayed against you; but if you are reconciled to God—if you are once more at peace with him—then you are in harmony with yourself, in harmony with his laws, and consequently happy with all things. He commands the elements to do you good. For you the winds are to make music, and the waves are to bring you the fruits of the earth, and all things shall WORK TOGETHER for your good.

It is true, as the Persian monarch says in his decree, "God maketh signs and wonders." It is his voice that has called forth the beauteous spring. The flower that germinates—the bud that bursts from the stem—the fragrance that floats in the air—the sweet warblings from gardens and forests that charm you, and the glorious heavens above you, are all evidences of his presence, and power, and goodness. There is just as much of God's mighty power present in making your living heart continue to beat this moment, as there was in making Lazarus' dead heart begin to beat again. God's signs and wonders are all around us. We are ourselves a part of them. Our history is full of miracles of mercy. Philosophers, in their pride, and to hide their own ignorance, call the tokens of the living God, phenomena. The Bible calls them his signs and wonders. Newton discovered orbs, and laid the line and the plummet on the very out skirts of creation; but this he could never have done had not the Creator's hand been there before him, and laid

His laws upon them, by which He guides them still. It was the hand of Daniel's God that mingled those beauteous colors which the same Newton was the first to analyze, and have since been made to paint the unerring portrait. God launched into being the suns and systems whose vast revolutions the astronomer now calculates with so much accuracy. God buried the vast Saurian tribes before man was created. He knows all the discoveries that science will make. He understands all the creeds that men will ever propound. He sees through all the cabinet councils that will ever sit in Parliament, in Divan, or Congress; and He has determined that the wrath of man shall praise Him, that the Gospel shall prevail, and His glory fill the earth.

FINALLY. In Daniel's fidelity to his conscience and his God, we have an instance of the sublimest MORAL HEROISM. It was not that Daniel was insensible to the favor of the king; it was not that he did not love life, or that he cared nothing for the privileges of his position as first of the presidents. The penalty threatened was death, and death in an aggravated form. Death is a terrible penalty. Death is the most unnatural of all things. It is something abhorrent to all living creatures. Man was not made to die; his very nature shrinks from death. Death, in itself, was not desirable even to the Apostle Paul. He did not desire to "be unclothed," but he desired "to be with Christ." He was willing to meet the foe, for the sake of the victory; he was willing to pass through the dark and stormy sea, that he might gain the shore of beauty and blessedness that stretched beyond it. Nature shrinks from death, but faith teaches the true Christian to say,

"O death, where is thy sting? O grave, where is thy victory? Thanks be unto God that giveth us the victory through Jesus Christ." It was a true and living faith, then, that enabled Daniel to triumph over the fear of death. His faith taught him that his God was able to deliver him, or to make his death, amid the ravenous wild beasts, the forerunner of endless life. Faith whispered to him, as he was led along and cast into the lions' den, If this is to be the manner of my death, then this den will be the vestibule of glory. His faith told him that death was not a sinking into nonentity—that it was not even a momentary suspension of the continuity of life. It is only a transition. When the Christian dies, he does not cease to be. When the eye that looks upon us with so much affection, and the lips that breathe our name are closed, our father or child has not ceased to be. Their eyes are open upon another and a brighter world. They have only begun to live. The evening twilight of this world closes only upon the eye of a believer as the morning twilight of glory bursts upon him, and begins to open into the brightness of eternal day. The flame that consumes the martyr's body is the chariot that wafts his soul to immortality.

The sublime moral heroism of Daniel was the result of his faith in God, and his faith in God was the result of his early religious education. The Christian principles in which he was educated sustained him through his eventful life.

May your lives be full of honor and happiness, and your deaths be for the glory of God, through Jesus Christ, to whom be praise forever. Amen.

LECTURE XVI.

DANIEL A STUDY AND MODEL FOR YOUNG MEN AWAY FROM HOME.

On Dan., vi., 28.

"So this Daniel prospered in the reign of Darius, and in the reign of Cyrus the Persian."

Young Men in Cities.—Advantages and Dangers.—Evils of Clubs and College Commons.—Perils of Young professional Men and of Clerks.—Crisis in a young Man's Life.—New Orleans not the worst City above Ground.—Young Men's Christian Association.—Daniel's Diligence.—A Model Statesman.—His Promptitude, Punctuality, Integrity, Temperance, Benevolence.—High Character of New Orleans Business Men.—Aim High.—"Tracts for the Times."—Our Savans not yet manufactured a Spider.—Every Age has its Peculiarities.—Young Men must be armed for the Battle of the Age.—Gross Materialism of our Times.—Namby-pambyism of our popular Press.—Bible.—Young Men are the only Men for the Times.—Air-gun Attacks.—Don't wear out your Certificates.—Not Churchmen nor Sectarians, but pious.—Not Crab-apple Christians, but active ones.—Importance of early religious Culture.—MOTHERS wanted.—Trust in Providence.—No Fanaticism in personal Religion.—God the young Man's best Patron.—Your Privileges superior to those of Daniel.—You must have a personal Acquaintance with Religion.—Farewell of the Series.

With this sixth chapter the historical part of the book of Daniel ends. We find no further use of the Chaldee language after this chapter. The subsequent part of the book being occupied with an account of Daniel's own visions, and not containing edicts of Chaldean or Persian kings, is written, as we should expect it to be, in Daniel's own language, and in just such Hebrew as we should expect such a man as Daniel, a well-educated Hebrew, living in the courts of Babylon and Persia in the time of Nebuchadnezzar and Cyrus, would use. It is easy to see that the object of the writer of this book has not been to give a regular and complete history, either of the Babylonish kings, of their successors, or of Daniel himself. Those, and only those, events are noticed which tend to exhibit Jehovah as working miracles, in order to preserve and, in due season, deliver his ancient covenant people out of their captivity. That there is an ethical and religious design in the narratives is most palpable; but we have shown that this is no reason for believing the whole history a mere fable. It is clear that the writer designed to commend a steadfast adherence to the principles and practice of piety and virtue, amid the trials and temptations to which the Hebrews were exposed in their captivity in Babylon. And in Daniel we have a most felicitous grouping of virtues, personal, private, and public, for the study and imitation of young men who are, as he was, *away from home*, and obliged to live in great cities. If extremes do not meet in our large towns and cities, they are certainly near neighbors. In such a city as London, Vienna, Paris, New York, or New Orleans, there is to be found something of every thing, and something of every thing of the best, and something of every thing of the worst. It is this fact that gives such importance to the entrance of young men into large cities, or to their assuming independent positions in them, even after they have been brought up there. For example, as to amusements, whether for the health of the body or the cultivation of the mind, a young man may find the worst or the best in a great city. The intellect may be enlarged, the perceptive powers quickened, habits of promptness and decision formed, and the mind be stored, by attendance on Lectures by men of the highest science and of approved moral characters and sentiments, and by intercourse with intelligent, high-minded, active business men. The very atmosphere of a busy community is inspiring, and should be elevating. This is one view of the matter. There is another, and a different one also. Young men in cities may quicken their talents at the expense of their virtue and reputation, by the coarser wit of clubs and societies where religion furnishes the best joke, and sobriety and chastity the loudest laugh. It may be put down as a safe, as a very important rule, that no youth at school or college, or away from home, should be allowed to lodge or board in commons; but always to take meals where a lady presides at the head of the table. I had rather a son of mine should grow up ignorant of the curriculum of university studies, than for him to live without the society of intelligent and pious females for three or four years. But let us take another illustration of the point in hand. A young man, away from home, and beginning life in a great city, desires to enter the learned professions. As such, he may be associated with the most high-minded, religious, straightforward lawyer or physician, or he may be placed with the very reverse; and instead of learning from his associates an honorable way to renown and fortune, he may be taught, by their example, and by a gradual training under the older members of the profession, to regard as the one object of his life and business, to draw the life-blood to the last drop from every unfortunate client or patient. Or if the young man enters a house of business, he may find himself with a firm who, both by theory and practice, inculcate every thing that is honest, noble, and of good report; or he may find his lot among those with whom profession is not principle—whose lengths, measures, and descriptions of merchandise are varied to suit customers—where Mammon is the only god served, and where clerks are complimented on the principle that gain is godliness—where honesty to the buyer is counted dishonesty to the seller—where the net profits shown by the ledger are counted of more consequence than the certain losses recorded in the Book of God. The dangers to which youths are exposed in large cities have often been pointed out, and in the most earnest and affectionate manner, from this pulpit. It does not come within my present scope to dwell upon them. This much, however, must now be said, that the entrance of a young man upon his life in a large city is a great crisis in his existence. It is then, if not before, that the trial comes that will show what stuff he is made of. It is then the question, to be or not to be, is pressed with an emphasis totally unknown before; to be or not to be, a virtuous man; to be or not to be, an honorable man; to be or not to be, a religious man—a man of God, thoroughly furnished unto every good work; to be or not to be, mindful of the principles of their parent; to serve or not to serve the God of their fathers: these are the questions which, of all others, he must decide on his entrance upon life in a city. Here are temptations to vice, facilities for gratifying a depraved taste, opportunities for profound secrecy, and refinement in the forms of sensuality; and here the gradations of the downward course of iniquity are so imperceptible, and yet their tendency so certainly fatal, both to body and soul, to happiness here and hereafter, that it is not without some appropriateness that our city is called "the modern Babylon." I do not admit that our city is as bad as its reputation abroad makes it. I do not believe it is any worse, not quite as bad as other cities in our own country, and certainly not equal in vice to the large cities of the Old World; still, a young man's life in New Orleans is full of perils. It is proper that the arrival of a youth from the country, or from a smaller town, or the starting out in life of one brought up among us, should be an occasion of deep anxiety. To one from the country every thing is new—the modes of doing business are new—the subjects of conversation are new. His associates and channels of news are different from those with which he has been accustomed. The churches, and modes of worship, and ministers, are all new. He is not acquainted with the pious people of the city. No wonder, then, that we have thought it important to have a Young Men's Christian Association formed in this city, that may sympathize with the young man from home, and throw around him a shield of protection and encouragement. The young man that now knows the *heart of a stranger* need be friendless no more. He is no longer left to the mercy of the vicious and ungodly. But so precious are his interests, and so perilous still is his condition, that it is no wonder his family at home follow him with deep solicitude. No wonder that his mother and sisters laid a Bible and some earnest religious books with his apparel, and that they follow him with letters, and look anxiously for his, and if his letters arrive irregularly, that they are troubled. Now, while the dangers of city life are imminent, they are not inevitable. A youth may be brought up in, or come to and reside in, our modern Babylon unharmed amid all its temptations, just as Joseph did in Egypt, and as Daniel remained in Babylon and Susa, amid all the temptations of the luxurious heathen courts of the Babylonish and Persian empires. Daniel so acted as to escape the corruptions that surrounded him, and to the end of a long life feared God and obtained his blessing. His conduct in the chief cities of the old Oriental empires supplies a moral for young men in our cities of the Western World. His character is now presented for your imitation; the points of resemblance are not without their force. The disparities are in your favor. He was carried to Babylon, a heathen city, as a captive. You come as a freeman to a city of Gospel privileges, a city where there are thousands that do not bow the knee to Baal. If, indeed, there be not a Lot and an Abraham here to intercede for the city, there are hundreds of pious Christian men and women in this city, whose example and prayers are worth more than the gold of Babylon. Daniel and his three friends were of the first families of Jerusalem. They were carried to Babylon when about seventeen or twenty years of age. Their age and temperaments, hopes and fears, trials and temptations, were, therefore, similar to your own. It will not be proper for me to repeat what has been already said in this series of Lectures. I can now do but little more than seize on a few of the more important points of his character. And,

I. Daniel is a model man for all young men on ac-

COUNT OF HIS DILIGENCE IN BUSINESS. You remember how he declined the royal table, and yet became more comely than the other captives, and how he was promoted to great honors. He served at least five royal masters: Nebuchadnezzar, Evil-Merodach, Belshazzar, Darius, and Cyrus, yet his unscrupulous persecutors could "find neither error nor fault in him"—no partiality, no selfish ness, no remissness, no harshness, no mismanagement of the public funds, nor of the public business in any way What a model for business young men, clerks, agents of commercial houses, and politicians. His success was doubtless owing, in part, to his diligence in acquiring knowledge. As a statesman under so many different monarchs and dynasties, it required effort to make himself acquainted with the diversified duties of his official station. He was the first president of the rulers of one hundred and twenty provinces, and *Rab Mag*, or chief of the college of learned men; consequently, he had to make himself familiar with the scientific and political knowledge of his times. He had no time to read novels and superficial Reviews, had there been such trash then in the metropolis. His intellect was expended in researches for knowledge as for hid treasures. Few statesmen have served so many masters without flattering any, or been so successful in the management of public affairs, or been so useful to the states over which they have presided. Samuel, Joseph, and Daniel are the best specimens of prime ministers that have ever appeared on earth.

In the administration of the royal laws, Daniel was diligent and prompt. At the appointed hour he was at his place *in the king's gate.* No one could accuse him of a want of punctuality—no one could charge him with impatience in hearing causes, nor of the want of deliberation in his decisions, nor of weakness in the execution of the judgments decreed; nor was there any deficiency in the revenue of one hundred and twenty provinces. As Secretary of the Treasury and Secretary of State, his enemies themselves being judges, there was nothing to be found against him. Uncertain markets, distracting competitions, a voluminous correspondence, the incessant cares and excitements of office—how must all these things have pressed upon him! yet his strong, well-balanced, prayer-sustained mind, took such a clear, comprehensive, wide-reaching control of the vast affairs of the dominant empire of the globe, that he was without fault. He so counseled his royal masters, as to preserve their dominions tranquil, loyal, and secure. As a student, as a subject, as a statesman, from early youth to old age, Daniel was remarkable for his habits of sobriety, industry, and piety; he was both diligent in business and fervent in spirit, serving the Lord. He was no idler, no loiterer, no lackadaisical youth; his industry was not to feed and pamper himself. Never did man spend less for his personal gratification who had so much at command. He never pandered to any guilty passions, nor luxuriated in the debaucheries of vice; he made no provisions for the flesh to fulfill the lusts thereof. Had he been guilty of such things, his enemies would not have failed to expose his guilt with malignant joy. He was not a worldly-minded man. The love of money was not found in him. His toil was not to indulge himself in low gratifications, nor to aggrandize himself or his relations. *He was thoroughly a man of business, and he was quite as thoroughly a man of God.*

Young men, it is your duty to be men of business, of high business talents and character. You know better than I can tell you, that loiterers, procrastinators, and tattlers, and busy bodies in other men's business, cannot succeed in this community. You already know that laziness is disreputable, that dilatoriness is disgraceful, that procrastination is a reproach. There is not a more industrious, honest, manly, high-minded, upright, prompt, whole-souled business community on the globe than we have here. Fix your mark high. Acquire at once a character for integrity, and for the quickness, punctuality, neatness, and high manliness of all your transactions. With the urgency of such motives upon you as the Gospel supplies, you must not be content with small things. In such a city as this, aim directly at becoming first-rate business men. Let it be a point of honor with you, whether you are in the lecture-room, or in the warehouse, or in the mechanic's shop, or in the profession of the law or of medicine, that you will seek for distinction, for integrity, and proficiency in your particular calling. The apostle has told us, "It is good to be zealously affected always in a good thing."

II. Daniel is the young man's model FOR EARNESTNESS IN HIS RELIGION. His whole life illustrates the criminality of indifference to such a subject as religion. I have sought to make these Lectures "Tracts for the Times," as it respects the duties of young men to their country and their God. I have sought to make you somewhat acquainted with some of the modes of attack upon your religious faith most to be feared, and to put you in some measure on your guard against the phases of infidelity and skepticism peculiar to our day. It is true that human nature is every where the same; and it is also true that the world, for at least some six or seven thousand years, has not furnished us with a single experimental fact going to show that it is possible, by any process of development, to make a world without a Creator; and surely the experiment has been continued long enough. And if now our *savans*, with all the light of the "Vestiges of Creation" and of the nebular hypothesis, are not able to make one spider, nor to make a human being out of a monkey, we may be excused for holding still to our old orthodox belief, that "in the beginning God created the heaven and the earth," "and all that in them is." Every age has its characteristics in philosophy, science, morals and religion. Our age is grossly material, and yet ethereal. For while we live amidst intense pursuits of the things that perish, our received opinions of common sense, and of man's relations and hopes, are violently attacked from the airy heights of a dreamy, impersonal, impalpable, *soi disant* philosophy. The poets, essayists, and historians of the age generally, and not a little of every species of our popular literature, is a mass of namby-pambyism that enfeebles the intellect, corrupts the imagination, and destroys the soul. And these are all the more dangerous because they are made chiefly by professed lovers of truth. By giving specious titles to things, and wrong names to errors, their batteries are masked, their shots are from air-guns that makeno noise, and their deathly blows are not seen till the victim is past hope.

In an age so impetuous and vigorous, the only men for the times are young men, who by education, discipline, and noble bearing, are up to the exigencies of their age. Such men are always Bible made; their characters are formed after Bible models, and their conduct regulated by Bible principles. In seeking a home, therefore, in a strange city, be sure to carry with you the evidences of your church membership, and call at once on the minis ter of the place whether God leads you. Don't put it off till you wear out your certificate by carrying it in your pocket. Engage at once in the Sabbath school and other approved agencies, by which to encourage and comfort the servant of God in whose congregation your residence may be. Never was there an age or a country where pious young men had such a destiny in their hands as in this age of the United States. It is intelligent, Bible-formed piety that will save this continent from paganism and papal priestcraft, and that only. Nothing else will do. Every possible motive urges you not to be bigots, churchmen, or sectarians, but earnest, intelligent, high-minded, whole-hearted Christians. In ages past, and even now, there are too many pious people living in the strait-jackets of little prejudices, and lying on the Procrustean beds of their own short and narrow creeds. But the Gospel is not a yoke of ceremonies or dogmas. It is liberty, life, and salvation. The age calls you not to be sour-faced, fault-finding, complaining followers of Christ, but cheerful, hopeful, active, earnest, pious disciples of the one and only great Redeemer. The great Napoleon was told that all that France wanted to make her the greatest nation in the world was MOTHERS. It is true that intelligent, pious, praying mothers are the greatest benefactors of any age or country. Never can you too highly appreciate the blessings of religious culture.

III. In conclusion, then, we desire you to take Daniel as your model. Study him in all the completeness of his character as a man, a prophet, and a statesman; as to his capacities and their improvement; his habits and business traits. Forget not his steadfast adherence to principle, seen in his life-long devotion to the law and service of his God; and that, too, amidst the most appalling persecutions. He served God in little things as perseveringly and as fully as in great things. With him true principle was ever and always the only expediency. Varied and oft repeated as were his trials, he had but ONE RULE, which was to obey his God unhesitatingly and cheerfully. The result he committed to Him whom he served. His enemies left no stone unturned by which to compass his ruin; but always did they fail. They flattered, they threatened, and they tried to overreach him; but no cause for his accusation could be justly found against him, either as to his activity and capacity, or honesty in business, nor as to his loyalty. It was at last only in regard to his religion that they dared to attack him. His heroism was of the noblest kind. It overcame the most appalling difficulties in the best of causes, and from the purest of motives. And was not Daniel right in his steadfast adherence to the law and service of his God? From whom had he his being? By whom had he been preserved all his life long, and exalted to favor in various kingdoms? To whom was he indebted for the revelations of the dream of Nebuchadnezzar as well as for the explanation of the handwriting on the wall? And are you not indebted to the Creator likewise for your existence and well being? Is not the God of Daniel your Maker, Preserver, and Benefactor, and will He not soon be your Judge? Have you not your health, education, reason, speech, and civil, social, and religious *status* from Him? Ought not the creature to worship the Creator? Ought not the beneficiary to praise the Benefactor? And ought not the sinner to seek reconciliation with his Sovereign, and acceptance with his Judge? There is then no fanaticism in religion like that of Daniel. It is the highest reason, and the only true heroism, to fear God and keep his commandments.

Like Daniel, then, let me urge you, in closing this series of discourses, to rely upon God with an unfaltering trust in his providence. Daniel's heroism was such as the world can neither give, nor appreciate, nor take away. *It was godly.* He was decided, open, and bold in his avowal of the God of his fathers as *his God.* He again and again declared that he could not deny or forsake the religion of his fathers. Nothing could induce him to conform to the fashionable, court religion of Babylon. And his professions were his principles. He had not a mere form of godliness, but also its spirit and power. He was a Jew inwardly. He belonged to the true circumcision. Hence he trusted in his God, and relied on Him in the face of the most appalling and cruel punishment. He believed in his heart, and confessed with his mouth, and put his trust in the true God, and he was not disappointed. He would not take any situation, nor keep any place, upon the condition either expressed or implied, that he must depart in the smallest matter from the injunctions of the law of his God. Like him, then, take care never to offend your conscience, never shrink from duty, because of difficulties; never tamper with convictions; never forget the words of the Lord Jesus, who has said: "Fear not them who can kill the body, but after that have no more that they can do, but rather fear Him, who, after He hath killed, hath power to cast into hell." Fix the resolve deep in your souls that you will abide by well formed convictions, cost what it may. If you must suffer persecution for confessing Christ, be it so. Confess Him cheerfully amidst all persecution that may arise to you on that account. Bear up against all temptations to deny Him, by remembering his gracious promise, that He will confess you before his Father and his holy angels. "Him that honoreth me, I will honor. He that despiseth me, shall be lightly esteemed." To be like Daniel, you must have a *personal* interest in the God of your pious fathers. You must, by sincere penitence and faith, appropriate Him to yourself as your God. And to do this, you must, like Daniel, be regular, punctual, fervent, and persevering in prayer and in the study of God's revealed will. The strength and rationality of Daniel's character is found in the divine *imprimatur* of his deliverance from the lions: *Because he believed his God.* His education had been a good one. He had been instructed in his early years in the law of his God, and he had kept himself from all defilement. He never read sickly, sentimental, moon-stricken novels and essays, nor gazed on licentious pictures, nor consorted with profligate "fast boys about town," nor done that which he would have been ashamed to tell his father, nor found where the approach of his mother's footfall would have made him take to flight. He was a diligent student of the Scriptures of God. But you have advantages even greater than he had. Your age and country are in advance of his. You are a freeman. He was a captive. You have Christ and his Apostles, in addition to Moses, the Psalms, and the Prophets, which he had. But all will be of no avail, but rather aggravate your guilt, if you believe not in the Son of God, and receive Him as the only Redeemer. Make God your portion. Serve Him with all your soul. Trust in Him, and to the end of the earth He will be your friend. And to God the Father, the Son, and the Holy Ghost be everlasting praise. Amen.

THE END.

www.ingramcontent.com/pod-product-compliance
Lightning Source LLC
LaVergne TN
LVHW010209110826
845151LV00002B/644

* 9 7 8 1 4 2 5 5 3 4 9 4 3 *